American Living Standards

AMERICAN LIVING STANDARDS

THREATS and CHALLENGES

Robert E. Litan
Robert Z. Lawrence
Charles L. Schultze
editors

THE BROOKINGS INSTITUTION
Washington, D.C.

Copyright © 1988 by
THE BROOKINGS INSTITUTION
1775 Massachusetts Avenue, N.W., Washington, D.C. 20036

Library of Congress Cataloging-in-Publication data

American living standards.

Includes bibliographical references and index.
1. Cost and standard of living—United States.
I.   Litan, Robert E.   .   II. Lawrence,
Robert Z.   .   III. Schultze, Charles L.
IV. Brookings Institution.
HD6983.A69   1988   339.4'7'0973   88-26238
ISBN 0-8157-5274-1 (alk. paper)
ISBN 0-8157-5273-3 (pbk. : alk. paper)

9 8 7 6 5 4 3 2 1

The paper used in this publication meets the minimum
requirements of the American National Standard for Information
Sciences—Permanence of Paper for Printed Library Materials, ANSI
Z39.48-1984.

Set in Caledonia with Univers display
Composition by Monotype Composition Co.
Baltimore, Maryland
Printing by R.R. Donnelley and Sons, Co.
Harrisonburg, Virginia
Book design by Ken Sabol

Foreword

The United States enjoys the highest living standards of any nation on earth, and for decades most Americans have taken it for granted that their material lives would continue to improve. But that assumption is now in jeopardy despite our recent success in avoiding both recession and inflation. The key to rising living standards is the rate at which productivity, or output per worker, grows. Since the early 1970s the growth of American productivity has slowed sharply, reducing the growth of wages and family income. During the 1980s American living standards have been sheltered from the consequences of that slowdown because the United States has spent more than it produced, borrowing the difference from abroad. But that situation is unraveling, and clearly the most difficult economic challenge facing the new president is what to do about the slowdown in the growth of American productivity, family income, and living standards.

This book documents what has been happening to American productivity growth and explores the causes of the slowdown and the implications for the nation's well-being. The authors examine the recent changes in the level and distribution of incomes among workers and families, the changes in the quality and distribution of jobs among industries and regions, and the trends in the quality of education. They project what will happen to American living standards over the next five to ten years under several sets of reasonable assumptions and offer suggestions about how to improve productivity performance.

Robert E. Litan and Robert Z. Lawrence are senior fellows in the Economic Studies program at the Brookings Institution; Charles L. Schultze is director of the program. Martin Neil Baily and Robert W. Crandall are also senior fellows in Economic Studies, and Margaret Mendenhall Blair is a senior research analyst. Frank Levy is professor of economics in the Public Affairs School at the University of Maryland, and Richard J. Murnane is professor of economics at the Harvard Graduate School of Education.

The editors are grateful to Caroline Lalire, Jeanette Morrison, Brenda B. Szittya, and Theresa B. Walker for editing the manuscript, and to Victor M. Alfaro and Anna Nekoranec for verifying its factual content. Felice Levy and Cynthia Crippen prepared the index.

This is the initial book published under the sponsorship of the new Brookings Center for Economic Progress and Employment. Brookings gratefully acknowledges financial support for the center from Donald S. Perkins, American Express, AT&T, Chase Manhattan Bank, Cummins Engine, Ford Motor Company, General Electric, Hewlett-Packard, Morgan Stanley, Motorola, Springs Industries, Union Carbide, Xerox, the Ford Foundation, Smith Richardson Foundation, the Institute for International Economic Studies, and Alex C. Walker Educational and Charitable Trust. In addition, Brookings acknowledges and thanks those trustees who have provided special assistance in the formation of the center: Donald S. Perkins, Walter Y. Elisha, James D. Robinson III, Henry B. Schacht, and Morris Tanenbaum.

The views expressed here are those of the authors and should not be attributed to the organizations whose assistance is acknowledged, or to the trustees, officers, or other staff members of the Brookings Institution.

BRUCE K. MAC LAURY
President

October 1988
Washington, D.C.

Contents

Tables

Figures

American Living Standards

CHAPTER ONE

Introduction

Robert E. Litan, Robert Z. Lawrence, and Charles L. Schultze

FOR THE first twenty-five years after World War II, productivity, real wages, and average incomes in the United States grew rapidly. American living standards were not only high, but they were increasing at a handsome pace. Not surprisingly under these circumstances, popular discussion and political debate concentrated on the *stability* of our economic system; economic performance was judged in terms of how well the nation did with respect to unemployment, inflation, and recession. The long-term rise in incomes and living standards was more or less taken for granted.

This complacence is no longer appropriate. Since 1973, the growth of American productivity and income per worker has slowed to a crawl. Ultimately, slower growth in productivity and income means slower growth in living standards. For a time we have been able to avoid or postpone some of these unpleasant consequences by various devices. But our ability to do so is coming to an end. The central economic problem for the country, therefore, and the one this book addresses by way of analysis and policy prescription, is the recent and prospective slowdown in the growth of American living standards.

Preventing a recession or a renewal of inflation remains a serious policy challenge whose successful accomplishment cannot be taken for granted. Over the past six years, our country has met this challenge. The rates of both inflation and unemployment are now at roughly half their double-digit peaks earlier in the decade. This performance is even more impressive since it occurred during a period in which both the budget and trade deficits swelled to unprecedented size, while interest rates and exchange rates fluctuated sharply. Now that the economy is approaching full capacity, policymakers face a stiffer challenge of maintaining stability, ensuring reasonably full employment without an accel-

We are grateful to Annette N. Brown and Ellen E. Pack for research assistance, and to Anita G. Whitlock for administrative support.

1

eration in inflation. With careful management of economic policy, however, economic stability can, not certainly but most probably, be maintained in the years immediately ahead.

Even if this challenge is successfully met, the United States will nevertheless face the deeper long-run problem of improving its recent disappointing productivity performance. As noted, the United States has for a time succeeded in avoiding some of the decline in the growth of living standards that goes with a decline in productivity growth. We have done so in three ways: more women are working, giving families two earners rather than one. A greater share of our income has been devoted to consumption—both private and public—rather than to investment. By 1987 net domestic investment in housing and business plant and equipment was down to 6 percent of national income, from an average of 8 percent in the three decades from 1950 to 1980. Most important, the United States has resorted to massive borrowing from abroad. By 1987, as a nation we were spending 4 percent more than we produced, incurring an equivalent amount of overseas debt.

Foreign investors, however, will not continue indefinitely to finance our accumulation of overseas debt. Indeed, for the sake of our own and our children's future, we should take steps to bring it to an orderly end. The growth of consumer and government spending must be brought back into line with the nation's productive capacity. In a similar vein, the recent reduction in the percentage of national output devoted to investment further diminishes the potential size of future productivity gains, and should be reversed, also requiring a temporary slowdown in the growth of consumer and government spending.

The imperative need to slow the growth of national spending poses critical challenges for economic policy. How can the nation avoid recession and manage an inflation-free transition from a state of national overspending, large trade deficits, and heavy overseas borrowing to a state of balanced national spending and production, balanced trade, and far less reliance on foreign creditors? By how much must the growth in American living standards be temporarily cut back in order to bring national spending back into line with production? Which way of doing so will be most conducive to maintaining the long-term health and growth potential of the economy? Can the nation achieve a more rapid rise in national productivity to minimize any required slowdown in the growth of spending? These are among the questions that the authors of this book address in the chapters that follow.

The Economic and Political Background

The behavior of the American economy in the 1980s presents a number of paradoxes.

By most of the usual standards the economy performed well in the recent past. A deep recession occurred in 1981–82, but six years of uninterrupted advance followed. Employment grew strongly and by mid-1988 the unemployment rate was only a little more than 5 percent, lower than it had been in fifteen years. A large part of the rise in inflation in the 1970s was wrung out of the economy by the 1981–82 recession. Although there are a few signs of trouble ahead, inflation remains relatively moderate and most observers do not expect a big upsurge in the near future. On all of the measures that relate to economic stability—especially unemployment and inflation—the American economy has been healthy.

Nevertheless, though jobs have been increasingly available, the growth of productivity and the closely associated growth in real wages of American workers have been disappointingly slow for some time. Starting in the early 1970s output per worker and the real income of the average American began to rise far more slowly than they had in the 1950s and 1960s. The decline in output per worker that began in the 1970s was sharp. Some recovery took place after 1979, but even then productivity growth continued at a much slower pace than it had in the 1950s and 1960s. The fall in the growth of output per capita was less severe—because the work force expanded faster than the population—but it was nevertheless substantial. Accompanying the fall in productivity growth was a fall in the growth of average incomes.

When the growth of income for the average worker is rapid, as it was in the 1950s and 1960s, even those who fall behind in the economic race can still achieve absolute advances in living standards. But when the average rate of income growth is sluggish, as it has been over the past fifteen years, then many of the individuals, firms, and communities who do worse than average will suffer absolute losses in their incomes and living standards. Unlike in good times—when unemployment is low and most people can find a job—there are many more losers. And since the cause of these concentrated losses is not easily understood (as a recession might be), there is a tendency to search for some flaw in the basic structure of the economy—"America is no longer creating enough good jobs."

Table 1-1. *The Growth of Output, Income, and Spending, 1950–87*
Percent a year

	Output[a]		Real Income[b]		Real domestic spending (per capita)	
Period	Per worker[c]	Per capita	Compensation per worker	Median family income	Total	Government and consumer
1950–73	1.9	2.1	2.6	3.1	2.2	2.1
1973–79	− 0.2	1.2	0.6	0.9	1.1	1.2
1979–87	0.8	1.2	0.5	0.3	1.6	1.8

Sources: Robert Z. Lawrence, "The International Dimension," in this volume, table 2-1; U.S. Department of Commerce, Bureau of Economic Analysis, national income and product accounts; and U.S. Congressional Budget Office, *Trends in Family Incomes: 1970–1986* (Washington, D.C., 1988), p. 102.
  a. Output is defined as net domestic product.
  b. Compensation and median income are adjusted to eliminate the effect of inflation. The U.S. Department of Commerce fixed-weight price index for consumer expenditures is used.
  c. Workers include the self-employed.

Despite sluggish improvement in per capita output and income over the last seven years, the growth of per capita spending has rebounded sharply (see table 1-1). On a per capita basis, growth in total national spending— by consumers, investors, and government—recovered about halfway back to where it was in the earlier postwar decades. Since the growth of investment spending slowed, the combined growth of spending of consumers and government rebounded almost back to the pace of the 1950s and 1960s. Federal taxes were reduced sharply in 1981, so that consumers had more to spend. Simultaneously, the government boosted defense spending without an offsetting cut in civilian programs. Finally, consumers and businesses began saving less and spending more of their incomes.

For all these reasons, living standards, insofar as they can be measured by the combination of consumer purchases and government services, grew rapidly in the first seven years of the 1980s. But the only way that the country as a whole could spend more than it produced was to import the difference from abroad and to finance it by borrowing from foreign creditors. In absolute size, the gap between spending and output was unprecedented. So was the trade deficit that made it possible.

In the long run, however, slower growth of productivity implies a slowdown in the advance of living standards; when the growth in output per worker rises at a slower pace, the amount available for purchase by consumers or by government must also grow more slowly. As long as foreigners are willing to lend to the United States on a large scale, the country can postpone the day of reckoning and continue to increase spending at an undiminished rate. This era, however, has already begun to end. Foreigners are increasingly unwilling to finance excess spending; their decreased demand for U.S. dollars has driven down the value of the dollar from its highs of several years ago; the lower dollar, by making U.S. exports less expensive abroad and raising the price of imports into this country, has set in motion a fall in the U.S. trade deficit and a concomitant decline in the inflow of foreign funds into the United States. As the trade deficit continues to fall, the growth of domestic spending will have to shrink to make room, within the limits of the nation's slowly growing industrial capacity, for the production of more exports and domestic substitutes for imports. Indeed, domestic spending will eventually have to come down even further. The United States will have to pay interest on the overseas debts it has accumulated. To do so the nation will have to run a trade surplus to earn the income for those interest payments. Domestic spending will thus have to fall below national output in order to leave enough output available for the inevitable export surplus.

With a little luck and careful management by the Federal Reserve, this nation can probably continue to postpone the necessary adjustments to its spending patterns, as symbolized by the federal budget deficits, without stumbling into inflation or recession. If the United States is waiting for a crisis before taking action, the signal may never come. Rather, the consequences of failing to act and of continuing to save only a pitifully small fraction of national income are likely to show up only slowly and imperceptibly as a steady erosion of the growth of U.S. living standards. The tragedy of national overspending and the budget deficit is that there has been no visible crisis. Had there been, the nation might already have done something about the problem.

In the field of national security the United States long ago learned that it should not wait until an enemy lands on the beaches of San Diego or Long Island before attending to national defense. There is time to learn and act on the same lesson as it applies to defending advances in national living standards.

Policy Options for the New President

To meet the need for reduced U.S. domestic spending, the new president will have to choose among four options. The first, and most politically tempting choice, is simply to postpone or minimize the necessary adjustment. That is, the United States could try to keep foreign funds flowing in at high levels to support continued overspending. The real exchange value of the dollar would have to be maintained and even increased above its current level. To make investment in the United States sufficiently attractive to foreigners, without an increase in interest rates of a kind that would put the economy into a recession, the United States might have to issue large amounts of U.S. government securities denominated in other currencies—yen, marks, or pounds. That would transfer the exchange risk from foreign investors to the U.S. government and might keep the demand for dollars high.

Assuming that a policy of supporting the dollar and maintaining the trade deficit at a high level could be carried out successfully (and it is not at all clear that it could), the United States could extend its national overspending. But such a policy would have serious adverse consequences for the long run by greatly increasing our overseas debts and the annual debt service burden. For example, if the United States could successfully postpone adjustment until 1995, keeping the balance of payments deficit and the inflow of foreign funds at its 1988 level of about $140 billion a year, and then begin adjusting over the subsequent eight years, U.S. debts owed to foreign creditors would exceed $2 trillion early in the next century. The annual interest bill required to service this debt would range between $140 and $160 billion, or more than 1 percent of GNP—indefinitely, year after year. Moreover, by relying more heavily on foreign creditors to finance our excess spending, postponement subjects the United States to a mounting risk of an economic crisis sometime in the future. Given America's huge debts, foreigners could suddenly lose confidence in the U.S. ability or willingness to maintain the value of the dollar, triggering a sharp rise in interest rates and raising the risks of recession.

Nevertheless the president might choose a second option—letting international financial markets bring down the dollar, thus eliminating the trade deficit. However, the president would be failing to take the necessary steps to reduce excess domestic spending. Consequently, the federal budget deficit would remain at its current projected level of about $150 to $160 billion a year and consumer spending would not be reduced through either tax increases or government spending cuts. At the same time, to avoid depressing investment spending the Federal Reserve would have to inject large volumes of new credit into the economy to replace the shrinking inflow of foreign funds.

Since U.S. output is already close to its potential level, the nation cannot maintain prior growth rates in all three elements of domestic spending—investment, consumption, and government spending—and simultaneously allow a lower dollar to expand exports and reduce imports without overheating the economy. Under the second option, therefore, total demand would exceed available supply, renewing domestic inflation and laying the foundation for another policy-induced recession to cool it off.

The third policy option is to maintain a large budget deficit by refusing to raise taxes or to cut government spending, but letting the Federal Reserve squeeze out the excess domestic spending through a very restrictive monetary policy. Such a course could produce a big increase in interest rates, keeping the exchange rate of the dollar higher than it otherwise would be, thereby slowing down the fall in the trade deficit. Monetary restriction would also produce a decline in domestic spending for investment purposes—housing construction and business plant and equipment. With some luck and very good monetary management such a policy might enable the United States to continue government and private consumption at high levels, but only by pushing already anemic levels of investment and saving even lower. This low-investment, low-saving option would put the nation on a course that would gradually but inevitably further diminish the growth of national productivity, incomes, and living standards.

Finally, the president might choose to make the necessary reductions in national spending by urging enactment of a program to eliminate the government budget deficit. The growth of consumer spending would be reduced through a tax increase and the growth of government spending would be cut as well, but investment spending would be maintained. Although this course of action would, for a time, mean a slower growth of consumer and government outlays, it is clearly superior to any of the other four approaches in securing the long-run advance of American living standards and maintaining the United States as a vigorous dynamic economy.

Fortunately, the nation has already made some progress in implementing this fourth approach. The overall (or consolidated) budget deficit has been reduced from a 1986 peak of $221 billion, or 5.3 percent of gross national product (GNP), to approximately $155 billion, or 3.2 percent in fiscal year 1988. However, with no further change in budgetary policy, and with no tax increase, the deficit will remain at $120 billion–

Table 1-2. *Historical and Projected Growth Rates of National Output and Spending*
Percent a year

Period	Output per capita	Government and consumer purchases per capita
Historical		
1950–73	2.1	2.1
1973–79	1.2	1.2
1979–87	1.2	1.8
Projected		
1987–95	1.7	0.7

Source: Lawrence, "International Dimension," in this volume, table 2-1; and authors' calculations.

$150 billion through 1993. National spending cannot be brought into line with national production unless the remaining deficit is eliminated.

The exact balance between tax increases and spending cuts needed to achieve that goal is more a political than an economic decision. But a review of the budget numbers shows that any serious attack on the deficit must include substantial tax increases as well as spending cuts. Although the budget deficit cannot and should not be brought into balance in a year—that would be too big a wrench for the economy—it could, without danger of an excessively rapid adjustment, be reduced at a pace of perhaps $40 billion a year, reaching zero in four years.

The reduction in the growth of per capita consumer and government spending that would be entailed during the next eight years by the preferred policy alternative is shown in table 1-2. The estimates optimistically assume that unemployment falls to 5.0 percent and output per worker improves a little; as a consequence, the annual growth in per capita output rises from 1.2 percent to 1.7 percent a year. The estimates in table 1-2 then assume that the balance of payments deficit (balance on current account) declines to zero by 1995; the merchandise trade deficit, which was $160 billion last year, is converted into a modest surplus in that year, sufficient to cover the annual interest payments on overseas debt.[1] For this to occur, domestic spending per capita will have to rise by less than the growth in output (GNP) per capita, to make room for the rise in exports and substitution of domestic production for imports.

1. The current account deficit consists of the trade deficit plus the net outflow of interest and dividend payments to foreigners (and a few other smaller items that are not important for the present purpose).

Table 1-2 assumes that the required reduction in the growth of spending will not come at the expense of business investment but will be concentrated among consumers and government. As a result per capita government and consumer spending combined can grow only at 0.7 percent a year over the next seven years (to 1995), a much slower rate of increase than at any time in the postwar period, and far below the growth rate of the last seven years. Once the adjustment is made, however, the per capita growth of national spending can rise again and proceed more or less in line with the growth of per capita output.

While eliminating the nation's overspending will not be easy, the adjustment does not mean an absolute reduction in living standards. The standard of living could still increase, although at a much slower rate than in the recent past. With this temporary reduction in the growth of current living standards, the United States can put its economy on a much sounder footing for sustained long-run progress.

If the nation's productivity growth could be substantially raised, then spending and production could be brought into balance by an improvement of supply rather than a reduction in consumption. However, it would take a major improvement in productivity—doubling the current 1 percent annual growth of output per worker—to allow American living standards to keep growing at the pace of the preceding eight years in the face of the short-term spending adjustment recommended here. The United States has been experiencing slow productivity growth for some fifteen years now, and no one can satisfactorily account for the slowdown or confidently suggest policies that would reverse it. Thus in the more likely event that a significant burden of adjustment remains, those who have been the beneficiaries of the national overspending of the past six years ought to bear that burden rather than pass it along—with interest—to the next generation.

In short, the picture of the recent economic past and the projected economic future has many shadings—some bright, some dark. The mixed assessment seems to be closely reflected in the opinions that most Americans hold about their own, and the nation's, economic fortunes. Survey after survey shows that most people are fairly satisfied with many aspects of their own recent economic history. In view of the economy's good overall performance on employment and inflation, and given the spending splurge of recent years, that opinion is not surprising. The same surveys, however, suggest that many Americans are concerned and uneasy about the longer-run prospects for the economy and thus for their children. Without being able to pinpoint the problems, they nevertheless sense correctly that some difficult, unpopular, and painful adjustments must be made.

Public discussions and popular concerns also reflect the effects on individuals and communities of the slowdown in the growth of American productivity and incomes. As noted earlier, when the growth of average income slows down and stays low for a long period, the number of losers—people who experience absolute declines in their standard of living—will rise substantially. Thus even as most people report that their economic conditions have improved in recent years, a growing minority of people feel that they have "lost out" in the economic struggle. The belief has spread widely that the number of "good middle-class jobs" has been declining.

The new president will have to face these economic realities and perceptions. Virtually all of them pertain directly or indirectly to American living standards: what has been happening to them, on average, and for different groups; how they will be affected by the economic adjustments that our country sooner or later will have to undertake; and what can be done to enhance the prospects for their improvement.

Summary of the Book

In chapter 2 of this book, Robert Lawrence observes that between 1950 and 1979, the United States lived largely within its means. Annual growth in per capita spending—private and public—was matched by increases in domestic production. But much has changed in the 1980s. In this decade, Americans maintained their spending growth at almost the pace of the three previous decades, but the growth rate of their incomes and production has dropped. Americans have satisfied about 25 percent of the growth in their living standards by borrowing from foreign creditors.

Lawrence calculates the impact on the average American of gradually bringing the patterns of national spending and production into balance. For example, if national output grows at an average rate of 2.5 percent a year, a reasonable mid-range assumption, per capita output in 1987 dollars would grow by a total of $2,288 through 1995. But achieving current account balance by 1995 will leave room for per capita spending to improve each year by a much lower amount; the balance would be devoted to other purposes: $707 per capita to additional net exports;

$141 per capita to interest on new foreign debt accumulated between now and 1995; $121 per capita to net fixed investment; and $413 per capita in losses from a decline in our terms of trade (a loss of purchasing power because of lower prices of American exports relative to the prices of imports). After all these subtractions are accounted for, per capita spending (or living standards) would rise by $906.

Lawrence demonstrates that growth in American living standards will be far more affected by an adjustment in national spending patterns than by any continued deterioration in U.S. competitiveness. Using historical relationships that measure the relative attractiveness of U.S. and foreign goods, he finds that past deterioration has lowered living standards by an insignificant amount—less than one-twentieth of a percent a year. If this deterioration continues, per capita spending will be lower in 1995 by a further tiny amount.

The case for adjusting future spending patterns—and thus temporarily accepting some lower growth in living standards—rests primarily on the judgment that the United States needs to increase its rate of savings. It is conceivable, even if far from certain, that the United States could, for some time, continue to run a large budget deficit, attract substantial inflows of foreign capital, and sustain a large trade deficit. If the trade deficit and the inflow of foreign funds into the United States were being used to raise the national rate of investment, then continued large deficits might not be a problem. But the United States has not applied its increased foreign borrowing to fund additional investment. To the contrary, real per capita fixed investment in 1987 was lower than in 1979. Accordingly, the United States must increase its savings rate and reduce dependence on foreign creditors. Thus, even if the United States could, it should not postpone the necessary adjustments.

Postponing adjustment could have other costs. Each year that the nation delays adjustment it adds greatly—more than $100 billion a year—to the outstanding stock of net foreign debt. Given the uncertain state of knowledge about how investors allocate their portfolios among various currencies, it is difficult to predict how investors' willingness to hold dollars will be affected by this buildup in debt. But continued large current account deficits, coupled with the United States' perceived refusal to deal with the budget deficit, would make the American economy vulnerable to a sudden disorderly flight from the dollar or a "dollar strike" at some time in the future, triggered perhaps by an unexpected outside event. This development would result in a sharp fall in the dollar and a large rise in interest rates, perhaps sufficient to trigger a recession. The Federal Reserve could then be reluctant to use its weapon of easy money because of the rise in import prices that would follow the large dollar decline (which could also worsen if monetary policy were relaxed). Moreover, even if a recession could be avoided—by some combination of good luck and skillful management—the rapid readjustments in national spending that would be required by the steep dollar decline would be far more abrupt and painful than the gradual adjustments in domestic spending recommended here.

In chapter 3, Robert Litan explores the dangers of a dollar strike and other possible causes of a future economic downturn, which clearly would reduce any advances in living standards below those projected by Lawrence. Litan begins by observing that, in the absence of a major shock, there is no reason why the economy cannot continue its current expansion. If accompanied by an appropriately expansionary monetary policy, a phased reduction in the federal budget deficit will not lead to recession.

Paradoxically, however, if meaningful deficit reduction measures are not taken, Litan argues, the economy is likely to face its greatest danger of a recession. Ignoring the need to reduce the deficit would postpone the necessary spending adjustments—at a time when the economy is operating at or close to its capacity—and thus signal to investors that the United States may have lost the ability to manage its financial affairs. In addition, continued large budget deficits will require the Federal Reserve to keep interest rates high to prevent inflation from accelerating. But by propping up the exchange value of the dollar, a high interest rate policy would prevent the trade balance from reaching long-run equilibrium, enlarging current uncertainties about the dollar's ultimate value. In such an environment a sudden flight from the dollar could be more likely.

Litan also considers other possible triggers of a recession, including another oil shock, drought, and another stock market collapse like the one of October 1987. He argues that a sudden run-up in oil prices, large enough to generate a recession, is unlikely. It is also improbable that another crisis in the financial markets would independently cause a recession. Rather, if another stock price collapse were to occur, it would probably reflect other triggering events, such as a sudden run from the dollar.

If a downturn occurs, how deep is it likely to be? Litan suggests that the answer depends on the nature of the shock that triggers it. He estimates that a moderate recession, similar to the three downturns between 1948 and 1958, would cost the nation approximately $500 billion in lost output, or roughly $2,000 a person. A severe recession, like the 1973–75 and 1981–82 oil shock contractions, would entail losses roughly twice as large.

Finally, Litan examines three key structural conditions in the economy that many believe may affect the depth and severity of the next recession. He concludes that the growth of private sector debt over the last decade could deepen the next downturn, but it is also possible that higher leverage among corporations will simply cause the negative effects of a future downturn to be distributed differently than in prior contractions, more on the corporate business sector and comparatively less on construction. Current weakness among the nation's depository institutions could worsen the next contraction, but the greater danger is that another recession will strain many more financial institutions and raise the long-run budgetary and social cost of forcing insolvent banks and thrifts to close or merge with healthier partners.

In Litan's view, the progress made in reducing the federal budget deficit may be the most important influence on the depth of the next downturn. If the economy enters a recession sometime soon—before further serious cuts in the deficit are made—policymakers may be reluctant to stimulate the economy through fiscal measures, which could prolong and worsen the contraction. A recession arising from a sudden flight from the dollar could inhibit the use of either monetary or fiscal policy, given the price-raising consequences of a steep dollar decline.

In chapter 4 Frank Levy looks at changes in the distribution of income among families and individuals, and among workers in different industries and with different educational levels. He begins by observing that average real incomes and hourly earnings have barely grown since 1973. Although some have attributed this disappointing performance to a rising share of poorly paid jobs in the service sector, Levy finds that the dominant underlying causes were macroeconomic events—the productivity slowdown and the two oil shocks of the 1970s.

At the same time, sharp differences occurred in earnings growth among different groups. Women of most ages and educational levels have increased their earnings (both because of higher wages and more hours worked); most men have not. Indeed, slightly more college educated males were employed in goods production in 1986 than in 1973, yet their average incomes stagnated during this period. Among both sexes, however, less educated workers have fared significantly worse than others. Younger men with a high school education or less suffered especially large income losses.

One of the paradoxes of the last fifteen years is that while earnings per worker have been stagnant, income per capita has risen markedly, from $9,926 (in 1987 dollars) in 1973 to $12,150 in 1987, a 22 percent increase. Levy explains the apparent contradiction by pointing to two significant changes. Female participation in the labor force has increased enormously, from 35 percent in the 1950s to 57 percent currently. At the same time, both men and women are postponing marriage. And when they do get married, they are having fewer children. With a larger fraction of the population working to support fewer children, income per capita has been able to rise much more rapidly than earnings per worker. This trend is unlikely to continue, however, since both the rise in the female labor force participation rate and the decline in the birth rate have leveled off. In the future, income per capita will probably grow no faster than earnings per worker.

Levy also finds several noteworthy changes in the distribution of family incomes between 1973 and 1986. Much of the recent concern about income distribution has centered on the alleged decline of the "middle class." If by the middle one means families with annual incomes between $20,000 and $50,000 (in 1986 dollars), then the assertion is true: fewer American families fell into this category in 1986 than in 1973. But this is only because the proportion of families earning more than $50,000 has risen, while the share below $20,000 has remained constant.

A closer look at the distribution of families with incomes below $20,000 reveals a more disturbing picture, however. The proportion of families earning less than $10,000 has increased. Such families account for an increasing share of American children, from 10 percent in 1973 to 16 percent in 1986. One-third of the nation's children now live in families with incomes below $20,000. At the same time the proportion of children in families with incomes above $50,000 has risen (reflecting more two-earner families). In sum, the standard picture of a shrinking middle class with growing concentrations at the top and bottom is not a good description of families taken together, but it is not a bad description of families with children.

What lies ahead? The answer depends on future productivity growth for the nation as a whole and the educational attainment for specific individuals. For example, if output per hour worked should grow at only

1.25 percent a year—roughly the rate of the last eight years—then 30-year-old college educated men in 1986 will only earn at age 50 about $1,700 more, on average, than their fathers with similar education levels earned in 1986. If productivity increases by 1.9 percent a year, the picture for this group becomes much brighter; at 50 the men's average earnings will exceed their fathers' 1986 earnings by $10,000. But even with more rapid productivity growth, men with only a high school education now entering the labor force cannot expect to earn at age 50 what high school educated 50-year-olds earn today.

Robert Crandall in chapter 5 turns to another distributional dimension—differences in wage and income growth across different regions of the United States. Part of the concern about the fortunes of the middle class centers on the closures of manufacturing plants in the so-called Rust Belt states of the North and East, as well as a weakening of income growth in those states.

The evidence Crandall reviews tells a different story. In fact, there has been a long-running shift of population, income, and firms from the Rust Belt to the Sun Belt states in the South and West since 1930. That trend continued for manufacturing in the 1980s, but it did not occur because the Rust Belt was "cursed" by containing an excessively high proportion of declining industries. From 1967 through 1985, growth in the Sun Belt was faster in almost *every* industry. Moreover, plant closures were not disproportionately located in the Rust Belt. States in that region of the country have been losing ground not because more plants have closed there but because they have been unable to attract *new* plants.

Crandall rejects several popular theories for the Rust Belt's declining appeal, including unionization and higher wages. In particular, if wage differentials were a strong motivating force for industrial relocation, one would expect to see a narrowing of the wage gap between the Rust and Sun Belts. In fact, manufacturing wage differentials have not changed much since 1967. Crandall also dismisses the attraction of raw materials located in the South and West as the explanation for recent population and income shifts. With changing production technologies and improvements in transportation, the location of raw materials is far less important than in earlier decades. Crandall concludes that the Sun Belt has become more attractive because of its weather, as well as because many of its states offer a better business climate.

He then turns to developments outside of manufacturing and finds that they are of equal, if not greater, importance in explaining regional differences. Indeed, the gap between per capita incomes in the Sun Belt and Rust Belt narrowed between 1930 and 1980, despite the fact that manufacturing wages in the Rust Belt remained relatively high, precisely because the Sun Belt states were successful in raising incomes through jobs in services rather than manufacturing. In the 1980s, the income gap between the two regions has again widened somewhat, but only because of the growth in nonmanufacturing industries located in New England and the Middle Atlantic states.

Disparities in economic performance across regions, reflected in the dispersion of unemployment rates across states, have widened since the 1982 recession. But Crandall finds that plant closures are not the reason. Instead, unusual instability in energy and agricultural markets and extraordinary fluctuations in interest rates have marked the 1980s. These conditions explain the increase in the greater regional dispersion of average incomes.

Crandall's analysis implies that if in the future macroeconomic policies create a more stable economic environment, the dislocations seen during this decade should moderate and disparities in the historical geographic trends should also continue. People will probably keep moving to the Sun Belt, and incomes in the states in this region should continue to approach those in the Rust Belt. Disparities in unemployment across states should also narrow.

If the United States is to improve economic performance on a sustained basis, the nation must increase productivity. Martin Neil Baily and Margaret M. Blair address part of this challenge in chapter 6 by focusing on the causes of the productivity slowdown since 1973 and the possibilities for reversing it.

Baily and Blair illustrate the dramatic effects of the slowdown with a simple exercise. They show that if productivity had continued to grow throughout the postwar period at the 3.25 percent rate recorded between 1948 and 1965, output in 1987 would have been about 50 percent higher than it was. To be concrete, the income of the median American family— roughly $30,000 in 1987—would have been about $45,000.

Pinning down the cause of the U.S. productivity slowdown, however, has been difficult, partly because it has been pervasive not only in different industries in the United States but throughout the major nations of the industrialized world as well. At the same time, Baily and Blair note a significant divergence in productivity growth rates across broad sectors of the economy since 1979. Manufacturing productivity has advanced at 3.3 percent a year, roughly its post-World War II norm and significantly higher than its 1973–79 performance. The productivity of the nonmanufacturing sector, however, has barely grown in the 1980s.

Baily and Blair report that when all is said and done, only about one percentage point of the 2.44 percentage point drop in the annual productivity growth rate since 1973 can be attributed to identifiable causes. Capital per worker did grow a little less rapidly, but that accounted for only a modest part of the productivity slowdown. A decline in educational quality did not play a material role. Nor can the slowdown be attributed to measurement error; productivity in the service sector, the area of the economy in which productivity is most difficult to measure, rose by 2.4 percent a year during the 1948–65 period, but advanced at only 0.1 percent annually from 1979 to 1987. Small contributions to the decline, however, can be attributed to the end of the population shift from farms to self-employed businesses and a rise in the costs of health and safety regulation.

Given the large unexplained part of the productivity slowdown, Baily and Blair turn their attention to failures by American business managers as a possible reason for the falloff in productivity growth. Many have alleged that American managers have increasingly neglected long-term research and investment, concentrating instead on short-run profits. No hard evidence indicates that this is true. Nevertheless, there is no escaping the fact that in many industries, firms located in the United States have lost ground in world markets.

Part of the reason, Baily and Blair suggest, may lie in the increasing volatility of the United States economy since 1973—periodic oil shocks, erratic movements in interest and exchange rates, and big swings in inflation. Any manager would have difficulty planning and making appropriate decisions for such an unpredictable long run.

But Baily and Blair also pin some of the blame for the troubles of American industry on a reluctance by many firms to compete aggressively for market share by cutting prices, a tactic that has worked well for Japanese manufacturers. One of the reasons why productivity in American manufacturing has rebounded in the 1980s is that, because of the overvalued dollar and recession earlier in the decade, firms in the United States have been forced to improve their performance simply in order to survive against the increasingly stiff challenges posed by their overseas competitors.

The wave of corporate mergers in the 1980s has also stimulated a

vigorous debate about the effectiveness of American business management. Some contend that takeover threats discipline managers and offer
incentives for them to increase productivity. Others see many mergers
as inefficient, wasting social resources.

Baily and Blair suggest that this debate is tangential to the productivity
issue. Mergers are more a symptom than a cause. Merger activity is
highly episodic—the 1980s merger boom is the fourth such wave since
the late 1800s. This wave-like behavior suggests that mergers represent
a response to basic structural shifts in the economy that make old
organizational forms obsolete and open up opportunities for new forms
to succeed. Although many takeovers will fail to improve the performance
of the firms involved, they nonetheless facilitate experimentation and
innovation in organizational design. Hence, proposals to limit takeovers
could inhibit productivity growth in the long run by locking firms into
old ways of doing things.

Instead, Baily and Blair offer a number of suggestions that, on the
basis of available evidence, would be far more likely to enhance productivity. These proposals include increased federal funding for technology
research, as well as a shift in emphasis toward encouraging the development part of research and development (R&D); continuation and
perhaps modification of the current R&D tax credit; elimination of the
current tax advantage of debt over equity; enhanced personal tax
deductions for worker retraining and mandatory transferability of employer-provided benefits such as health-care coverage to encourage labor
mobility. In addition, Baily and Blair urge a review of American
intellectual property laws to see if new ways can be found to ensure that
innovators reap the rewards from their new products and production
processes.

At the same time, Baily and Blair caution against measures to limit
foreign investment. Such investment introduces new technology and
managerial techniques. We in the United States also have much to learn
from Japan's success. American managers must improve their ability to
learn from their foreign competitors, adapting and improving upon other
countries' technology. American firms could reap greater benefits by
paying closer attention to incremental improvements in technology as
their Japanese counterparts do, rather than betting their scarce R&D
funds heavily on finding a single major breakthrough. Our antitrust
administrators, meanwhile, can learn that bigness is not necessarily bad
and that there are benefits when groups of companies support one another
to reduce risk.

It is far from clear, however, that government-directed industrial policy—by directing traffic and specifying directions for research—guarantees success. Economic policymakers in other countries, notably Great Britain, have misjudged market forces. The safest, and most appropriate, role for government is to provide broad, general support of technology development, leaving to the marketplace the job of sorting out the winning and losing industries.

Precisely because so much about previous productivity performance remains unexplained, Baily and Blair conclude by outlining a number of ways in which our understanding of this issue might be improved. In particular, they suggest giving priority to research into industrial structure and organizational design. Theoretical research should be directed at explaining empirical realities rather than elaborating on mathematical possibilities. Empirical research should stress international comparisons of institutional performance—why some other countries have been successful with approaches to industrial organization and government policy that are much different from ours.

Better management will be enhanced by a better work force. The nation's well-being stems importantly from the skills of its people. These are, in turn, heavily influenced by their education and training. Unfortunately, as Richard Murnane reports in chapter 7, the quality of American education, as measured by students' performance on tests, declined from the mid-1960s through the mid-1970s. Although there is little quantitative evidence thus far that the deterioration significantly helped to diminish productivity growth after 1973, the effects of poor schooling may show up in the future. In any event, there is little doubt that a well-trained work force is essential over the long run to maintaining a first-class economy. As a result, Americans face the challenge of altering the direction of U.S. educational policy to maximize the potential of the work force of the future.

Current educational policy is not moving in this direction. Too much of the effort to reform the schools, however well intentioned, has been directed at merely improving the ability of students to read and to perform routine arithmetic. In a dynamic economy in which new technologies are constantly bringing new products to market and changing the way products are made and services delivered, this approach to educating the future labor force is not the ideal one.

Instead, the United States should be teaching children the crucial skills necessary for success on the job—the ability to use reading and mathematical skills to solve problems in the workplace. Moreover, these skills must be taught not only to the select few who choose to go on to professional careers but on a highly practical level to the entire student population. In short, the United States must have as its national educational objective the teaching of problem-solving skills to all students.

Unfortunately, the United States currently falls far short of meeting this objective. A sizable number of American students, while able to read and perform basic arithmetic exercises, have not shown an ability to solve multistep problems of the sort that workplaces require. Children from poor families or from minority backgrounds fare worst of all, and they are the ones who will constitute a growing proportion of the labor force of the future.

Although by explicit policy choice the role of the federal government in setting educational policy has been limited, federal policymakers can help promote important national educational goals. Murnane recommends six affirmative measures.

The Head Start program has shown significant promise and should be extended to as many eligible children from poor families as possible (only 20 percent of the 2.4 million poor children are currently served). The summer training and education program (STEP), designed to enhance the reading and mathematics of disadvantaged children during the summer months, has a similar positive report card and should be enhanced. Federal funding of compensatory education programs—aimed at school districts serving poor children—is desirable especially if the funds can be precisely targeted on those who particularly need them; according to Murnane, the recent increase in funding levels and refinements in targeting are justified. Given evidence that American students fall behind their Japanese counterparts in mathematics as early as the fifth grade, summer training institutes for math teachers should be open not only to high school teachers but to those from junior and primary schools as well. Incentives for inducing college math majors to teach should be upgraded; perhaps federal tuition grants should be given in exchange for minimum commitments to teach in urban schools for a specific period.

Perhaps most important, Murnane recommends revising school curricula and tests to focus more extensively on literacy and problem-solving skills. He demonstrates that curricula and the content of tests are intertwined and self-reinforcing. If the United States wants its future labor force to be trained in problem solving, then tests must be designed to measure those skills, thus offering incentives to teachers to teach them. To facilitate this process, Murnane urges the federal government to fund the development of exemplary grade-specific exercises that focus on problem solving. He also suggests that the federal government keep track of students' progress toward acquiring these skills.

Finally, Murnane points to evidence casting strong doubt on the wisdom of several widely discussed education reform proposals. Merit pay programs for teachers, for example, have not so far proved successful in improving student performance. In fact, they may detract from the teamwork by teachers that is often necessary for success. Longer school periods—either days or hours each day—have not proved cost beneficial and are unlikely to do so unless new material is added to school curricula. And simply introducing computers into the classroom is not a remedy if, as is often the case, it results in more drill and practice of basic reading and computation skills.

Murnane's recommendations are designed to ensure that a greater number of students acquire the problem-solving skills needed for their future success in the workplace. But he cautions that even better educational instruction will not materially improve the job prospects of many children from poor families, where the resources and environment conducive to educational progress are often lacking. In the end, poor families need more income if they are to provide the environment that can facilitate the educational progress of their children.

Conclusion

American economic policy faces two principal challenges: national overspending and sluggish productivity growth. The country must move promptly to eliminate the national overspending that has characterized the recent past. Most mainstream professional thinking is fairly unified on what must be done. Because the required course of action is—in the short run—a painful one, neither the public nor most political leaders are anxious to hear the consensus of the experts. Attacking the problem of America's sluggish rate of productivity growth, however, is less beset by political difficulties. In fact, political leaders eagerly seek suggestions. But, although many experts have offered proposals, there is little professional consensus about what to do. Ironically, for the problem on which professional economic advisers offer widely agreed-on advice, political leaders have not listened. For the problem on which political leaders eagerly seek advice, the experts have little agreed-on advice to offer.[2]

Nevertheless, we hope this book in some way helps to relax both the political and economic constraints on dealing with the two problems we discuss: overspending and productivity growth. We offer arguments to soften the political opposition to the solution of the overspending problem. We summarize the professional consensus on ways of speeding up productivity growth and identify the aspects of this problem that need further research.

---

2. This situation resembles, but is not exactly the same as, what Alan S. Blinder has labeled Murphy's law of economic policy: "Economists have the least influence on policy where they know the most and are most agreed; they have the most influence on policy where they know the least and disagree most vehemently." Alan S. Blinder, *Hard Heads, Soft Hearts: Tough-Minded Economists for a Just Society* (Addison-Wesley, 1987), pp. 1–2.

CHAPTER TWO

The International Dimension

Robert Z. Lawrence

AMERICAN living standards are determined by three factors. First, and most important, our living standards depend on national production. Second, we can for a time spend beyond our own production by borrowing from abroad—importing more goods and services than we export and financing the resulting balance of payments deficit by issuing obligations to foreign investors. But we cannot keep this up forever; eventually we will be forced to bring our living standards back into line with national production and indeed to produce more than we spend in order to pay interest on the debts we have accumulated. Finally, our living standards can be affected by the terms at which we exchange exports for imports. The more favorable our terms of trade—the higher the price of our exports relative to the price of imports—the better off we can be.

This chapter addresses primarily the implications of reversing the buildup of foreign debt in the 1980s, which increased by a record $160 billion in 1987. Reversing this trend—that is, bringing national spending in line with national production—will be manageable, but costly. Under reasonably optimistic assumptions, if net foreign borrowing were to end by 1995, living standards for the average American are projected to improve by a total of 5.7 percent between 1987 and 1995, only one-third of their growth in the past eight years. Future living standard growth could be either higher or lower than this projection if the annual growth in output per worker exceeds or falls short of the mid-range projection of 1.0 percent.

America's competitiveness, or trade performance, difficulties are small by comparison. A loss of competitiveness implies that the prices of

I am indebted to Edward M. Bernstein, Edward F. Denison, Peter Hooper, Stephen Marris, and Joseph A. Pechman for helpful advice. I also benefited from presenting seminars at the Brookings Institution. I thank Amy Salsbury for research assistance and Evelyn Taylor for text processing.

American goods in world markets must fall to finance imports. A fall in the price of exports relative to the price of imports (the terms of trade) adversely affects American standards of living because we must give up more resources to obtain a given amount of imports. The analysis here shows that between 1973 and 1987 the United States required a continuous fall in the terms of trade to maintain a constant trade balance. But the required decline was relatively small. A persistence of these trade performance problems would depress living standards by a total of less than half a percent over the next seven years.

A central choice for the nation in the years immediately ahead will be how fast, if at all, it is prepared to change its spending patterns and thus reduce its reliance on foreign creditors. The analysis of this chapter suggests that the payments of interest from accumulating more debt are not the most important cost associated with more borrowing. The principal costs of delaying adjustment will be the dislocation caused by the need to move U.S. workers into export industries and the difficulties of reducing U.S. government and private spending. These costs are greater the more rapidly such shifts must be made. The wisest course is for the United States itself to make the adjustment in its own spending at a reasonable pace rather than to have that course forced on it at some unpredictable time and pace by foreign creditors.

The United States in the Global Economy

The economic relations between the United States and the rest of the world have changed dramatically since the beginning of the postwar period. During the 1950s and 1960s the U.S. economy was preeminent globally and was virtually self-sufficient. America was clearly number one: U.S. GNP (gross national product) per capita in 1950 was double that of Europe and was six times greater than Japan's. U.S. economic performance was strong. Between 1950 and 1973 per capita incomes rose at an annual rate of 2.1 percent. Although growth was sometimes interrupted by recessions, and inflation presented a recurrent problem, faith in sustained growth over the long term proved justified. Structural changes, like the population shift from rural areas, were viewed as vital elements of progress. Essentially, America's economic fate was determined at home: most of what the United States consumed it produced, and exports and imports combined accounted for less than 10 percent of GNP.

Since the 1970s, however, the U.S. economy has been much less dominant globally. By 1975 growth in the rest of the developed world had considerably narrowed the U.S. lead in living standards. GDP (gross domestic product) per capita in Germany and Japan was 83 and 68 percent, respectively, of the U.S. level.[1] It was not that the U.S. performance was disappointing; rather it was that the other industrial countries had extraordinarily high growth rates as they swiftly introduced advanced U.S. technology into their own economies. All through this period the involvement of the United States in world trade grew steadily. By 1974 the sum of American exports and imports had grown to almost 20 percent of GNP. As a result, foreign events such as OPEC pricing decisions, Russian grain purchases, and Japanese automotive innovation deeply affected the U.S. economy. In the 1980s, principally because of a large government budget deficit, U.S. net national savings fell from more than 8 percent of net national product (NNP) to 3 percent. With domestic spending outpacing production, the United States ran large trade deficits financed by foreign borrowing.

Economic conditions have had an important effect on American attitudes toward international trade. During the 1950s, when growth was strong and the United States enjoyed a position of relative dominance and independence, Americans viewed the world with confidence. Sure of their lead, business and labor agreed that free trade would benefit the nation. America's concerns about Europe and Japan focused on their economic weakness, and the United States promoted economic development in those areas as a means of containing Soviet expansion.

Since 1973 the U.S. economy has performed less well. Growth has been retarded by three recessions and a slump in the rate of productivity advance. In the minds of many Americans, the increased internationalization of the economy in the 1970s and 1980s and its own weaker performance are causally linked. Many now question the ability of the economy to sustain the rise in living standards recorded in the past, and they blame U.S. international economic relations for these diminished prospects. The erosion in America's technological lead, growing international interdependence, rising international indebtedness, and the

1. Irving B. Kravis, Alan Heston, and Robert Summers, *World Product and Income: International Comparisons of Real Gross Product* (Johns Hopkins University Press, 1982), p. 19. GDP is GNP plus the net earnings from capital investments abroad (or minus the net flow of earnings to foreigners).

severe trade difficulties have dramatically changed U.S. attitudes. Some now see foreign economic development as a threat rather than a benefit to U.S. prosperity, and they advocate restrictions on trade and investment. More specifically, the concerns about U.S. international economic relations center on the rise in U.S. international indebtedness and on U.S. trade performance:

Spending patterns. As a result of its borrowing in this decade, the United States has emerged as the world's largest net debtor nation. There is fear that this trend is not sustainable—that foreigners at some point will cease lending or demand repayment, producing potentially severe disruptions in the U.S. economy.[2] Even if foreign creditors continue to finance America's borrowing, U.S. debt-servicing requirements will become increasingly burdensome, requiring a larger portion of U.S. output and dragging down U.S. living standards.

Trade performance. Recently a number of concerns have arisen that U.S. living standards could be jeopardized by developments in international trade.[3] Several reasons have been cited. In a world with mobile capital and technology, firms located in low-wage countries can underprice those located in the United States.[4] A second concern is that American firms no longer produce the best and latest products and are losing important markets to European and Japanese competitors. Eventually, it is feared, the United States will be reduced to selling only agricultural and other natural-resource-intensive products or be forced to lower wages and profits. Finally, because many foreign governments support targeted industries with subsidies, selective procurement, and trade protection, foreign producers have a distinct advantage over Americans. Foreign policies capture benefits for their nationals at American expense.

The balance of this chapter appraises these concerns about U.S. international economic relations and considers their implications for U.S. living standards. It first measures the effect of trade performance on

2. See, for example, Peter G. Peterson, "The Morning After," *Atlantic Monthly*, October 1987, pp. 43–69. The prospects and implications of such a dollar strike are explored in detail by Robert Litan in chapter 3.

3. See, for example, John M. Culbertson, "The Folly of Free Trade," *Harvard Business Review*, vol. 64 (September–October 1986), pp. 122–28.

4. Another concern, according to Dornbusch, is the spending patterns of the newly industrializing countries (NICs)—they export manufactured goods mainly to the United States but import proportionately more from Europe and Japan—which creates a "triangle" problem requiring continual dollar devaluation. See Rudiger Dornbusch, "Further Dollar Depreciation," *NBER Reporter* (Winter 1987–88), pp. 8–11.

living standards. It argues that low foreign wages, a loss in the U.S. technological lead, or foreign industrial policies will reduce U.S. living standards if they force Americans to earn less on exports and to pay more for imports. When used with caution, therefore, the terms of trade (the ratio of export to import prices) offer an important clue about the impact of trade on U.S. living standards. This insight is then used to distinguish between the effect on U.S. living standards of domestic factors (productivity and employment growth) and of international factors (changes in the terms of trade, net foreign borrowing, and net foreign earnings). Next, an econometric analysis provides an estimate of the contribution of poor U.S. trade performance to changes in the U.S. terms of trade. Then follows a quantification of the effect of future changes in U.S. spending patterns on living standards. The concluding section discusses policy implications.

The Effect of International Developments on the Growth of Living Standards

There are two principal ways in which developments in the international sector of an economy can affect living standards. The first is tied to a nation's spending and saving behavior. In a world where both goods and finances can cross borders, a country can temporarily consume beyond its means by borrowing from abroad, initially raising its living standards relative to its own productive capabilities, and then lowering its rate of spending when, as inevitably occurs, the inflow of foreign funds dries up.[5] The second revolves around long-run alterations in a country's competitiveness, or trade performance. To the extent a nation can improve the terms on which it exchanges its exports for the imports it wants—its terms of trade—that country's living standards will improve, and, of course, vice-versa.

When a country, deliberately or unwittingly, embarks on a course of spending more than it produces, a complex chain of events is set in motion. The United States in the first half of the 1980s provides an example. Stimulated by large structural deficits in the federal budget,

---

5. Through international trade and borrowing a country can also invest more than its own national savings by importing capital from abroad. So long as the investment projects have a rate of return higher than the cost of overseas borrowing, the results will be a long-run improvement in the country's living standards.

domestic spending rose sharply relative to national output and income—in other words, national saving declined. The United States was able to obtain the additional goods it wanted by running a trade deficit and financing it with overseas borrowing.

Interest rates and the dollar exchange rate adjusted to make this spending pattern possible. When national savings declined while business and consumer demand for borrowed funds remained at a high level, the competition for borrowed funds drove U.S. interest rates above those in other world financial centers. Because foreign investors—Japanese life insurance companies, German pension funds, and so on—could get better returns by investing in the United States than they could get at home, they were eager to lend some of their own savings to us. But to invest in the United States they needed dollars, and their demand for dollars, added to normal commercial demand, drove up the exchange value of the dollar above the level that would have kept U.S. exports more or less in line with imports. The increasingly expensive dollar penalized U.S. exports, reduced the price of imports, and led to a large trade deficit.

All this affected American living standards in a number of ways. The principal effect was to enable the United States temporarily to push domestic spending above domestic production and so to enjoy living standards higher than were warranted by national productivity. Americans also gained as the dollar appreciated—our terms of trade improved, and each dollar of U.S. exports bought more imports. But on the downside, our nation incurred obligations to pay interest and dividends in the future to the foreign investors who financed the balance of payments deficits.

Ultimately, foreigners will not continue, without substantial increases in our interest rates, to finance our excess spending, especially when their funds are devoted not to investment in productive assets but to consumption. In short the spending pattern of the 1980s has to unwind. The nature and magnitude of the consequences of this coming reversal for American living standards are discussed later in this chapter.[6]

As outlined above, the main forces that drive a nation's balance of payments into a large surplus or deficit position are changes in its spending and saving behavior. Despite this fact, there is a widespread

---

6. The same essential story can be told in reverse for countries like Japan and Germany, which for some years now have been spending substantially less than national production and investing the difference abroad.

belief that trade deficits arise, not from national spending patterns, but from a deterioration in the trading advantages of American industries. For example, foreign products become cheaper than items made in the United States because of low wages or government subsidies, or they become more desirable because of better foreign quality controls and improved technology.[7] In fact, such changes in the relative trade performance of American industries will only affect the trade balance in the short run. The trade deficit may rise temporarily, but the loss of foreign markets will put downward pressure on U.S. wages and prices, and, more important, will tend to depress the exchange value of the dollar. U.S. export prices to foreign buyers will fall and U.S. import prices will rise to the point where the trade deficit turns around and moves back to an equilibrium determined by the country's fundamental spending-saving behavior. In the process, however, the deterioration in the terms of trade, which requires selling more exports to buy a given volume of imports, will exert a downward influence on American living standards. This is the second main way in which the international sector of our economy affects the growth of our living standards.

America's trade performance, and its terms of trade, can be favorably or adversely influenced by factors other than the quality of its export- and import-competitive industries. If, for example, the economies of major U.S. customers begin to grow rapidly, the demand for U.S. exports will rise sharply, and eventually—after a temporary period of trade surplus—the U.S. terms of trade will improve. The spurt in demand for U.S. exports will enable the nation to raise its prices, mainly through an exchange rate appreciation that can now take place without throwing America into a trade deficit. The reverse occurs if economic growth among major U.S. customers falls off, as in fact happened in Europe during the 1980s.

These relationships are illustrated in figure 2-1, which sets a moving average of the U.S. terms of trade (excluding oil and agricultural prices)

7. Cheaper foreign goods may help or hurt U.S. living standards. Lower import prices will *raise* U.S. living standards, although not all Americans may benefit—domestic manufacturers of those products may be forced to lower their wages—and in the short run there may be adjustment costs. Lower prices of products competing with U.S. exports worsen our terms of trade and thus reduce our living standards. See, for example, John R. Hicks, "An Inaugural Lecture," *Oxford Economic Papers*, vol. 5 (June 1953), pp. 117–35; and Jagdish Bhagwati, "Immiserizing Growth: A Geometrical Note," *Review of Economic Studies*, vol. 25 (June 1958), pp. 201–05.

Figure 2-1. *U.S. Current Account versus Moving Average of Fixed-Weight Terms of Trade, 1961–87*[a]

Three-year moving average
of fixed-weight terms of trade

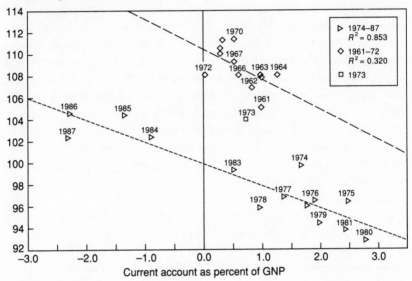

Current account as percent of GNP

Source: U.S. Department of Commerce, Bureau of Economic Analysis, national income and product accounts data tape.

a. Terms of trade are the ratio of the fixed-weight deflators for nonagricultural exports and nonoil imports of goods and services.

against the trade balance in goods and services as a share of GNP. Downward movements of the curve itself correspond to declining trade performance. If our goods and services become less attractive to foreigners, we need to lower their prices to achieve any given amount of net foreign earnings; that is, the terms of trade must fall to achieve any given trade balance. Leftward or rightward shifts along the curve reflect changes in spending patterns. The curve should slope down to the right. That is, higher trade surpluses are associated with lower terms of trade. The larger the trade surplus, the more we are lending to foreigners, the more goods we have to sell to foreigners, and therefore the lower our prices have to be.

The figure is drawn with two regression lines fitted to the data. The first captures the relationship between 1961 and 1972, the second between 1974 and 1987. A clear downward shift in the relationship seems to have occurred in the mid-1970s: in the 1960s a given trade surplus (measured as a share of GNP) was associated with higher terms of trade than in the 1980s. This suggests that U.S. competitiveness declined over the period. In addition, as the dramatic leftward movement along the lower regression line indicates, there have been major expenditure shifts in the 1980s—in this case, reduced national saving. Our terms of trade nevertheless temporarily improved for a few years because we increased our net foreign borrowing. To put it differently, because we were borrowing more, we needed to sell less to foreigners and to buy more from them, which increased the relative price of U.S. goods. This adjustment was stimulated by the strong dollar during the first half of the decade, which improved U.S. terms of trade by making American goods relatively more expensive.

In summary, and contrary to widely believed notions, a deterioration in the trade performance of America's industries will not, in the long run, generate a large trade deficit. But, as was evident in the 1970s, such a deterioration in trade performance will, by worsening America's terms of trade, depress the growth of its living standards.

The trade deficit is principally determined by our spending and saving behavior. As happened in the 1980s, by borrowing from abroad we can temporarily live beyond our means and in the process get some further advantage through a temporary improvement in the terms of trade. But the process cannot continue. Eventually we will have to give back our gains in spending and in the terms of trade, and indeed will return even more than we originally got, since we must pay the interest on the overseas debts piled up during our spending spree.

Finally, implicit in the foregoing analysis is a twofold characterization of changes in a country's terms of trade. Changes in national spending and saving behavior can lead to short-run changes in the terms of trade that eventually tend to reverse themselves.[8] In addition, longer-run changes in the terms of trade can occur when a country's trade performance improves or deteriorates relative to the trade performance of other countries.

Therefore, an assessment of U.S. international economic relations on U.S. living standards must consider both the terms of trade and spending patterns. Each is examined in the sections that follow.

---

8. The terms of trade changes need not be symmetric. If a country increases its foreign debt, then even after it stops borrowing, it must run a trade surplus to earn the interest it has to pay on its debts. To do so its export prices must be made "permanently" cheaper, relative to its import prices—that is, at the end of the process, its terms of trade must be somewhat lower than they were at the beginning.

Domestic and International Components of U.S. Living Standards

In a closed economy, domestic production alone provides the resources for domestic spending. Living standards will thus depend only on the growth of factor inputs and the efficiency with which they are used to produce goods and services. In an open economy, however, other factors can affect living standards. The previous analysis identified three of them: (1) foreign borrowing can allow current spending to differ from current production; (2) U.S. citizens may receive a net inflow of profits and interest (net capital income) from abroad or may, on balance, remit profits and interest to foreigners; and (3) the terms on which the United States exchanges exports for imports—its terms of trade—can change, and in so doing have an influence on our living standards.[9]

The national income accounts provide various constant-price measures that are helpful in isolating these effects.[10] Table 2-1 uses these measures to break down changes in U.S. net domestic spending (spending on private and public consumption and investment) into changes in its components: domestic production, net capital income, the effects of changes in the terms of trade, and net foreign borrowing.[11] (All these data have been adjusted to constant [1982] prices to exclude the effects of inflation.)

Essentially the story told in table 2-1 is that, until very recently, the growth of U.S. per capita spending in the period since World War II

---

9. Terms of trade losses provide an *upper bound* estimate of the potential damage that changes in trade might inflict on U.S. welfare; the ratio of export to import prices does not account for improvements in export industry productivity. If it takes less labor and capital to produce a given export, even though it sells at a lower relative price, living standards may be improving. In addition, import price measures may not accurately capture the benefits from increased variety afforded by imports.

10. Net national product (NNP) adds net foreign factor payments to net domestic product; command NNP adjusts NNP for changes in the international buying power of exports as measured by import prices; and net national purchases equals the real net national product plus net foreign borrowing. For further discussion, see Edward F. Denison, "International Transactions in Measures of the Nation's Production," *Survey of Current Business*, vol. 61 (May 1981), pp. 17–28.

11. This formulation understates the benefits of international factors: (1) technological innovations abroad may be emulated by domestic producers and show up as an improvement in domestic productivity; (2) domestic output will reflect increased efficiencies due to specialization; (3) the implicit price deflators used in the GNP accounts may vary slightly from those calculated with fixed weights.

Table 2-1. *Contributions to per Capita Net Domestic Spending Annual Growth Rates, 1950–87*

Percent a year

Item	1950–73	1973–79	1979–87
Net domestic product[a]	2.07	1.18	1.20
Plus Net investment income[b]	0.05	0.13	−0.15
Plus Terms of trade[c]	0.16	−0.38	−0.04
Plus Net foreign borrowing[d]	−0.07	0.16	0.57
Equals Net domestic spending	2.21	1.09	1.58
Consumption and government[e]	2.05	1.16	1.78
Net fixed investment	0.16	−0.07	−0.20

Sources: U.S. Department of Commerce, Bureau of Economic Analysis (BEA), national income and product accounts, and unpublished BEA data for 1987. Data adjusted to constant 1982 prices.

a. The growth of production per capita differed in the various periods from the growths of production per worker because of changes in the ratio of population to work force:

	Net domestic production per worker	+	Ratio of employment to population	=	Net domestic product per capita
1950–73	1.93		0.14		2.07
1973–79	−0.19		1.37		1.18
1979–87	0.80		0.40		1.20

b. Net national product (NNP) − net domestic product. See footnote 10 of text for explanation.

c. Command NNP − NNP.

d. Net national purchases − command NNP.

e. Includes inventories.

has been dominated by the pattern of growth in U.S. per capita production. From 1950 to 1973 the 2.2 percent annual growth in spending per capita was virtually the same as the growth in per capita domestic production. On balance, the factors associated with international trade played little role. After 1973 the growth in U.S. production per capita slowed down substantially, from 2.1 to 1.2 percent a year. From 1973 to 1979 there was a similar fall in the growth of per capita spending. During this period several important developments occurred in the foreign sector that affected domestic spending, but they offset each other. The sharp increase in OPEC oil prices coupled with lower prices for agricultural exports worsened our terms of trade, but that was more or less compensated for by increased earnings on investment overseas and a small increase in net borrowing from abroad.[12]

Between 1979 and 1987, however, the growth of per capita spending for the first time substantially exceeded the growth of per capita production, 1.6 percent versus 1.2 percent. And this was achieved, as

12. In fact, what occurred was a *decrease* in our own net foreign lending to other countries, which has the same effect on the growth of domestic spending as an *increase* in net borrowing from abroad.

detailed earlier, by a large rise in overseas borrowing, the mirror image of which was the rise of the U.S. trade deficit. As is evident from the figures in the bottom two rows of table 2-1, this surge in national spending relative to production did not come about through increased investment. Indeed net investment per capita actually declined. What occurred was a large rise in consumer and government spending, financed by the overseas borrowing. The former was stimulated by the large 1981 tax cuts and the latter by the swift buildup of the defense budget. To the extent one can use the combination of consumption and government purchases as a very crude proxy, current living standards rose sharply during the period despite the low growth of American productivity.

Terms of Trade

A consensus has emerged that the main reason for looking at U.S. competitiveness is a concern about U.S. living standards (rather than about the trade balance or the size of the manufacturing sector). But though many commissions have gathered an immense amount of information on the various reasons for poor U.S. trade performance, specific numerical estimates of the net effect of all these factors on living standards have been absent. In this section I attempt to fill this gap.

As explained earlier, changes in American spending behavior will lead to changes in the U.S. balance of payments, which in turn generate changes in the terms of trade. Long-run improvements, or deterioration, in American trade performance also produce changes in the terms of trade. The data in table 2-1 suggest that in the postwar period alterations in the terms of trade have not, on balance, played a significant role in explaining changes in the growth rate of American living standards. But that result might simply reflect the fact that the several forces affecting the terms of trade—spending behavior and trade performance—have offset each other.

With the aid of econometric analysis, I have determined how U.S. exports and imports have responded to changes in U.S. and foreign income growth and to changes in export and import prices. The details of that analysis are supplied in appendix A; the results can be summarized as follows.

—If the prices of U.S. and foreign tradable goods are assumed not to change relative to each other, each 1 percent rise in foreign income raises U.S. exports (excluding agricultural products) by about 1.9 percent, while each 1 percent rise in U.S. income raises U.S. imports (excluding oil) by a slightly greater amount, 2.2 percent. Between 1972 and 1987 (also between 1980 and 1987) U.S. growth rates averaged 0.1 to 0.2 percent a year less than those in the rest of the world. This implies that, at constant relative prices, the growth of U.S. imports would have outpaced the growth of exports by about 0.5 percent a year. Thus a continuing decline in U.S. export prices relative to import prices—that is, a decline in U.S. terms of trade—appears to have been necessary for the United States to avoid a steady worsening of its trade balance, even though the growth of foreign economies has been slightly faster than its own. In this sense, it can be said that America's trade performance has been declining for some time.

—The decline in the U.S. terms of trade required to maintain a steady balance in American international accounts (excluding oil and agriculture) appears, fortunately, to be quite small—according to the estimates from the econometric analysis, about 0.4 percent a year (assuming, of course, that no other factors, such as changes in spending-saving patterns, were at work).

—The effect of a 0.4 percent annual decline in the U.S. terms of trade on the growth of American living standards—roughly proxied by the growth of domestic spending—is trivial. Nonoil imports are about 12 percent of GNP. If the terms at which the United States buys those imports deteriorate at 0.4 percent a year, the effect on overall American living standards will be to lower their annual growth by less than one-twentieth of 1 percent a year.

Thus, although the trade performance of U.S. industries has deteriorated over the last several decades, its magnitude and impact have been very small. Of course, if economic growth in the rest of the world should slacken in the future while U.S. growth remained the same, the decline in the terms of trade and the associated depressing effect on American living standards would be somewhat larger.

The econometric analysis on which these conclusions is based is necessarily imprecise and subject to error. Even if the relationships among export and import volumes, national economic growth rates, and relative prices continue unchanged in the future, the analysis may not have correctly identified the strength of those underlying relationships from the welter of forces affecting trade flows. Nevertheless, the conclusions reached above are still quite robust. For example, even if the changes in the U.S. terms of trade required to keep American international payments in a stable balance were underestimated by a factor of two or three, the consequent effect on American living standards would still be small.[13]

Two additional considerations strengthen this conclusion. First, there is reason to believe that a strong element of catch-up accounted for much of the decline in U.S. terms of trade. As American technology was diffused abroad, foreign goods became better (and sometimes superior) substitutes for U.S products. But for Europe and Japan most of that catch-up has been completed. Though this effect will continue for developing economies, they account for a relatively smaller share of U.S. trade. Second, it should be stressed that the terms-of-trade impact is an *upper-bound* estimate of the unfavorable effect of changes in trade performance on living standards. It fails to capture the growth in export industry productivity achieved from increased specialization and the gains in welfare from a greater variety of imported products.

The finding here that trade performance has a relatively small effect on living standards conflicts with the prediction made by Lester Thurow that the dollar must fall and U.S. import prices rise by fairly large amounts because U.S. productivity growth is slower than that in the rest of the world.[14] But his analysis is flawed. If higher foreign productivity growth is absorbed by higher foreign wages and profits, prices will remain unchanged and no devaluation will be necessary. If higher foreign productivity is passed through into lower prices of foreign products in foreign currencies, a *nominal* depreciation in the dollar (or fall in the U.S. price level) will be required to maintain trade balance. In that case,

---

13. How trade affects national welfare through the rents captured by workers is not considered here. Katz and Summers have shown that for the United States such wage premiums are generally larger in export than in import competing industries. Thus, under conditions of balanced trade, U.S. labor in export industries derives additional benefits from trade not reflected in the terms of trade. Lawrence F. Katz and Lawrence H. Summers, "Can Inter-Industry Wage Differentials Justify Strategic Trade Policy?" (Harvard University and National Bureau of Economic Research, April 1988). See also Paul R. Krugman, "The U.S. Response to Foreign Industrial Targeting," *Brookings Papers on Economic Activity*, 1:1984, pp. 77–131. (Hereafter *BPEA*.)

14. According to Thurow, "If American productivity grows at 1 percent per year and the productivity of our industrial competitors grows at 4 percent per year, the American dollar must fall by approximately 3 percent per year to maintain a balance in America's balance of trade. With 12 percent of GNP imported . . . [this] causes American standards of living to fall by .04 percent (.12 times .03) per year forever." Lester C. Thurow, *The Zero Sum Solution: An Economic and Political Agenda for the 80's* (Simon and Schuster, 1985), pp. 93–94.

import prices in dollars would not rise and thus U.S. living standards would be unaffected.

Although foreign productivity growth that is concentrated in industries which compete with U.S. export firms could affect the real exchange rate, uniform productivity growth (the case implicitly considered by Thurow) need have no such effect. In fact, in the simplest case higher productivity increases a country's income and its imports. The *foreign* (not the U.S.) real exchange rate and terms of trade would actually have to fall to induce a compensatory increase in demand by the rest of the world for foreign exports.[15]

Current Account Adjustment and Living Standard Prospects

Between 1981 and 1987 the United States fed its appetite for spending by importing much more than it exported and borrowing the difference from foreign investors. As long as foreigners are willing to lend to America on a large scale, it can postpone the day of reckoning and spend more than it produces. But the splurge has already begun to end. Foreigners have become increasingly unwilling to finance the U.S. current account deficit. Between 1985 and 1987 their decreased demand for U.S. dollars drove down the value of the dollar. The lower dollar, by making U.S. exports less expensive abroad and raising the price of U.S. imports, set in motion a fall in the U.S. trade deficit and a concomitant decline in the net inflow of foreign funds.

If the trade deficit continues to move toward balance, U.S. domestic spending will have to shrink to fit within the limits of domestic production. Indeed domestic spending will eventually have to come down even more than this. The United States must pay interest on the overseas debts accumulated while its current account has been in deficit. To do so, *it will have to run a trade surplus* in order to earn the income with which to make those debt service payments. Domestic spending will thus have to fall *below* domestic production.

To bring spending into line with production, the U.S. economy will have to engage in considerable belt tightening. Goods once available for

---

15. This relationship between productivity and the terms of trade was examined many years ago when Great Britain was worried about rapid American productivity growth. See, in particular, Hicks, "An Inaugural Lecture." Subsequent articles have pointed out that, in general, the result is more indeterminate. A survey is provided in Richard E. Caves, *Trade and Economic Structure* (Harvard University Press, 1963), pp. 152–60.

domestic use will be exported or used to substitute for imports. To sell these U.S. products abroad, a weaker dollar will be required. This decline in the dollar will further lower U.S. buying power. All told, U.S. living standards will be reduced through three effects: first, by the need to bring spending back into line with production; second, by the permanent interest burdens that will have to be serviced; and third, by the declining purchasing power of the dollar necessary to generate the trade flows required to bring spending into line with production less net foreign interest payments.

The Model

These effects can be estimated, under varying assumptions, with the aid of a simple model. That model is described in appendix B. Essentially it operates as follows:

First, GDP is calculated on the assumption that the recent trend rate of growth in productivity (output per worker) continues, that the labor force increases at the rate forecast by the Bureau of Labor Statistics, and that employment rises slightly faster than the labor force over the next several years, to bring the unemployment rate down to 5 percent.

Second, a system of equations that explains U.S. exports and imports is used to determine the behavior of the current account under different exchange rate assumptions. The model forecasts both the dollar values of imports and exports. Using various assumptions about pricing practices, it takes account of changes in the terms of trade to determine the associated changes in export and import volumes.

Third, since domestic spending is equal to GDP minus the trade balance in goods and services, it is possible to project the course of total spending, given the path of GDP and the volume of exports and imports.[16]

Finally, by assuming that investment spending remains a constant share of GDP, it is possible to project the maximum feasible growth rate of consumer and government spending combined (which, as noted earlier, is used as a crude proxy for living standards).

Three sets of estimates were constructed; a mid-range, a pessimistic, and an optimistic estimate. Over the whole period 1987–95 all three

16. The price and volume of U.S. oil imports are treated separately, assuming conservatively that oil imports grow at twice the rate of U.S. GDP and that oil prices rise in step with other U.S. prices.

estimates assume that U.S. GDP grows at an average rate of 2.5 percent and foreign GDP at 2.8 percent.

The mid-range estimates assume (1) that each 1 percent increase in U.S. growth raises our imports by 2 percent, while each 1 percent growth in foreign income raises our exports by 2 percent; (2) that each 1 percent change in the relative price of U.S. products shifts export and import volumes by 1.2 percent; and (3) that four-fifths of any change in exchange rates shows up in the prices of U.S. exports and imports.

The pessimistic estimates assume that the responsiveness of export and import volumes to relative price change is smaller than in the mid-range case; that U.S. exports rise less in response to foreign economic growth than U.S. imports respond to U.S. economic growth; and that 100 percent of any change in exchange rates shows up in changes of export and import prices.

The optimistic estimates use parameters chosen so that the current account could be balanced by 1995 with the dollar at its level of December 1987. The estimates assume greater responsiveness of exports and imports to changes in prices, larger U.S. export response to foreign economic growth, and (like the mid-range case) an 80 percent pass-through of exchange rate movements into export and import price movements.

Obviously, this is not a credible model of the complete economy. It is not designed for distinguishing variables like inflation and interest rates that influence spending decisions and are determined jointly with exchange rates. Instead, its purpose is simply to determine the resources available for total spending given a particular path for the current account and output. Identifying the spending paths provided by the model under different scenarios makes it possible to explore the policies that might be required to bring demand into line with the economy's potential.

Results

Between 1987 and 1995 all projections assume that U.S. population grows at 0.8 percent annually. Thus the 2.5 percent growth in GDP results in GDP per capita rising by 1.7 percent a year. As shown in greater detail below, it is possible, given this growth, both to improve U.S. living standards and eliminate the current account deficit over eight years. In the mid-range case, to reduce the current account to balance by 1995 requires that domestic production outpace consumption by about 1 percent of GDP annually. This leaves 0.7 percent per year for per capita increases in living standards. Under the optimistic scenario—that

Table 2-2. *Current Account Scenarios with Constant 1987 Real Exchange Rates, 1987–95*
Billions of current dollars

Year	Current account	Net investment income	Debt as percent of GDP
		Mid-range	
1987	− 160.00	14.50	9.17
1988	− 130.17	2.50	11.14
1989	− 109.40	− 7.26	12.41
1990	− 125.30	− 15.47	13.72
1991	− 143.20	− 24.87	15.08
1992	− 154.91	− 35.61	16.45
1993	− 166.81	− 47.22	17.75
1994	− 178.78	− 59.73	18.97
1995	− 190.66	− 73.14	20.10
		Pessimistic	
1987	− 160.00	14.50	9.17
1988	− 149.68	2.50	11.54
1989	− 148.35	− 8.73	13.51
1990	− 176.35	− 19.85	15.64
1991	− 208.79	− 33.08	17.93
1992	− 236.70	− 48.74	20.35
1993	− 267.70	− 66.49	22.82
1994	− 302.08	− 86.57	25.35
1995	− 340.19	− 109.22	27.92
		Optimistic	
1987	− 160.00	14.50	9.17
1988	− 103.28	2.50	10.61
1989	− 55.90	− 5.25	10.90
1990	− 57.05	− 9.44	11.13
1991	− 57.35	− 13.72	11.26
1992	− 48.46	− 18.02	11.25
1993	− 36.00	− 21.65	11.01
1994	− 19.23	− 24.35	10.52
1995	2.70	− 25.79	9.77

Sources: Author's calculations using unpublished BEA data for 1987 and appendix B.

is, the current account balance requires no decline in the dollar from its levels at the end of 1987—an annual growth in living standards of 0.8 percent is possible. Under the pessimistic scenario just 0.1 percent per year would be available for higher living standards.

1987 EXCHANGE RATES. The first set of simulations holds real exchange rates at their levels of December 1987. As reported in table 2-2, given the mid-range parameters, the U.S. current account does not achieve balance. Driven by the lagged impact of earlier exchange rate changes, the current account deficit declines from $160 billion in 1987 to $109 billion in 1989.[17] Thereafter, however, it drifts upward. Although export volumes rise by 17.2 and 12.4 percent in 1988 and 1989, respectively, the nominal current account deficit gradually rises as a share of GDP once the exchange rate changes between 1985 and 1987 have completed their effects. Reflecting these deficits, by 1995 U.S. net foreign debt exceeds $1.622 trillion (about 20 percent of GDP), and U.S. net interest payments rise to $73 billion (0.9 percent of GDP). Because of these rising payments to foreigners, real GNP grows at a slower rater after 1991 (2.08 percent) than does real GDP (2.0 percent).[18]

With the pessimistic parameter set, the current account deficit shows little improvement through 1989 and thereafter rises fairly rapidly as a share of GDP. By 1995 U.S. net foreign debt is $2.25 trillion (27.9 percent of GDP).

Under the optimistic assumptions, however, the current account achieves balance by 1995 with a net foreign debt of $0.8 trillion (9.8 percent of GDP) and net foreign interest payments of $25.8 billion (0.32 percent of GDP). What is significant is that *both* the high price elasticities and high foreign income elasticity are required to achieve this result.[19]

CURRENT ACCOUNT BALANCE. A zero current account may or may not be optimal for the United States. In principle, the ideal current

17. The 11.3 percent dollar depreciation between (annual average) 1986 and (annual average) 1987 affects trade flows and U.S. import prices in 1988. The additional change of 6.6 percent (between 1987 average and 1987 year end) affects trade flows and prices in 1989.

18. Several other analysts have recently reached similar conclusions. Ralph Bryant estimates that real exchange rates as of December 1987 would lead to a U.S. current account deficit of $108 billion in 1989. Thereafter the deficit would rise to $127 billion by 1991. See Ralph C. Bryant, "The U.S. External Deficit: An Update," Brookings Discussion Papers in International Economics 63, January 1988, table 3. Cline projects a deficit of $110 billion in 1989 that rises to $140 billion by 1992. See William R. Cline, "Medium-Term Prospects for the U.S. External Current Account" (Washington, D.C.: Institute for International Economics, March 1988). See also Nigel Gault, "The U.S. Current Account: A Current Policy Baseline," in Alfred Reifman and Craig Elwell, eds., *The Dollar and the Trade Deficit: What's to Be Done?* report 88-430E (Congressional Research Service, 1988), pp. 84–96.

19. The optimistic assumptions are that both imports and exports have price elasticities of 1.5 and foreign income elasticity for U.S. exports is 2.3. If export and import income elasticities of 2.0 are combined with price elasticities of 1.5, 1987 exchange rate levels are not compatible with the current account balance. In this case, the current account is brought down to $75 billion in 1990 and remains in the region of $85 billion thereafter.

Table 2-3. *Scenarios to Achieve Current Account Balance, 1987–95*
Billions of current dollars

Year	Exchange rate[a]	Current account	Net investment income	Debt as percent of GDP
		Mid-range		
1987	100.0	− 160.00	14.50	9.17
1988	94.9	− 130.17	2.50	11.14
1989	90.0	− 73.83	− 7.26	11.74
1990	89.3	− 41.88	− 12.80	11.65
1991	89.3	− 38.13	− 15.94	11.45
1992	89.3	− 31.98	− 18.80	11.19
1993	89.3	− 23.65	− 21.20	10.80
1994	89.3	− 12.73	− 22.97	10.27
1995	89.3	1.27	− 23.93	9.59
		Pessimistic		
1987	100.0	− 160.00	14.50	9.17
1988	94.9	− 149.68	2.50	11.54
1989	90.0	− 122.48	− 8.73	13.03
1990	85.4	− 115.93	− 17.91	14.14
1991	76.0	− 103.14	− 26.61	14.82
1992	76.0	− 20.02	− 34.34	14.16
1993	76.0	− 14.41	− 35.84	13.45
1994	76.0	− 7.40	− 36.92	12.67
1995	76.0	1.25	− 37.48	11.84

Source: See table 2-2.
a. Real exchange rate as calculated by Morgan Guaranty for fifteen industrial countries expressed in foreign currency per dollar.

account depends on appropriate saving and investment levels in the United States and the rest of the world. Nonetheless, it is of some interest to examine what exchange rate levels are required to achieve a zero current account.

As reported in tables 2-3 and 2-4, within the mid-range and pessimistic parameters, further exchange rate depreciation is needed to bring the current account into balance. The mid-range parameters, combined with a total depreciation of 10.7 percent spread over three years, lead to current account balance by 1995. With the pessimistic parameters, a real dollar decline of 24 percent between 1988 and 1991 is required to achieve current account balance by 1995. In the mid-range and pessimistic cases, U.S. net foreign debt in 1995 is 9.6 and 11.8 percent of gross domestic product, respectively.

LIVING STANDARDS. The assumptions about labor force and productivity growth imply that real GDP per capita grows at 1.7 percent a year

Table 2-4. *Percent Growth Needed to Achieve Current Account Balance under Various Scenarios, 1988–95*

Year	Export volume	Import volume	Manufacturing value added
		Mid-range	
1988	17.17	−3.10	4.00
1989	18.25	−3.70	3.90
1990	11.12	1.42	3.63
1991	6.44	5.03	3.41
1992	5.65	4.50	2.25
1993	5.65	4.50	2.25
1994	5.65	4.50	2.25
1995	5.65	4.50	2.25
		Pessimistic	
1988	17.20	−2.99	3.91
1989	18.32	−3.61	3.80
1990	10.89	1.73	3.59
1991	10.89	1.78	3.60
1992	18.30	−4.35	2.89
1993	5.22	4.89	2.29
1994	5.22	4.89	2.29
1995	5.22	4.89	2.29
		Optimistic	
1988	21.33	−5.15	3.35
1989	15.24	−0.89	3.26
1990	6.62	5.65	3.33
1991	6.62	5.65	3.33
1992	6.62	4.50	2.18
1993	6.62	4.50	2.18
1994	6.62	4.50	2.17
1995	6.62	4.50	2.17

Source: See table 2-2.

between 1987 and 1995, or by $2,288 in 1987 dollars for the period as a whole. But because all these scenarios entail some adjustment in the U.S. current account relative to GDP, real per capita spending will grow more slowly than this.[20] Tables 2-5 and 2-6 illustrate the implications of various scenarios for U.S. living standards.

The most rapid rise in living standards occurs with the least adjustment in the current account and with the "pessimistic" parameters. That is because there is less adjustment of the traded goods sector to changes

20. In all cases, I assume real per capita investment rises at 1.65 percent a year and derive real per capita living standards (private consumption plus government expenditures) as a residual.

Table 2-5. *Index of per Capita Consumption plus Government Spending (Living Standards) under Different Scenarios, 1987–95*
1987 = 100

Year	Constant 1987 exchange rates			Current account balance	
	Mid-range	Pessimistic	Optimistic	Mid-range	Pessimistic
1987	100.0	100.0	100.0	100.0	100.0
1988	99.6	99.6	98.8	99.6	99.6
1989	100.0	100.1	98.7	98.7	98.7
1990	102.0	102.2	100.5	99.3	99.4
1991	104.0	104.4	102.3	101.0	99.9
1992	105.3	105.8	103.4	102.1	97.6
1993	106.6	107.3	104.4	103.3	98.7
1994	108.0	108.8	105.5	104.5	99.9
1995	109.3	110.3	106.5	105.7	101.0
Addendum	*Average annual growth in per capita spending (percent)*				
1987–95	1.12	1.23	0.79	0.70	0.12

Source: See table 2-2.

in prices and incomes, so more room exists for domestic consumption. Thus, table 2-6 illustrates that *if exchange rates remain at their December 1987 levels* and the pessimistic set of elasticities apply, per capita living standards (private and public consumption) improve by $1,641 (1.23 percent per year) through 1995. Of course, this pace of spending can be sustained only by an increase in U.S. international indebtedness, $254 per capita. With the mid-range parameters, a constant dollar produces more adjustment, so living standards improve more slowly, 1.12 percent a year or a total of $1,483 per capita by 1995.

Bringing the current account to zero over the next seven years would reduce the growth of living standards considerably. With the optimistic parameters, no further declines of the dollar are required to improve the current account since faster foreign growth (or an improvement in the attractiveness of U.S. products) suffices to generate the required export growth. Nonetheless, living standards rise by just $1,037 per capita (0.8 percent annually) by 1995. The corresponding increase for the mid-range parameters is $906 per capita (0.7 percent annually). For the pessimistic parameters it is just $156 per person.

In sum, U.S. living standards will be reduced by three major adjustments if national spending is brought into line with national production by 1995. Regardless of the parameters assumed, reduced borrowing from abroad will lower the average American's spending by about $700. Net interest payments to foreigners will cost between $147

Table 2-6. *Average per Capita Changes in Living Standards under Different Scenarios, 1987–95*
1987 dollars

Item	Actual (1979–87)	Constant 1987 real exchange rates		Current account balance		
		Mid-range	Pessimistic	Optimistic	Mid-range	Pessimistic
Net domestic product	1,500	2,288	2,288	2,288	2,288	2,288
Plus Net investment income	−183	−275	−373	−147	−141	−178
Plus Terms of trade	−56	−247	−407	−259	−413	−1155
Plus Net foreign borrowing	723	−162	254	−724	−707	−677
Equals Net domestic purchases	1,984	1,604	1,762	1,158	1,027	278
Consumption and government	2,240	1,483	1,641	1,037	906	156
Net fixed investment	−256	121	121	121	121	122

Source: See table 2-2. See table 2-1 for explanation of terms.

and $178 per person. And per capita losses due to the decline in the terms of trade could range between $259 and $1,155.[21]

DEINDUSTRIALIZATION. Each of the adjustment scenarios just outlined entails not only a considerable shift in U.S. spending patterns but also a substantial change in the U.S. production structure. Since most trade occurs in goods, the projections imply a major expansion in the manufacturing sector. For example, in the mid-range case, U.S. exports rise at an average annual rate of 9.5 percent a year between 1987 and 1995 (see table 2-3). The U.S. trade balance in manufactured goods shifts from a deficit of $123 billion in 1987 to a *surplus* of $79 billion in 1995. To support an export boom of this magnitude, the U.S. manufacturing sector will have to grow at an annual rate of 3.0 percent, compared with the rise of 2.5 percent for GDP as a whole. Measured in 1982 dollars, manufacturing output as a share of GNP is projected to rise from 22.1 percent in 1987 to 23.1 percent in 1995. These projections are not that much different under either the pessimistic or optimistic parameters. In all cases, manufacturing is projected to perform well, compared with its relatively poor record during the first half of the 1980s.

CAPACITY GROWTH. Whereas some fear that U.S. industry will shrink

21. In aggregate terms over the eight years, taking the 1987 population of 243 million, this works out to roughly $170 billion as the effect of reduced borrowing, between $36 billion and $43 billion as the effect of additional interest, and between $62.2 and $280 billion as the effect of the terms of trade.

in the years ahead, others fear it cannot grow sufficiently to provide the export capacity that will be required to reduce the trade deficit. But in fact, these simulations indicate that if domestic spending is kept in check so that the aggregate demand for U.S. goods and services grows in line with the economy's potential, there will not be a serious capacity constraint in manufacturing in general and in most U.S. export industries in particular.

Capacity growth will not be an immediate problem for U.S. industry in the aggregate. Assume that the 1978–80 peak rates of capacity utilization, as measured by the Federal Reserve Board index, represent full capacity, and that once the 1978–80 peak rates are reached, capacity must rise at the same rate as production. In the mid-range scenario, industrial production grows at a 4.0 percent annual average rate between 1988 and 1989 and 3.1 percent annually between 1989 and 1991. As of July 1988, however, U.S. capacity utilization in the manufacturing sector of 83.5 percent remained below its 1978–80 peak (of 86.5 percent). To remain within or below this peak level requires an aggregate expansion of U.S. production capacity of just 0.6 percent annually between 1987 and 1989. Thereafter, between 1989 and 1992 an annual rise of 3.1 percent is required. This is quite in line with the 2.9 percent annual increase recorded between 1980 and 1985.

In more disaggregated simulations, some bottlenecks do appear. These are evident in the rubber, chemicals, aerospace, and paper industries. The capacity growth they require is above the rates recorded between 1980 and 1985. Together, these industries accounted for about 25 percent of U.S. manufactured exports in 1984. Nonetheless, adequate capacity appears available in most of the capital-goods sectors, such as electric and nonelectric machinery, which provide the bulk of U.S. exports.

In sum, although some bottlenecks may limit export growth, the United States should have adequate industrial capacity for an adjustment to current account balance by 1995. However, a major decline in the dollar more substantial than the mid-range projection of 10.7 percent, acceleration in exports for another reason, or a failure to keep domestic spending in line with the room available could produce more significant bottlenecks, with their inflationary consequences.

ADJUSTMENT TIMING. In the long run the United States must bring its spending into line with production. But why should this be accom-

Table 2-7. *Comparison of Thrifty's and Splurge's Spending Patterns*
Dollars

	Tom Thrifty		Steve Splurge				
Year	Income	Spending	Income	Spending	Amount bor-rowed	Inter-est paid	Debt out-stand-ing
1	20,000	20,000	20,000	20,400	413	13	413
2	20,000	20,000	20,000	20,400	426	26	838
3	20,000	20,000	20,000	20,400	440	40	1,278
4	20,000	20,000	20,000	20,400	454	54	1,732
5	20,000	20,000	20,000	20,400	468	68	2,200
6	20,000	20,000	20,000	19,517	−483	70	1,787
7	20,000	20,000	20,000	19,517	−483	57	1,362
8	20,000	20,000	20,000	19,517	−483	44	922
9	20,000	20,000	20,000	19,517	−483	30	468
10	20,000	20,000	20,000	19,517	−483	15	0
All	200,000	200,000	200,000	199,585	. . .	417	. . .

plished in the next five years? What are the costs to the nation of delaying adjustment?

The answer is that delay now will require a greater adjustment in the future. One measure of the costs of delay is represented by interest payments on additional borrowing. If the real exchange rate is held at its levels at the end of 1987, with the mid-range parameters, the current account deficit is projected to grow from 2.0 in 1989 to 2.4 percent of GDP in 1994, reflecting an improvement in the trade balance as a share of GDP that is more than offset by an increase in net factor payments to foreigners of about 0.7 of a percent of GDP. From 1987 to 1995 total U.S. indebtedness to foreigners is projected to rise by $1.36 trillion.

The implications of this level of additional borrowing can be illustrated by a simple example, using a real interest rate of 3.2 percent. Compare two consumers who both earn $20,000 a year, roughly the level of per capita income in the United States in 1988: Tom Thrifty, who earns and spends $20,000 each year; and Steve Splurge, who also earns $20,000 but borrows enough to raise his consumption spending to $20,400 a year and to pay for the interest costs of servicing his debts. Assume, as for the United States, that Splurge can borrow at 3.2 percent interest in this world of no inflation. As shown in table 2-7, maintaining these habits for five years leads Splurge to consume $2,000 more than his frugal counterpart. As a result, by the end of the fifth year, he owes $2,200 (or 11 percent of his income). His interest payments in the fifth year are $68

(0.34 percent of income) and his "current account deficit" is $468 (2.34 percent of his income).

Now assume that beginning in the sixth year Splurge decides to repay his debt in five annual installments. Given the added interest costs, these payments will amount to $483 annually. During the payback period, Splurge will be able to spend only $19,517 a year as against the steady $20,000 spent by Thrifty. Over the entire ten-year period, while Thrifty will spend $200,000, Splurge will be able to consume $199,585, or just 0.21 percent less. In essence, borrowing at 3.2 percent is not very costly. Indeed, Splurge does not seem particularly profligate and, even at its peak in the fifth year, his debt burden seems eminently manageable.

The adjustment would be only somewhat more painful, however, if his creditors were less obliging. For example, if the interest rate were doubled to 6.4 percent, at the end of five years Splurge would spend an additional $225 on interest over the full period and his yearly spending during the payback period would be $19,472 a year rather than $19,517. All told, this would require him to consume 0.32 percent less than Thrifty over the decade—a cost that is still rather small.

The costs to Splurge go up further, if, after five years, his creditors insisted on repayment over two years rather than five. During his repayment years (6 and 7), his spending could be only $18,947 a year; the 7.1 percent decline from year 5 to year 6 could represent a difficult adjustment. Still, over the full seven-year time period, Splurge's total spending of $139,694 would be just $306 (or 0.21 percent) lower than Thrifty's.

The foregoing example has been constructed to be very similar to a five-year postponement by the entire United States in its current account adjustment. The United States is a rich country. Accumulating interest obligations of about half a percent of GDP (or an additional net foreign debt of 10 percent of GDP) would also be manageable. If the United States can choose to repay these obligations steadily, about as rapidly as they were accumulated, it is hard to get upset about the delay in repayment. Indeed, the example suggests that delaying adjustment may be quite appealing, particularly if it can be shifted from one leader to his successor or from one generation to the next.[22]

---

22. Edward Gramlich pointed out that, although reduced national saving ultimately lowers living standards, this reduction could take at least ten years to appear. See Edward M. Gramlich, "How Bad Are the Large Deficits?" in Gregory B. Mills and John L. Palmer,

Adjustment for a household, however, is more easily coordinated than that of an economy the size of America's. As the experience during the buildup of the current account deficit in the first half of the 1980s showed, expenditure switching of even small relative magnitudes can entail considerable dislocation for important segments of the economy. But if the adjustment process can be extended so that it is gradual, the shifts can probably be absorbed by the economy without great additional cost. If the adjustment occurs during a crisis and is very rapid, it may be more traumatic.

To give a sense of the size of that adjustment, consider a scenario in which adjustment is delayed until 1994 (as in the mid-range scenario with 1987 exchange rates). Then assume that the U.S. current account shifts from a deficit of about 2.4 percent of GDP to balance within a two-year period. Unlike the example above, this scenario requires borrowing to cease rather than repayment of net foreign debt. Assume further that macroeconomic policymakers are sufficiently adept to keep the economy at full employment, growing at 2.2 percent annually during the adjustment.

The "sudden adjustment" scenario, under these conditions, means a decline in the dollar of 12.9 percent in 1994. This gives rise to large shifts in resources. With the mid-range parameters, over two years the trade balance swings by 3.8 percent of GDP as export volumes rise by 27.4 percent and import volumes fall by 2 percent. Value added in manufacturing due to trade rises 29.4 percent, whereas value added due to domestic absorption falls 3.0 percent. The inflationary pressures on the economy are also extremely large: nonoil import prices rise 19.2 percent, and export prices are up 12.5 percent. Moreover, to keep aggregate demand growing at the economy's potential, domestic absorption (the sum of consumption, investment, and government spending) rises by just 0.6 percent over two years. If investment remains a constant share of GDP, per capita living standards fall by 1.7 percent over the two-year period.

The foregoing scenario, however, is unrealistically optimistic. The size and speed with which resources must be shifted and the degree to which inflationary pressures must be suppressed make it unlikely that the adjustment process would occur without a significant increase in the U.S.

---

eds., *Federal Budget Policy in the 1980s* (Washington D.C.: Urban Institute Press, 1984), p. 64.

unemployment rate. Moreover, coordinating the adjustment with offsetting changes abroad would be particularly difficult. To achieve the necessary reduction in spending without inflation would probably require a contractionary aggregate demand policy in the United States and an expansionary policy abroad. It is extremely unlikely these shifts could be achieved without a U.S. recession. In fact, as discussed by Robert Litan in chapter 3, that is the principal reason why a dollar strike by foreign competitors in the future could be so damaging.

In sum, early adjustment is more attractive the higher the rate of interest, the greater the value placed on smooth growth, and the greater the preference for having living standards rise steadily. *However, the main costs of postponing adjustment are those associated with the dislocation caused by the adjustment process itself rather than the costs of borrowing and the time profile of the consumption path.* Adjustment sooner rather than later lessens the likelihood that dislocation costs will be major because resources must be reallocated rapidly. By the same token, adjustment should be undertaken gradually. It would be foolish to apply sudden adjustment shock to ourselves simply to avoid it being imposed by others.

Facilitating the Adjustment

The mid-range scenario here suggests that, given exchange rates as of December 1987, the U.S. current account would decline to about 2.4 percent of GNP and then remain in that range. Similarly, current projections imply that the U.S. budget deficit is likely to decline to the point where the federal debt will rise about as fast as GNP. Since the twin deficits do not appear to be growing, some have questioned whether additional adjustment is necessary.[23] The argument that the U.S. current account should be reduced rests on the judgment that the U.S. national savings rate is too low, rather than on the belief that the present current account deficit is unsustainable. Once an appropriate savings rate is achieved, the level of the current account becomes a secondary issue. If the existing inflow of foreign funds into the United States were being used to raise the national rate of investment, then continued current

23. While inflation distorts measures of the levels of the federal budget deficit and the U.S. net international position, there is much less inaccuracy in the measures of *changes* in these variables over the 1980s.

Table 2-8. *Net Savings and Investment Flows as a Percentage of GNP, 1950–87*

Period or year	Net private domestic savings (1)	State and local surplus (2)	Federal deficit (3)	Net domestic savings available for domestic investment: (1)+(2)−(3) (4)	Net private domestic investment (5)	Net domestic savings shortfalls (5)−(4)= net capital inflows (6)
1950–59	7.5	−0.2	−0.1	7.8	7.5	−0.3
1960–69	8.1	0.0	0.3	7.8	7.1	−0.7
1970–79	8.1	0.8	1.7	7.2	6.9	−0.3
1980	6.4	1.0	2.2	5.2	4.9	−0.3
1981	6.6	1.1	2.1	5.6	5.5	−0.1
1982	5.5	1.1	4.6	2.0	2.0	0.0
1983	5.7	1.4	5.2	1.9	3.1	1.2
1984	6.8	1.7	4.5	4.0	6.6	2.6
1985	5.7	1.6	4.9	2.4	5.1	2.7
1986	5.3	1.3	4.8	1.8	5.1	3.3
1987	4.1	1.2	3.5	1.8	5.1	3.3

Sources: U.S. Department of Commerce, Bureau of Economic Analysis, *National Income and Product Accounts of the United States, 1929–82, Statistical Tables* (Washington, D.C., 1986), tables 1.1, 5.1; BEA, *Survey of Current Business*, vol. 67 (July 1987), tables 1.1, 5.1; and unpublished BEA data for 1987.

account deficits would not be a problem. But that is not happening. As reported in table 2-8, America is borrowing to sustain a share of investment that is no greater than in the past. We are better off by borrowing from abroad than we would be if we were forced to match the drop in national savings rate with an equivalent reduction in national investment. Less domestic capital formation means lower wages and tax revenues. But that does not mean our current spending patterns are optimal.

There are legitimate questions about the reliability of the data underlying this analysis. Robert Eisner, in particular, has questioned the relevance of measures of the federal budget deficit that fail to take inflation into account; and Robert Lipsey and Irving Kravis have emphasized problems of comparing U.S. savings rates with those in other countries.[24] Also, it is well known that data on the U.S. net international investment are not measured accurately, because U.S. direct foreign investment assets abroad are valued at historic rather than current costs. But though the precise level of the federal budget, U.S. savings, and

24. See Robert Eisner, *How Real Is the Federal Deficit* (Free Press, 1986); and Robert E. Lipsey and Irving B. Kravis, *Saving and Economic Growth: Is the United States Really Falling Behind?* Research Report 901 (New York: Conference Board, 1987).

the U.S. net investment position may be uncertain, there is little doubt that all these variables have declined markedly in the 1980s. If America's national savings rate was just right in the late 1970s, it is too low today. Indeed, to provide for the baby-boom generation in their retirement, our savings rate should be rising rather than falling.

Assuming U.S. spending is eventually brought into line with income, an important question is which *components* of spending should be reduced the most. The exercise in the previous section assumed that private and public consumption, rather than investment, will bear the brunt of the adjustment. In fact, U.S. policymakers face three options. The first is to take no major actions to reduce domestic spending at all. In this case, unless the dollar appreciates, it is likely that when the stimulus from the external sector is combined with strong domestic demand, U.S. inflation will rise and eventually contractionary policies will be adopted. The second option is to reduce spending through tighter monetary policy. The high interest rates associated with this approach would discourage investment. While consumption and government spending could be stronger over the short run, less investment would mean lower incomes in the future. The third option is to rely primarily on tighter fiscal policy to concentrate the spending reduction on private and public consumption. That would be achieved by tax increases (which reduce consumer spending) and cuts in government spending. This approach would lead to relatively lower interest rates and thus higher investment and income over the long run.

There are two ways to avoid this adjustment. The first is simply to delay belt tightening until foreigners refuse to continue financing the trade deficit. That response may seem attractive in the short run, but, as just shown, it will make the required adjustment larger and more costly when foreign patience runs out (or when the interest burden accumulates).

The second and more appealing response would be to increase U.S. productivity growth and improve the attractiveness of U.S. products, thereby raising income growth to match a higher spending path. Our optimistic scenario makes clear, however, that improved trade performance alone will not do the trick. Even if foreigners suddenly found U.S. products very attractive (if they removed barriers to U.S. exports, or if their incomes grew more rapidly), the need to make goods and services available for export would impose a severe constraint on the growth in domestic living standards unless U.S. productivity growth improved.

Reducing the pain of the adjustment by raising productivity growth will not be easy, as Martin Neil Baily and Margaret M. Blair remind us in chapter 6. There are no panaceas to replace the need to work harder and more efficiently. Nonetheless, as this analysis demonstrates, domestic productivity growth is the key to our future living standards. While more open foreign markets and faster foreign growth will allow the United States to adjust with relatively smaller declines in the exchange rate, the overwhelming determinant of our living standards will depend in the long run, as it always has, on the productivity of the domestic economy.

The simulations suggest that about 1 percent of GDP a year over seven years would be required to bring the current account to balance by 1995. A return to the productivity growth of the period 1950–73 of 1.9 percent a year (versus the 1.0 percent projected here) would permit this adjustment to take place while simultaneously allowing living standards to rise over the next eight years as rapidly as they have over the past eight years.

The necessary spending adjustments in the years ahead will increasingly integrate the United States into the global economy. While the past seven years have seen a rapid increase in import penetration into the U.S. market, the next decade will be marked by a significant rise in the share of U.S. production going for exports. At the end of this process, U.S. interdependence with the global economy will be far greater than when it set off on the borrowing spree in the early 1980s.

America cannot ignore this changing global reality. Efforts to recapture the past by retreating into isolation by means of trade barriers, capital controls, and restrictions on foreign investment are doomed to failure. Such measures will simply compound the inevitable slowdown in the growth in living standards by lowering economic efficiency. Instead, America must meet the challenge of its changing global role head on, by adapting its institutions to ensure that it competes effectively in the global economy.

Conclusion

Between 1950 and 1973 almost all of the improvement in the U.S. standard of living resulted from higher domestic production. Between

1973 and 1987 domestic production was again the principal determinant of living standard growth, but after 1981 U.S. spending was also boosted through increased foreign borrowing while between 1973 and 1980 U.S. buying power was reduced because of lower terms of trade and decreased net foreign factor payments. The terms of trade changes were partly due to higher oil prices, but they also reflected deteriorating U.S. trade performance. Although the causes of this deterioration are not readily measured, together, they required a real annual depreciation of the dollar of about 0.4 percent annually to keep U.S. exports and imports of goods and services growing at similar rates. Since imports were about 10 percent of U.S. GNP during this period, a real depreciation of this magnitude would have lowered U.S. living standards by 0.04 percent annually.

Between 1979 and 1987 Americans increased their per capita spending on private and public consumption at the rate of 1.6 percent a year. Since annual growth of per capita production averaged only 1.2 percent, increased borrowing accounted for 0.4 percent annual growth in living standards. Unfortunately, the United States has borrowed to fund consumption rather than investment. Per capita real fixed investment in 1987 was lower than in 1979.

In the absence of an improved productivity growth, America's future living standards will have to grow more slowly in order to bring national spending into line with production. Given likely projections for labor force and productivity growth between 1987 and 1995, per capita production will increase at an annual rate of 1.7 percent, or $2,288 (in 1987 prices). If national spending is brought into line with national production by 1995, however, not borrowing from abroad will cost the average American about $707. Additional net interest payments to foreigners will require another $141 to $178 per capita while losses due to the terms of trade could range between $259 and $1,155 per capita. After taking account of all these subtractions from total production, per capita spending on public and private consumption would rise between $156 and $1,031 (or between 0.1 and 0.8 percent a year).

A continuation of poor U.S. trade performance would further reduce U.S. spending power, but by a relatively small amount—just $8 per person (or 0.04 percent) annually. Thus the need to adjust the U.S. current account is a far more serious threat to U.S. living standards than poor U.S. trade performance.

The case that the U.S. current account should be reduced rests on a judgment that the U.S. national savings rate is too low, rather than the belief that likely future paths for the current account are unsustainable or that a dollar crisis is inevitable. If higher U.S. savings and the existing inflow of foreign savings were being profitably invested in the United States, the existing level of the current account deficit would not be a problem. In the absence of higher domestic savings, the United States is better off being able to borrow from abroad than reducing domestic investment.

Provided domestic spending is kept in check, the United States should have adequate industrial capacity to adjust toward higher exports and lower domestic consumption. However, the decline in U.S. spending growth required over the next decade will require much greater discipline than Americans have ever displayed in either their public or private spending decisions.

The major costs of postponing adjustment are mainly those associated with the dislocation caused by the adjustment process itself rather than by the interest costs of borrowing. Because resources must be reallocated rapidly, early adjustment lessens the likelihood that dislocation costs will be major. It would be inadvisable, however, to adjust U.S. spending very rapidly simply to avoid a dollar shock imposed by others. It would also be unwise to achieve the adjustment by reducing domestic investment. The key challenge for U.S. policy in the years ahead is to adjust U.S. spending without penalizing domestic capital formation. This would be best achieved by relying primarily on tighter fiscal policy—through tax increases that reduce consumer spending and through cuts in government spending.

With improved trade performance we could avoid lowering the relative price of U.S. goods to sell more abroad. Balancing the current account by 1995 entirely through faster foreign growth or more open foreign markets rather than through an additional decline in the dollar of about 10 percent would improve living standards by four-fifths of a percent in 1995. But improved trade performance alone is insufficient. Even if foreigners find U.S. products more attractive, closing the current account requires giving up goods and services for export that might otherwise be consumed at home. The only way to actually avoid the difficulties of future spending adjustment without belt tightening is to produce more at home. It will take roughly 1 percent of GDP a year to bring the current account into balance by 1995. If productivity growth could be raised to the 1.9 percent annual average rate achieved between 1950 and 1973, living standards could rise as rapidly between 1987 and 1995 as they did between 1979 and 1987 *and* simultaneously the current account could be brought into balance.

Appendix A: Terms of Trade and Living Standards

As already noted, if changes in U.S. competitiveness had an adverse effect on U.S. living standards, they did so over the medium term, not by producing a larger U.S. trade deficit or higher U.S. unemployment, but by requiring the United States to increase the resources relinquished to obtain a given quantity of imports. In reality, however, except in the period 1973–79, changes in the U.S. terms of trade have not had a major influence on U.S. living standards.

This appendix takes a more detailed look at the linkage between U.S. terms of trade and national living standards. It uses econometric techniques to distinguish between the effects on the terms of trade of changes in the levels of the current account from the effects of changes in the relative prices required to achieve given levels of trade flows.[25] Econometric analysis is also required to learn the extent to which poor U.S. trade performance has eroded U.S. living standards. It has been argued in many reports that U.S. trade performance has suffered because of declining relative product quality, weak process innovation, slow investment, poor labor management relations, and misguided government policies. But for the most part, the arguments have been qualitative. This appendix estimates the combined importance of these factors for U.S. living standards.

In a seminal paper, Houthakker and Magee fitted conventional equations that explained import and export volumes by relative prices and economic activity.[26] Using data from the period 1951–66, they found that each 1.0 percent increase in U.S. GNP raised U.S. imports by 1.5 percent. In contrast, each 1 percent growth in foreign incomes raised U.S. exports by just 1 percent. These estimates implied that the U.S. trade balance would decline even if the rates of growth in the United

25. Because the U.S. trade balance was very different in 1973 and 1980, one cannot use the terms of trade alone to gauge U.S. trade performance. In 1973 nonoil imports of goods and services exceeded nonagricultural exports of goods and services by $9.0 billion (or 0.7 percent of GNP). In 1980 nonagricultural exports exceeded nonoil imports by $21.6 billion (or 0.8 percent of GNP).

26. H. S. Houthakker and Stephen P. Magee, "Income and Price Elasticities in World Trade," *Review of Economics and Statistics*, vol. 51 (May 1969), pp. 111–25.

States and the rest of the world were equal. Moreover, the United States could maintain trade balance only by growing at two-thirds the pace of other countries or by its allowing its export prices to decline relative to import prices.[27]

Used with caution, equations such as these offer useful statistical summaries of the historical relation between the variables. They allow one to control for the impact of relative price effects and to examine whether historically the United States could have maintained a constant trade balance without a real dollar devaluation. The coefficients on the activity variables in the equations should not, however, be interpreted as narrow estimates of the income elasticity of demand. In addition to income effects, these coefficients will pick up the effect of changes in industrial capacity, product quality, variety, reputation, and other non-price factors entering international competition.[28] When used for predictive purposes, the failure to model these variables explicitly could be a major drawback, but for historical analysis these equations make it possible to focus on the role of terms of trade changes (and thus of changes in living standards) in maintaining any given level of the trade balance.

The Houthakker-Magee equations can be updated by estimating sets of equations for both U.S. exports of nonagricultural goods and services and U.S. imports of nonoil goods and services.[29] These equations, reported in table 2-9, explain trade flows in terms of activity and relative price variables (all expressed in logarithms so that parameters may be interpreted as elasticities). Exports are explained by growth in the rest of the OECD (that is, Canada, Europe, and Japan, each weighted by its 1980

27. There are problems in interpreting the coefficients in these equations as structural parameters. The typical function explaining import and export behavior is based on the assumption of imperfect substitution and infinite supply elasticities at home and abroad. Although this procedure may be justified given the assumptions made, for goods that are close substitutes the specification fails to identify supply and demand variables. In addition they fail to model changes in absorption behavior that could shift the relation between these variables over time. For a more complete discussion see Robert Z. Lawrence, "Toward a Better Understanding of Trade Balance Trends: The Cost-Price Puzzle," *BPEA*, 1:1979, pp. 192–212; and Morris Goldstein and Mohsin S. Khan, "Income and Price Effects in Foreign Trade," in Ronald W. Jones and Peter B. Kenen, *Handbook of International Economics*, vol. 2 (Amsterdam: Elsevier Science Publishers, 1985), pp. 1041–1105.

28. Since these variables are likely to change fairly steadily, the equation will attribute them to the income variable that has a strong trend component or will capture them in a trend term if it is entered explicitly.

29. Oil imports and agricultural exports are excluded because of their unusual behavior.

Table 2-9. Trade Equations, 1968–87[a]

Equation	Period	Dependent variable[b]	YFOR[c]	YUS[d]	RPX[e]	RPM[f]	REX[g]	T[h]	D81	D82	D83	D84	D85	D86	D87	Standard error	Durbin-Watson
1	1972–87	QXNAG	1.85 (30.1)	...	−1.01 (−8.0)	...	...	...	...	...	...	...	...	...	...	0.023	1.83
2	1972–80	QXNAG	1.92 (29.1)	...	−1.64 (−7.0)	...	...	...	0.08	0.044	0.062	0.110	0.096	−0.02	−0.06	0.013	1.9
3	1972–86	QXNAG	1.57 (2.5)	...	−1.68 (−6.3)	...	...	0.01 (0.55)	...	...	...	...	...	...	...	0.015	1.7
4	1968–87	QMNO	...	2.17 (29.4)	...	...	−1.22 (−17.0)	...	...	...	...	...	...	...	...	0.025	2.2
5	1968–80	QMNO	...	2.18 (11.6)	...	...	−1.27 (−4.9)	...	0.002	−0.037	−0.009	−0.006	−0.03	0.005	0.02	0.029	2.2
6	1968–87	QMNO	...	2.42 (59.3)	...	−0.96 (−19.6)	...	...	...	...	...	...	...	...	...	0.024	2.9
7	1968–80	QMNO	...	2.16 (13.8)	...	−0.80 (−6.7)	...	...	0.032	0.052	0.07	0.12	0.10	0.10	0.10	0.025	3.5
8	1968–80	QMNO	...	2.06 (5.2)	...	−0.83 (−5.0)	...	0.0004 (0.3)	...	...	...	...	...	...	...	...	...
9	1968–87	QMNO	...	2.0 (7.6)	...	−0.97 (−20.5)	...	0.01 (1.6)	...	...	...	...	...	...	...	0.023	...

a. Annual data; all variables in logs. The numbers in parentheses are t-statistics.
b. QXNAG = volume of exports of goods and services besides agriculture; QMNO = volume of nonoil imports of goods and services.
c. GNP in Canada, OECD Europe, and Japan weighted by U.S. 1980 exports.
d. U.S. GNP in 1980 dollars.
e. Relative U.S. export prices from OECD.
f. Ratio of U.S. nonoil fixed-weight price index to U.S. nonoil, nonfood wholesale prices.
g. Real exchange rate for fifteen industrial countries from Morgan Guaranty, a subsidiary of J. P. Morgan and Co.
h. Time.

share in U.S. exports) and current and two-year lags on the relative price of U.S. exports as estimated by the OECD. Imports are explained by U.S. GNP and the current and two-year lags on the real exchange rate as estimated by J. P. Morgan.[30]

The equations have been estimated through both 1987 and 1980 to examine the stability of the coefficients. On the import side, the coefficients remain stable when the 1980s are added. They indicate that each 1 percent rise in real U.S. GNP raises import volumes by 2.17 percent, and that each 1 percent appreciation or depreciation of the dollar increases or reduces import volumes by 1.22 percent.[31] As the stability of the coefficients suggests, when the import equation fitted through 1980 (equation 5) is used to forecast import volumes (given the actual changes in real U.S. GNP and the real exchange rate through 1987), it tracks import growth with remarkable accuracy. In 1987, a full seven years out of sample, the error is just 2 percent. Over the period as a whole, the mean absolute error of 1.65 percent compares favorably with the within-sample standard error of 2.9 percent.

Fitted over the period 1972–87, the export equation (1) indicates that each 1 percent increase in foreign growth raises U.S. exports by 1.85 percent. Over the period 1972–80 (equation 2), the income coefficient is slightly higher (1.92) but not significantly different. The estimates of export price responsiveness change in the 1980s. Whereas through 1980 each 1 percent rise or fall in relative U.S. export prices reduced or increased exports by 1.64 percent, the full period estimates yield a coefficient of 1.01. The use of the coefficients estimated through 1980 lead to an underprediction of exports when U.S. export prices were high in 1984 and 1985 and an overprediction when they fell in 1986 and 1987.

As the dollar strengthened, the price responsiveness of U.S. exports declined. One explanation is that the composition of U.S. exports changed, becoming more heavily weighted with products having low price elastic-

30. Since U.S. export prices, particularly those of manufactured goods, seem to conform for the most part to standard markup behavior, it is appropriate to use relative export prices and to interpret the export equation as a demand schedule. But many firms selling U.S. imports appear to be price takers. Using the relative import price, therefore, fails to capture changes in profit margins. Accordingly, I use the real exchange rate as a proxy for both supply and demand side considerations.

31. The real exchange rate has a substantial effect on import volumes for a three-year period. The coefficients on the current one-year and two-year lagged real exchange rate are all highly significant in equations estimated from the periods 1967–80 and 1967–87.

ities of demand. When the dollar was within 10 or 15 percent of its 1980 level, the United States was able to sell a wide array of price-sensitive products, but at its 1985 levels all it could sell were products that could not be readily obtained elsewhere—for example, Boeings and supercomputers. Indeed, between 1980 and 1986 the share of high-technology products in U.S. manufactured export goods increased from 35 to 43 percent.[32] This explains why the export responses to the lower dollar in 1985 and 1986 were relatively small and implies that, as the dollar returns to the 1980 levels and price-sensitive U.S. products again become exportable, the response might be expected to rise.

It is significant that the income elasticities for U.S. exports (1.85) and imports (2.17) differ. This suggests that the Houthakker-Magee effect persisted during the estimation period, though in a more muted form than found in the 1950s and 1960s.[33] Given the average annual (logarithmic) growth rates of 2.69 and 2.88 in the United States and the rest of the world between 1972 and 1987, at constant real exchange rates import volumes would have outpaced exports by 0.51 percent annually.[34]

How big an annual real exchange rate change would have been required to keep exports and imports growing at the same rate? This question can be answered only by making some assumptions about pricing decisions. The most adverse impact on the terms of trade occurs when export and import prices remain fixed in their domestic currencies—that is, if each 1 percent real devaluation lowers export prices in foreign currency by 1 percent and raises import prices in U.S. dollars by 1 percent. Using this assumption, one can make some rough calculations. Assuming (again, the conservative) estimates of price elasticities of 1.0 for exports and 1.22 for imports, a real annual depreciation of 0.42 (logarithmic) percent would have been required to maintain balance

---

32. National Science Board, *Science and Engineering Indicators, 1987* (Washington, D.C., 1987), p. 313.

33. In the Helkie and Hooper model used by the Federal Reserve Board, relative changes in industrial capacity are explicitly modeled. The authors find no difference between U.S. and foreign income elasticities. See William L. Helkie and Peter Hooper, "An Empirical Analysis of the External Deficit, 1980–86," in Ralph C. Bryant, Gerald Holtham, and Peter Hooper, eds., *External Deficits and the Dollar: The Pit and the Pendulum* (Brookings, 1988), pp. 10–56.

34. U.S. imports would grow annually at (2.17 × 2.69) 5.84 percent, while exports would grow just (1.85 × 2.88) 5.33 percent.

starting from a position of initial balance. Over a fifteen-year period, a decline of 7.1 percent in the real exchange rate would be required.[35]

From 1980 to 1987, annual average growth rates in the United States and the rest of the world were 2.24 and 2.33 percent, respectively. At constant real exchange rates, therefore, U.S. imports would have increased 0.55 percent more rapidly than exports. Using the coefficient from the equations reported in table 2-9, this suggests that, had the United States not changed its spending patterns between 1980 and 1987, to have exports and imports rise at similar rates the real exchange rate would have had to decline by 2.5 percent (or 0.35 percent annually). This figure probably overstates the depreciation required: (1) for reasons given earlier, exports are likely to be more price elastic at lower dollar levels; and (2) the foregoing analysis does not account for positive effects operating on the current account through increased earnings from net direct foreign investment and improvements in U.S. agricultural export prices.[36]

Nevertheless, the 2.5 percent decline in the U.S. terms of trade can be translated into a loss of living standards. In 1980 nonoil imports of goods and services were 11.7 percent of U.S. GNP. Assuming that real exchange rates are fully passed through into export and import prices, the overall effect of poor trade performance in the 1980s would have been to reduce U.S. living standards by roughly 0.3 percent (2.5 × 0.117) over the seven-year period, or 0.04 percent annually. This estimate, too, overstates the effect of changes in competitiveness on U.S. living standards. It fails to account for the improvements in living standards resulting from increased export specialization and the availability of a greater variety of imports.[37]

In sum, although many have pointed to the problems that poor trade performance presents for U.S. living standards, few have provided

35. Of course, the actual change in the real exchange rate was influenced by other factors, such as changes in the desired level of the current account balance (reflected in national investment and saving decisions) and oil and agricultural prices.

36. The analysis by Helkie and Hooper models relative capacity growth rates to capture the competitiveness effect. Because of this effect U.S. nonoil imports were raised 4.5 percent between 1980 and 1987 and nonagricultural exports reduced by 7.5 percent. See Helkie and Hooper, "Empirical Analysis," p. 16. This suggests that, with price elasticities of 1.2, a devaluation of 1.4 percent annually would have been required to maintain balance.

37. Examining welfare in terms of fixed base-year weights also ignores the ability to substitute away from higher-priced products.

evidence on how large these effects might be. The actual behavior of the U.S. terms of trade suggests that these effects are relatively small. Econometric estimates show that declining competitiveness in the 1980s has lowered the annual growth of our living standards by less than one-twentieth of a percent of GNP annually.

Appendix B: The Model and Common Assumptions

This appendix sets forth the key elements and assumptions of the model used in the text to simulate different living standard scenarios:

1. U.S. demand for nonoil imports of goods and services and foreign demand for U.S. exports are a function of relative prices and incomes. No other terms appear in the equations. Real exchange rate changes are fully passed through and affect prices and trade flows with a one-year lag.

2. Trade flows in manufactured goods are estimated separately. Income elasticities of 2.0 and price elasticities of 1.3 are assumed in the mid-range case and 1.5 in the optimistic case. Prices operate with a one-year lag.

3. Real oil import prices remain constant, and the volume of oil imports has an elasticity of 2.0 with respect to GDP.

4. U.S. net transfers remain at their 1987 nominal levels. Changes in U.S. net foreign investment position equal the U.S. current account and are financed at 7.8 percent a year.

5. Real U.S. domestic absorption (consumption plus investment plus government spending) is determined by subtracting the real current account balance from real GNP. Real domestic absorption of manufactured goods is determined by using a regression that relates domestic absorption of manufactured products to real domestic absorption.[38]

6. Manufacturing value added due to changes in imports and exports is calculated by assuming that each dollar of nonmanufacturing exports or imports of goods and services requires or replaces 20 cents of value

---

38. Period 1970–87:

$$Labman = 2.0\,LCIG82 - 0.022T,$$
$$(11.8) \qquad\qquad (5.6)$$
Standard error = 0.014

where $Labman$ = log of absorption in manufacturing; T = time trend.

added in manufacturing. Each dollar rise in manufactured exports raises manufactured value added by 58 cents; each dollar rise or fall in manufactured imports reduces or increases manufactured value added by 58 cents.[39]

7. The share of each U.S. industry directly and indirectly embodied in U.S. exports and imports is assumed to remain constant. Similarly, each industry's share in manufactured goods produced and absorbed domestically is assumed constant. Industry growth rates are calculated by using the input-output table estimates of the importance of export and domestic demand in domestic production for each industry.

8. Industry growth rates are compared to current Federal Reserve Board capacity utilization rates. No additional capacity is required until utilization rates reach 1978–80 highs. Thereafter, capacity expands at the same rate as production.

9. This model equation system can be represented as follows (all variables are in logarithms):

(1) $$Qx = Epx \left[Px/(Prow/E) \right] + Eyx(Yrow)$$
(2) $$Qm = Epm \left(Pm/P \right) + Eym(Y),$$

where Qx and Qm are the quantity of exports of goods and services and imports of goods and services respectively; Px, U.S. export prices; P, domestic prices, Pm, U.S. import prices; and Y and $Yrow$, U.S. and foreign incomes; E, the foreign currency price of dollars; $Prow$, foreign prices in foreign currency,

(3) $$Px = (1 - Ptx) P$$
(4) $$Pm = Ptm (Prow/E)$$

where Ptx and Ptm indicate the degree to which changes in U.S. domestic prices and foreign prices are passed through into foreign currencies, and E the dollar price of foreign currencies.[40]

---

39. The effect of nonmanufacturing trade on manufacturing output is deduced by using estimates from Kan Young, Ann Lawson, and Jennifer Duncan, "Trade Ripples across U.S. Industries: Effects of International Trade on Industry Output and Employment," in U.S. Department of Commerce, *Implications of Internationalization of the U.S. Economy*, (Washington, D.C., 1986), pp. 47–120. The manufacturing coefficients are derived from Robert Z. Lawrence, *Can America Compete?* (Brookings, 1984).

40. Net factor payments are a function of the net international investment position and interest rates: $NF = rD$.

10. The alternative parameters are as follows:

(a) Mid-range: $Ptx = Ptm = 0.8$; $Epx = Epm = 1.2$; $Eyx = Eym = 2.0.4$.[41]

(b) Pessimistic: $Epx = Epm = 1.0$; $Ptx = Ptm = 1.0$; $Eyx = 1.85$; $Eym = 2.17$.

(c) Optimistic: $Epx = Epm = 1.5$; $Ptx = Ptm = 0.8$; $Eyx = 2.33$; $Eym = 2.0$.[42]

11. All simulations assume the U.S. economy grows at 2.8 percent annually through 1992 and 2.2 percent a year thereafter; foreign incomes ($Yrow$) rise at 2.8 percent throughout the period. Domestic prices (P) in the United States and the rest of the world ($Prow$) rise 4.6 percent annually. Oil prices rise at the rate of U.S. inflation and the volume of oil imports rises twice as fast as U.S. income. The rate of interest on net foreign debt is a constant 7.8 percent. Whereas foreign growth is assumed to be close to its average over the past decade, the U.S. growth path merits some explanation. In 1987 the U.S. unemployment rate was 6.1 percent, or somewhat above the level consistent with stable inflation. It is assumed here that the unemployment rate falls to 5.0 by the end of 1992; given a trend growth of potential output of 2.2 percent, that implies annual output growth between 1987 and 1992 of 2.8 percent,[43] and 2.2

41. Helkie and Hooper indicate a 1 percent depreciation of the dollar will raise U.S. nonagricultural export prices in dollars by 0.21 percent ($Ptx = 0.79$). Similarly, import prices in dollars will rise by 0.91 percent (that is, $Ptm = 0.91$). However, these equations do not track recent U.S. import prices in 1986 and 1987 with much precision. For further discussion, see Richard Baldwin, "Some Empirical Evidence on Hysteresis in Aggregate U.S. Import Prices," Columbia University and the National Bureau of Economic Research, November 1987; and Peter Hooper and Catherine L. Mann, "The Persistence of the U.S. External Deficit," March 1988. A more extensive survey of pass-through studies can be found in Goldstein and Kahn, "Income and Price Effects in Foreign Trade." See also Richard Herd, "Import and Export Price Equations for Manufactures," OECD Working Paper 43 (Washington, D.C., Organization for Economic Cooperation and Development, June 1987).

42. The same results would be obtained if we assumed an elasticity of 2.0 for U.S. exports (Eyx) with foreign growth at 3.3 instead of 2.8 percent annually.

43. This reflects the following regression using annual data from the period 1980–87:

$$PGDP = 2.38 + 2.12\,DU,$$
$$(8.5) \quad (8.84)$$

Standard error $= 0.76$; $\bar{R}^2 = 0.93$; Durbin-Watson $= 2.38$

where $PGDP$ is the percentage change in real GDP and DU the change in the unemployment rate. In the simulations, the intercept that captures trend growth is marked down from 2.38 to 2.2 to reflect slower labor force growth.

percent thereafter. These numbers reflect the projected 1.2 percent annual increase in the labor force forecast by the U.S. Department of Labor. I assume a 1.0 percent annual increase in GDP per worker, the rate recorded between 1979 and 1987.[44] Given the 0.83 percent annual population growth projected by the U.S. Bureau of the Census, this implies that U.S. GDP per capita will rise at 1.65 percent annually between 1987 and 1995.

44. This is a broader measure of productivity (including government and agriculture) than the nonfarm business measure used normally.

CHAPTER THREE

The Risks of Recession

Robert E. Litan

IN CHAPTER 2 Robert Lawrence outlines the structural changes in store for the U.S. economy over the next several years and the implications of those changes for American living standards. For analytical convenience, he assumes that output will soon reach its potential level and remain there. Even under this condition, both Lawrence and Frank Levy in chapter 4 project that American living standards are likely to grow more slowly in the decade ahead than in the previous seven years.

But this projection could be too optimistic. After nearly six years of uninterrupted economic growth, many Americans are fearful that the economy will soon fall into recession. Clearly, an economic downturn would reduce the growth, if not the level, of American living standards below any of the paths projected in earlier chapters.

This chapter takes a detailed look at the risks of recession. It asks two principal questions. Is a contraction inevitable given the length of the current expansion? And if a recession does occur, how will it be affected by the rapid buildup of private and public debt over the past decade?

My answers are cautiously optimistic. In the absence of major shocks, such as another explosion in the price of energy like those of the 1970s, there is no reason why the economy cannot continue its expansion, even if the federal budget is tightened over the next several years. Paradoxically, the economy is more in danger of entering a recession if the deficit is not reduced. If the budget deficit remains high while the trade deficit declines, the Federal Reserve will have to engineer an increase in interest

I wish to thank Joseph Pechman and George Perry for helpful comments on earlier drafts, as well as Jonathan E. Lubick for research assistance.

Table 3-1. *Duration of Economic Expansions and Contractions in the United States, 1854–1982*

Period	Number of cycles	Expansions[a]		Contractions[a]	
		Mean	Standard deviation	Mean	Standard deviation
1854–1919	16	27	10	22	14
1919–45	6	35	26	18	14
1945–82	8	45	28	11	4

Source: Victor Zarnowitz, "The Regularity of Business Cycles," Working Paper 2381 (Cambridge, Mass.: National Bureau of Economic Research, September 1987), p. 5.
a. Number of months.

rates to prevent inflation; doing so with the precision needed to avoid either recession or inflation would be difficult.

The recent substantial increases in private sector debt, as well as the fragility of many financial institutions, could worsen the effect of a recession on individuals, firms, and institutions. Increased debt service burdens in the corporate sector in particular could deepen the next downturn. The greater concern, however, is that if the nation is "shocked" into a recession before the federal budget deficit is reduced, policymakers may be frozen into inaction for fear of making the deficit problem even worse. In that event, any recovery from the recession could be delayed and its pace slowed.

In sum, the challenge for economic policymakers is to take preventive measures against an economic contraction before a crisis precipitates one. The chapter concludes by discussing some policy options to meet this challenge.

Is a Recession Inevitable?

Since the end of World War II, the United States has experienced eight recessions, or periods in which real GNP has declined for at least two successive quarters. As shown in table 3-1, the postwar recessions as a group have been relatively short-lived compared both with postwar expansions and with recessions in earlier periods. The average postwar downturn has lasted eleven months, only half as long as the sixteen recessions between 1854 and 1919, while the average postwar expansion has lasted nearly four years.

As the current expansion stretches out into its sixth year, well past the length of previous upturns, concern grows that another recession is likely, if not inevitable. Historical experience, it is said, demonstrates that regular business cycles are endemic to market economies.

In fact, however, economic fluctuations in the United States and abroad have stubbornly resisted any predictable characterizations, especially in the postwar era. Expansions in the United States have varied significantly in length, as indicated by the large standard deviations shown in table 3-1. Although economic forecasters have been reasonably successful in predicting short-run trends in key economic variables—GNP, inflation, and unemployment—they routinely miss turning points, or shifts from recession to expansion and vice versa.

A few postwar expansions did sow the seeds of future recession by creating inflations or other imbalances in the economy that brought forth restrictive fiscal or monetary policies. But, as shown in table 3-2, most of the downturns since 1945 were fundamentally caused by outside shocks—government retrenchment at the end of a war (Korea, Vietnam) or large increases in the prices of oil and other raw materials that simultaneously led to both inflation and reduced demand.

Outside shocks and shifts in policy can also interact. The jump in oil prices triggered by the Iran-Iraq war and the Iranian revolution in 1979 prompted the Federal Reserve to impose credit controls to restrain the resulting inflation, which led to the recession of 1980, and later to a restrictive monetary policy, which pushed the economy into recession again in 1981–82.

What lies ahead? In the absence of a serious shock, policymakers are unlikely to tighten either fiscal or monetary policy enough to induce a recession. Still, any one of several possible shocks could trigger a downturn. I shall review the possibilities in turn.

The Outlook with No Shocks

It is useful to begin by considering the economic outlook in the absence of shocks, but under two different fiscal policies. One policy, shown in table 3-3, would be to take no further action to reduce the federal budget deficit, which as of mid-1988 was projected by the Congressional Budget Office (CBO) to remain above $120 billion a year through fiscal year 1994. The second policy would gradually eliminate the budget deficit by fiscal year 1993, the target date for budget balance called for by the 1987 Gramm-Rudman-Hollings Act (GRH), shown in the third line of the table.

Table 3-2. *Recessions in the United States since 1945*

Dates	Length (months)	Decline in real GNP (percent)	Annual inflation rate (CPI) two quarters preceding the recession	Trigger
November 1948– October 1949	11	−1.4	8.0	Demand slowdown; shift toward contraction in fiscal policy (end of war economy)
July 1953– May 1954	10	−2.6	2.4	Demand slowdown (end of war economy)
August 1957– April 1958	8	−2.7	4.2	Restrictive monetary policy
April 1960– February 1961	10	−0.1	1.3	Restrictive fiscal policy; steel strike
December 1969– November 1970	11	−0.1	5.8	Auto and General Electric strikes; restrictive monetary policy (to stem Vietnam inflation)
November 1973– March 1975	16	−4.9	9.4	Oil price shock
January 1980– July 1980	6	−2.2	14.3	Oil price shock; credit controls
July 1981– November 1982	16	−3.0	10.8	Restrictive monetary policy, coupled with delayed effects of the 1979–80 oil shock

Sources: Otto Eckstein and Allen Sinai, "The Mechanisms of the Business Cycle in the Postwar Era," in Robert J. Gordon, ed., *The American Business Cycle: Continuity and Change* (University of Chicago Press, 1986), pp. 43–45; and *Economic Report of the President*, various issues.

Despite some fears to the contrary, the federal budget can be balanced by fiscal year 1993 without inducing a recession. For example, suppose policies were introduced to eliminate the $148 billion deficit for fiscal year 1989 projected in the CBO August 1988 baseline in equal annual installments of $37 billion over four years. At this pace, federal stimulus to the economy would be withdrawn at the rate of roughly 0.7 percent of GNP in 1989, declining to less than 0.6 percent in 1993. Given a fiscal policy multiplier of about 1.5,[1] the GRH reductions imply that in a *worst case*—that is, without offsetting monetary stimulus—GNP growth would

1. Ralph C. Bryant and others, eds., *Empirical Macroeconomics for Interdependent Economies* (Brookings, 1988), p. 72.

Table 3-3. *Actual and Projected Federal Budget Deficits, Fiscal Years, 1960–93*

	Actual averages				Projected				
Deficit	1960–69	1970–79	1980–87	1988	1989	1990	1991	1992	1993
In billions of current dollars									
Federal deficit—CBO baseline (August 1988)	-6	-35	-157	-155	-148	-136	-131	-126	-121
Standardized employment deficit (August 1988)[a]	-8	-29	-108	-141	-135	-129	-128	-120	-111
Federal deficit—Gramm-Rudman-Hollings	n.a.	n.a.	n.a.	-144	-136	-100	-64	-28	0
As share of potential GNP									
Projected federal deficit—CBO baseline (August 1988)	0.8	2.2	4.3	3.3	2.9	2.5	2.3	2.1	1.9
Projected standardized employment deficit (August 1988)	1.2	1.8	2.9	3.0	2.7	2.4	2.2	2.0	1.7
Federal deficit—Gramm-Rudman-Hollings	n.a.	n.a.	n.a.	3.0	2.7	1.8	1.1	0.5	0.0

Source: U.S. Congressional Budget Office, *The Economic and Budget Outlook, Fiscal Years 1989–1993, A Report to the Senate and House Committees on the Budget—*pt. 1 (Washington, D.C., 1988, p. 104); U.S. Congressional Budget Office, *The Economic and Budget Outlook: An Update, A Report to the Senate and House Committees on the Budget* (Washington, D.C., 1988), pp. xi, 6; and *Economic Report of the President, February 1988*, p. 337.

n.a. Not available.

a. The standardized employment deficit assumes that unemployment remains at the lowest rate consistent with stable inflation. This rate varied between 5 and 6 percent from 1960 through 1987. In 1988 and 1989 it is projected to be 5.7 percent, falling to 5.5 percent by 1993. The projected deficit figures are calculated from the annual changes (adjusted for tax reform and other special factors); projected in CBO's August 1988 *Update* report, p. 6.

be about 1 percentage point slower than otherwise, but still distinctly positive in the absence of negative shocks.[2]

In any event, this worst case is unlikely to come to pass. In fiscal 1987 the fiscal deficit as a share of potential GNP declined by 1.7 percentage points—double the deficit reduction just discussed—and yet the economy continued to grow.[3] There are two reasons why the economy can expand while the federal budget is tightened. First, in the period ahead the trade deficit is likely to be declining, and unless the budget deficit is reduced, aggregate demand is likely to grow too rapidly. Thus, to some extent, deficit reduction will be eliminating *excessive* demand. Second, deficit reduction beyond that point will permit the Federal Reserve to pursue a more stimulative monetary policy to offset the deflationary effects of a tighter fiscal policy. Lower interest rates do more than encourage private investment. Over the long run, they also reduce the worldwide demand for dollar-denominated assets and thus permit a drop in the exchange value of the dollar, further encouraging U.S. exports.[4]

A lower exchange value of the dollar—a possibility with or without deficit reduction—would, of course, worsen inflation, but probably not so much as to lead to recession. One reasonable scenario is that budget deficit reduction will cause a further 10 percent real drop in the dollar (from its December 1987 level) against the currencies of the Group of Ten (G-10) industrial countries over the next three years,[5] a decline that

2. The $37 billion annual deficit reductions in the above example depart somewhat from the annual cuts called for by GRH, namely $36 billion each year from 1989 through 1992 and $28 billion in 1993. The difference is that the CBO August 1988 baseline projected deficit for fiscal year 1989 of $148 billion is $12 billion larger than the GRH target of $136 billion in that year. Even if the cost of resolving the savings and loan crisis (discussed further later) should increase the deficit as much as $10 billion a year through fiscal year 1993, the additional taxes required to fund these expenditures would not materially alter this outlook.

3. U.S. Congressional Budget Office, *The Economic and Budget Outlook: An Update,* A Report to the Senate and House Committees on the Budget (Washington, D.C., 1988), p. 6.

4. Many analysts have suggested that budget deficit reduction might actually *increase* the value of the dollar by easing fears of foreign investors that excessive fiscal stimulus would worsen U.S. inflation. While this could very well be true in the short run, over the long run lower interest rates in the United States inevitably would depress the demand for dollar-denominated assets unless monetary authorities in other countries responded by easing their monetary policies, too. In that event, stronger growth abroad, rather than dollar depreciation, would encourage U.S. exports.

5. Comprises Canada, Japan, France, West Germany, Italy, the United Kingdom,

Robert Lawrence projects in chapter 2 will eventually eliminate the U.S. current account deficit. If, as assumed in that chapter, foreign exporters pass forward into their U.S. prices 80 percent of this depreciation—a higher rate of pass-through than in recent years—the U.S. price level would rise a little less than 1.0 percent, or about 0.3 percent a year over the three-year period.[6] Some, but probably not all, of this price increase would lead to higher wages and thus would become permanently embedded in the inflation rate. In addition, some U.S. companies would raise the prices of their domestically produced goods to match the import price increases. These effects would be likely to diminish over time so that the long-run inflation rate would increase at around 0.3 percent a year. Given quarter-to-quarter fluctuations in inflation that often substantially exceed this level, it is highly doubtful that the monetary authorities would risk a recession to counteract such a relatively small increase.

Consider now the alternative scenario—that no further deficit reduction measures are taken and the structural federal deficit continues to remain in the range of 2 to 3 percent of GNP, well above its historical average for high-employment years (table 3-3). Could the Federal Reserve manage monetary policy so as to avoid both inflation and recession? In the absence of any major shocks, the most reasonable answer to this question is "yes, but not easily." Over the next several years, the U.S. trade deficit is likely to be declining, perhaps not smoothly but surely. Exports will be rising rapidly, and domestic production will be substituting for imports. With no further reduction in the budget deficit, and at current interest rates, total spending in the economy would be growing faster than the economy's productive capacity. Because, as shown in table 3-4, the economy is not far now from its capacity levels (as measured by prior peaks in capacity utilization), the Federal Reserve would have to pursue

---

Belgium, Netherlands, Sweden, Switzerland, and the United States (eleven countries because Switzerland was added later).

6. Because imports account for 12 percent of GNP, an 8 percent rise in import prices would raise the price level 0.96 percent. The computation of the rate of "pass-through" depends on the price index for imports. Measured by the fixed-weight GNP import index, prices of nonoil imports rose 15 percent between early 1985 and the end of 1987; the rise was almost 20 percent according to the Bureau of Labor Statistics import index. By comparison, the dollar fell 40 percent in real terms during this period, indicating a pass-through rate between 38 and 50 percent. See William R. Melick, "U.S. International Transactions in 1987," *Federal Reserve Bulletin*, vol. 74 (May 1988), pp. 280–83.

Table 3-4. *Capacity Utilization Rates, U.S. Industry, 1973, 1980, 1988*
Percent

Industry	1973 peak	1978–80 peak	July 1988
Manufacturing	87.7	86.5	83.7
Primary processing	91.9	89.1	87.3
Advanced processing	86.0	85.1	82.0
Durable goods	91.8	89.8	81.6
Metal materials	99.2	93.6	84.6
Nondurable goods	91.1	88.1	88.2
Textile, paper, and chemical	92.8	89.4	89.3
Energy materials	94.6	94.0	86.3

Source: Federal Reserve, statistical release, G.3 (402), Washington, D.C., August 16, 1988.

an increasingly restrictive monetary policy and raise interest rates significantly to cut spending.

Quite apart from its negative effect on investment and long-term economic growth, this approach raises the risks of economic instability. Managing the monetary conditions appropriate to a high-pressure economy—one operating near its potential—is never an easy task. When it involves making major changes in economic structure through rising interest rates, the problem is considerably more difficult. Because changes in interest rates affect the economy only gradually, the Federal Reserve would have to make them well in advance of the actual overspending they were meant to discourage. The monetary authorities would then face higher risks of making one of two mistakes: reacting too little, too late, and thus permitting substantial inflation, or overreacting with too much restriction, and thus pushing the economy into recession.[7]

Possible Shocks

An economy is always susceptible to recession from unpredictable shocks that may boost prices and sharply curtail supplies of key materials or products. Of the possible shocks that have prompted recent concern, two—a "dollar strike" and another stock market collapse—may in some way be related to whether and how the United States attacks the federal budget deficit problem. The other two, a drastic oil supply interruption or an unexpectedly large price increase from the 1988 drought, bear no relation to policy measures.

7. As spelled out in the following pages, this risk is compounded by the additional difficulties that would arise for the Federal Reserve if investors were suddenly to reduce their demand for dollars in a period of high current and prospective budget deficits.

THE PROSPECTS OF A DOLLAR STRIKE. Chapter 2 demonstrates how the United States has been able in this decade to increase consumption more rapidly than output by borrowing record sums from foreign investors. But that reliance on foreign creditors has roused concern that the supply of foreign capital could sudddenly dry up, throwing the U.S. economy into recession. Any number of events, real or perceived, could trigger a dollar strike: a failure by the United States to reduce its budget deficit, a perception by foreign investors that the United States will become less hospitable to their capital; or a drift by the United States toward protectionism, to name just a few. Fearing the inflationary consequences of a plummeting dollar, whatever the cause, the Federal Reserve could be expected to tighten monetary policy sharply. Tight money could slow or halt the dollar's drop, but only at the cost of much higher interest rates, while the lower dollar would eventually strengthen U.S. exports and reduce imports. Those results would occur only after some time had elapsed and in the meantime the higher interest rates could depress demand first in the United States and then, in a chain reaction, in the rest of the world.

Such a "hard landing" scenario for the dollar has been feared by some observers for several years. In fact, from its peak in the first quarter of 1985 through July 1988 the exchange value of the dollar declined 41 percent in real terms against a basket of ten of the leading currencies in the world, or by approximately the same amount and at the same rate that one prominent analyst had warned would result in recession.[8] Yet the hard landing has not occurred. Figure 3-1 illustrates that notwithstanding concerns that a lower dollar would raise U.S. interest rates, both short- and long-term rates *fell* through the first quarter of 1987. Since then, both rates have risen, but both still remain well below 1985 levels. Significantly, throughout this period the U.S. economy has remained strong despite the temporary increase in interest rates in 1987 and the upward movement of rates again in the spring and late summer of 1988.

Currency intervention by foreign central banks, especially those in Japan and Germany, through the spring of 1988 helped brake the dollar's decline and thus prevent significant increases in U.S. interest rates. As shown in figure 3-2, foreign central bank investments in dollar assets in

8. See Stephen Marris, *Deficits and the Dollar: The World Economy at Risk* (Washington, D.C.: Institute for International Economics, 1985).

Figure 3-1. *Exchange Rates to Dollar and U.S. Interest Rates,*
1985:1–1988:1[a]

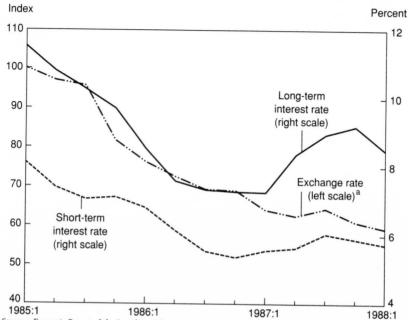

Sources: *Economic Report of the President*, February 1988, p. 371, and *January 1987*, p. 365; and *Federal Reserve Bulletin*, various issues.
a. Dollar to multirate, 1985 = 100.

the United States accounted for substantial proportions of the U.S.
current account deficit in about half the quarters during 1986–87. In
addition, foreign central bank investments in Eurodollar assets, or dollar-
denominated assets outside the United States, also supported the dollar.
Table 3-5 reports the annual increases in foreign exchange reserves held
by foreign central banks during 1985–87, expressed in dollars. Although
not all of these reserves are in dollars, a substantial portion are, given
the dollar's role as a reserve currency. As shown in the table, total
reserves held by the central banks of the Group of Seven (G-7) major
industrialized countries—excluding the dollar assets held in the United
States—rose $36 billion in 1986 and $103 billion in 1987.

By the summer of 1988, the dollar strengthened without central bank
intervention. Indeed, central banks were selling dollars to keep the dollar
exchange rate from rising in response to wider differentials between U.S.
interest rates and those offered in Japan and Europe that attracted private
investors to dollar assets. But in the event of a real dollar strike it is by

Figure 3-2. *U.S.Current Account Deficit and Change in Net Foreign Official Assets in the United States, 1986:1–1987:4*[a]

Billions of dollars

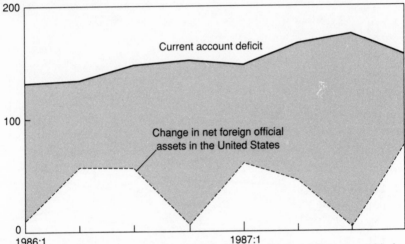

Sources: *Economic Report of the President, February 1988*, pp. 364–65; and *Economic Indicators*, prepared for the Joint Economic Committe by the Council of Economic Advisers, 100 Cong. 2 sess. (Washington, D.C., June 1988), pp. 36–37.

a. At annual rates.

no means clear that monetary authorities abroad would be willing to intervene again on a massive scale, and if they did, whether the intervention would work.

U.S. budget policy could have a decisive effect on whether the economy would suffer from a dollar strike—that is, endure *both* a steep fall in the dollar and a significant rise in U.S. interest rates. Investors here and abroad are well aware that, as shown in table 3-6, unless the federal deficit is reduced, the structural deficit through 1988–93 will remain well above the historical norm—as a share of potential GNP, almost double the average of previous years of comparably high employment. With a credible deficit reduction program in effect, a declining trade deficit and a shrinking inflow of foreign capital do *not* imply rising interest rates in the future even if the dollar should begin to fall again. Under these circumstances, financial markets would be unlikely to take the dollar's drop as a signal for higher interest rates, but rather as a precursor of the shrinking U.S. demand for foreign funds in the wake of a declining trade deficit. This logical sequence appears to explain the events of 1986 and 1987, when the structural budget deficit was falling

Table 3-5. *Annual Increases in Foreign Exchange Reserves Held by Central Banks Outside the United States, 1985–87*[a]
Billions of dollars

Item	1985	1986	1987
G-7 countries[b]	6.9	36.2	103.4
G-10 countries[c]	13.3	41.8	119.2
All industrial countries	19.3	46.4	148.5

Source: International Monetary Fund, *International Financial Statistics, Yearbook 1987* (Washington, D.C., 1987), p. 59; and IMF, *International Financial Statistics, June 1988* (Washington, D.C., 1988), p. 42.

a. Foreign exchange reserves are normally reported in special drawing rights (SDR). Dollar equivalent computed at the dollar/SDR.

b. Comprises Canada, Japan, France, West Germany, Italy, and the United Kingdom.

c. G-7 plus Belgium, Netherlands, Sweden, and Switzerland.

and both the dollar *and* interest rates declined at the same time (figure 3-1).

Failure to reduce the federal budget deficit substantially, however, could magnify the risks of a dollar strike. It could signal to investors that the United States has lost the ability to manage its financial affairs: if the deficit cannot be substantially reduced when the economy is operating at close to its capacity, then when will the deficit problem ever be attacked? Moreover, by requiring the Federal Reserve to maintain high interest rates to keep inflation from accelerating, continued inaction on the budget deficit would prevent the dollar exchange rate from falling to a level consistent with long-run equilibrium current account balance. In such an environment, the dollar will be exposed to a larger, sudden fall. And if a dollar strike should occur, the large demands on credit markets caused by the high budget deficit could lead to an even sharper increase in interest rates, raising the risks of a recession.

In short, budget deficit reduction may not avert a dollar strike, but it certainly can mitigate any rise in interest rates that a steep drop in the dollar would otherwise entail, and thus help keep the economy on a continuous path of growth.

ANOTHER FINANCIAL CRISIS. The stock market crash of October 1987 and continuing concerns about the fragility of many depository institutions (discussed later in the chapter) have generated fears that another financial shock could trigger a recession by causing consumers and businesses to lose confidence in the economy and thus to pull back their spending. Indeed, some analysts have even forecast a rerun of the Great Depression,

Table 3-6. *Structural Federal Deficit in High-Employment Years,*
Selected Years, 1956–93[a]

Percent unless otherwise specified

Year	Actual unemployment rate	NAIRU	Standardized employment federal budget surplus (deficit) as percent of potential GNP
1956	4.1	5.1	0.6
1957	4.3	5.1	0.6
1962	5.5	5.3	−0.5
1964	5.2	5.5	−0.8
1965	4.5	5.6	−0.4
1966	3.8	5.6	−1.6
1967	3.8	5.6	−2.3
1968	3.6	5.6	−4.3
1969	3.5	5.6	−0.9
1970	4.9	5.6	−0.7
1971	5.9	5.7	−1.9
1972	5.6	5.8	−1.7
1973	4.9	5.8	−1.7
1974	5.6	5.9	−0.8
1978	6.1	5.9	−2.4
1979	5.8	5.9	−1.6
Average for all years	4.8	5.6	−1.3
Projected average for 1988–93	6.0	5.6	−2.3

Sources: U.S. Congressional Budget Office, *Economic and Budget Outlook: Fiscal Years 1989–1993*, pp. 44, 104; and *Economic Report of the President, February 1988*, p. 293, table 3-3.

a. A high-employment year is one in which the actual unemployment rate was no more than 0.2 percentage points above the nonaccelerating inflation rate of unemployment (NAIRU) as calculated by the Congressional Budget Office.

which technically began before the stock market crash of October 1929, but clearly became worse as confidence fell along with stock prices.[9]

In fact, however, the U.S. economy has shown itself over the past year to be highly resilient in the face of one of the sharpest stock market declines in American history. Consumer spending dropped in the fourth quarter of 1987 at an annual rate of 2.1 percent (the first quarterly drop since 1981), consistent with the view that consumption depends in part on consumers' wealth.[10] But consumption rebounded in 1988 and through

9. See Christine D. Romer, "The Great Crash and the Onset of the Great Depression," NBER Working Paper 2639 (Cambridge, Mass.: National Bureau of Economic Research, June 1988).

10. There is some support for the estimate that a one-dollar decline in the value of the

Table 3-7. *Stock Market Declines and Recessions in the United States, 1948–87*

Dates of stock market declines	Decline in Standard and Poor's 500 index from peak to trough (percent)	Did recession follow?	Time from beginning of stock decline to beginning of recession (months)
October 1948–June 1949	14	Yes	1
January 1953–September 1953	11	Yes	6
July 1956–February 1957	11	No	. . .
July 1957–December 1957	17	Yes	1
December 1959–October 1960	9	Yes	4
December 1961–October 1962	22	No	. . .
January 1966–October 1966	17	No	. . .
December 1968–June 1970	29	Yes	12
January 1973–December 1974	43	Yes	10
December 1976–March 1978	15	No	. . .
February 1980–April 1980	11	Had already started	−1
April 1981–July 1982	19	Yes	3
October 1983–July 1984	10	No	. . .
August 1987–December 1987	27	No	. . .

Sources: Ekstein and Sinai, "Mechanisms of the Business Cycle in the Postwar Era," pp. 43–45; and Data Resources, Inc. database.

June was up at a 3.4 percent annual rate. Equally significant, private investment and export growth in 1988 have been strong. Through the second quarter real GNP was advancing in 1988 at a 3.3 percent annual rate, dropping the unemployment rate close to 5 percent, its lowest level in ten years.

The strong postcrash performance of the U.S. economy is not as surprising as it may seem. As shown in table 3-7, since 1945 falling stock prices have "predicted" eight recessions. On six other occasions when stock prices plummeted, the economy continued to expand.

Shortly after the October 1987 crash, analysts began drawing parallels between it and the October 1929 stock market debacle. News stories and commentators, noting the similar recovery in stock prices through April of 1930 and 1988, predicted (or feared) that the stock market would

---

stock market should depress consumer spending by about four cents for about a year. At this rate, the $1 trillion drop in the stock market in the fall of 1987 should have depressed consumer spending by about $40 billion. See *Economic Report of the President, February 1988*, p. 42; David E. Runkle, "Why No Crunch from the Crash?" *Federal Reserve Bank of Minneapolis Quarterly Review*, vol. 12 (Winter 1988), p. 2.

again begin falling in the spring, just as it did in 1930.[11] Presumably, the economy would then also enter a tailspin.

These predictions, too, have proved false. The parallels between 1929 and 1987 have been misleading for two fundamental reasons. First, the depth of the Depression was largely due to the failure of the Federal Reserve to provide sufficient liquidity to consumers and firms immediately following the October 1929 stock market crash and in the months and years thereafter. Currency and demand deposits actually *fell* 23 percent between 1930 and 1933.[12] In contrast, the monetary authorities pumped reserves into the banking system in the weeks after the October 1987 stock market crash and have since steadily expanded the money supply.

Second, because bank deposits were not federally insured until 1933, the federal government had little way of preventing worried depositors from withdrawing deposits from their banks. Indeed, between 1930 and 1933 nearly 9,000 of the nation's 25,000 banks closed their doors, and the banking system was in the midst of a full-fledged run when President Roosevelt took office. Since deposit insurance was instituted, however, federally insured depository institutions have not experienced a run, despite significant increases in bank and thrift failures in recent years.[13] Significantly, in the weeks following the stock market crash of October 1987, deposits in banks and thrifts *increased* markedly, as consumers fled to safe, federally insured assets.

In sum, even another fall in stock prices need not trigger or foreshadow a recession. The Federal Reserve's actions in 1987 demonstrate that even if it must temporarily sacrifice some stability of the dollar, the first order of business for the monetary authorities in the midst of financial market turmoil is to provide the necessary liquidity to avert a domino-like sequence of bankruptcies. If another stock market collapse occurs, it will more likely simply reflect underlying economic forces that would themselves cause an economic downturn. For example, any dollar strike scenario is likely to be associated with a steep decline in stock prices as well. But then the fall in stock prices would signal rather than cause the oncoming recession.

11. See, for example, Randall Smith, "Market Seers Fret over Analogies to '29–'30 despite Economic Vigor," *Wall Street Journal*, March 31, 1988.

12. U.S. Bureau of the Census, *Historical Statistics of the United States: Colonial Times to 1970*, pt. 2 (Washington, D.C.: Department of Commerce, 1975), p. 992.

13. In 1985, state-insured savings and loans in Ohio and privately insured thrifts in Maryland experienced runs after scandals at major institutions in each state were uncovered.

THE DROUGHT. During the late spring and early summer of 1988, many of the nation's agricultural states were hit by a severe drought, which sharply reduced output of feed and food grains. Although the price-increasing effects of the drought are not expected to show up fully until 1989, recent press reports suggest that the drought eventually will raise retail food prices 3-5 percent, which, given the 16 percent weight of food prices in the consumer price index, means a one-shot increase in consumer prices of 0.5–0.8 percent.[14] By comparison, food prices shot up about 10 percent in both 1973 and 1974 (relative to the economywide rate of inflation in 1972) when bad weather caused a major drop in crop production.[15]

If the consensus projections for the inflationary effects of the drought in 1988 prove correct, the higher food prices themselves need only lead to a one-shot increase in the price level. Only to the extent that they induced substantial increases in wage rates would this be likely to generate a sustained increase in the rate of inflation. A rise, of say 0.3 percent a year in the price level, is unlikely by itself to induce an acceleration of wage increases large enough to cause the Federal Reserve to take offsetting action through more restrictive monetary policy. And even if the Federal Reserve did see the need for some tightening, the magnitude of the restrictive effort required to contain inflationary pressures of this modest size would not be sufficient to put the economy into recession.

THE PROSPECTS OF ANOTHER OIL SHOCK. The oil shocks of 1973 and 1979 induced recession in the United States for three reasons. First, by sharply raising the price of oil, foreign oil exporters in effect imposed a stiff tax on American firms and businesses, dramatically increasing the flow of U.S. dollars to other oil-producing nations while depressing the ability of Americans to purchase domestically produced goods and services. Second, the tight monetary policy adopted by the Federal

14. Although the drought had a severe effect on crop production, its impact on food prices should be lessened by substantial government food surpluses built up earlier when prices were lower. In addition, raw grains account for a small fraction of the overall cost of most food items. See, for example, Bruce Ingersoll, "Rise of 3% to 5% in Food Prices Seen as Result of Drought, U.S. Agency Says," *Wall Street Journal*, June 22, 1988. For a projection of the impact of the drought, see *Economic and Budget Outlook: An Update*, pp. 16–17.

15. *Economic Report of the President, February 1988*, p. 313.

Reserve to keep the increase in oil prices from generating an upward price-wage spiral also depressed private spending. And third, after the first oil shock of 1973 federal policymakers attempted to cushion consumers by imposing price controls on domestic oil, which led to shortages and thus interruptions in the availability of key energy supplies. Although it is not likely that price controls would be reimposed, a third large increase in the price of imported oil would again reduce consumer and business purchasing power and probably prompt the monetary authorities to sharply curtail money supply growth. Both effects would probably produce another recession.

How likely is a third oil shock? Oil price movements over the past fifteen years have proven to be notoriously difficult, if not impossible, to predict. Few experts foresaw the Arab oil embargo in 1973, which led to the quadrupling of oil prices from $3 to $12 a barrel in 1973–74. The same was true in 1979, when the Iranian revolution and the Iran-Iraq war temporarily reduced world supply and unleashed a rash of speculative buying, which pushed oil prices near $40 a barrel. And finally, most experts failed to forecast that oil prices would plunge after 1981 to the $14–$18 a barrel price range of the past several years.[16]

Oil prices are so difficult to predict because they are influenced by so many factors, each of which is itself unpredictable. For example, at the beginning of the decade, many analysts were projecting that oil prices would continue to increase throughout the 1980s.[17] But these forecasts generally assumed that the world economy would grow steadily throughout the decade and that oil production in countries outside the Organization of Petroleum Exporting Countries (OPEC) would not rise significantly. Both assumptions proved incorrect. The United States and other industrialized countries either grew slowly or suffered deep recessions in the early 1980s. Slow growth, together with the doubling of oil prices in 1979-80, reduced oil consumption. Equally important, oil production by non-OPEC countries has risen steadily since the first oil price shock in 1973, as shown in figure 3-3. The combination of falling world demand and rising non-OPEC supply proved too much for the OPEC members to withstand and thus the cartel has cracked.

No one knows what lies ahead. Oil price optimists point to the rising

16. See Dermot Gately, "Lessons from the 1986 Oil Price Collapse," *BPEA*, 2:1986, pp. 237–71.
17. Ibid., pp. 249–50.

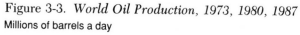

Figure 3-3. *World Oil Production, 1973, 1980, 1987*

Millions of barrels a day

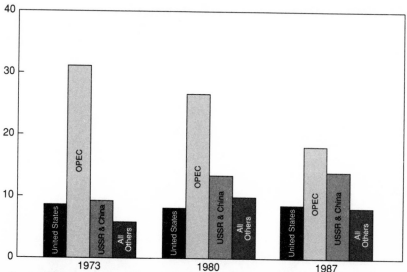

Source: U.S. Department of Energy, Energy Information Administration, *Monthly Energy Review, March 1988,* DOE/EIA-0035 (Washington, D.C., 1988), p. 113.

production levels outside OPEC as evidence that oil markets will remain relatively stable. Because the OPEC countries are the "swing" producers in the world, the high non-OPEC production levels have effectively idled much of OPEC's production capacity. The Department of Energy estimates that in 1987 excess production capacity worldwide hit 9.7 million barrels a day, roughly triple the level in 1980.[18]

Oil price pessimists, on the other hand, are concerned that non-OPEC production will not be able to match increases in consumption, especially in the United States, where oil imports have increased in recent years. Indeed, as shown in table 3-8, U.S. oil imports in 1987 had surpassed their level in 1973. Perhaps more ominously, U.S. domestic oil production has failed to increase over the past fifteen years even though oil prices in real terms have more than doubled. The table shows that the United States is likely to become even more dependent on oil imports, projected to make up between 50 percent and 64 percent of total U.S. oil

18. U.S. Department of Energy, Energy Information Administration, *Annual Energy Outlook 1987: With Projections to 2000,* DOE/EIA-0383 (Washington, D.C., 1987), p. 3.

Table 3-8. *U.S. Oil Consumption, Production, and Imports, Actual,*
1973, 1979, 1987, and Projected, 1990–2000
Millions of barrels a day

Item	Actual			Low-import[a]			High-import[b]		
	1973	1979	1987	1990	1995	2000	1990	1995	2000
Domestic consumption	17.3	18.5	16.6	17.6	18.3	18.3	17.9	20.0	22.2
Domestic production	11.0	10.2	10.0	9.8	9.3	9.1	9.4	8.3	7.9
Imports	6.3	8.5	6.5	7.8	9.0	9.2	8.5	11.7	14.3
Ratio of imports to consumption	0.36	0.46	0.39	0.44	0.49	0.50	0.47	0.59	0.64

Sources: *Monthly Energy Review, March 1988*, pp. 38–39, 115; U.S. Department of Energy, Energy Information Administration, *Annual Energy Outlook 1987: With Projections to 2000*, DOE/EIA-0383 (Washington, D.C., 1987); and author's projections. Figures are rounded.

a. The low-import scenario assumes that real GNP grows 2.8 percent a year through 1990 and then 2.2 percent annually thereafter; that oil prices increase 4 percent a year; that the income elasticity of oil demand is 0.8; that short-run (one-year) and long-run (ten-year) price elasticities of demand are -0.04 and -0.4, respectively; and that domestic supply for 1995 and 2000 is consistent with the EIA's "high price–low growth" scenario (supply for 1990 is interpolated).

b. The high-import scenario assumes that GNP grows 2.8 percent a year through 1990 and then 2.7 percent annually thereafter; that real oil prices increase 1 percent a year; that the income elasticity of oil demand is 1.0; and that domestic supply for 1995 is consistent with EIA's "low price–high growth" scenario (supply for 1990 is interpolated).

consumption by the year 2000, depending on the rate of GNP growth and annual increases in real oil prices.

Although it certainly will increase the exposure of the United States to the harmful effects of a future oil shock, the growing U.S. dependence on oil imports will not necessarily increase the likelihood of such a shock. Oil prices are set in a world market, not by the United States. Given the substantial excess production capacity around the world, a severe interruption in oil supplies would probably be required to trigger explosive price increases like those of 1973–74 and 1979–80. Although such an interruption is unlikely, the continuing tensions in the Middle East make it impossible to ignore the risk.

Severity of a Future Recession

However important the question of what may bring about the next economic downturn, even more important is how deep the downturn would be. Table 3-9 catalogues the short-run effects of projected recessions, of varying degrees of severity, assumed to begin in the first quarter of 1990. The three recession scenarios correspond roughly to the mild U.S. recessions of 1960–61 and 1969–70, the three moderate recessions between 1948 and 1958, and the two severe oil shock recessions of 1973–75 and 1981–82 (see table 3-2).

The projected GNP losses for the three recession scenarios range between $108 billion and $1.18 trillion, or between $432 and $4,708 per

Table 3-9. *Estimated Effects of a Recession in 1990*[a]

Billions of 1990 dollars unless otherwise specified

Effect	Recession		
	Mild	Moderate	Severe
Length of contraction (quarters)	3	4	5
Percentage drop in GNP (peak-to-trough)	-0.1	-2.2	-4.0
Total loss in GNP[b]	108	529	1,177
Per capita loss in GNP (1990 dollars)[c]	432	2,116	4,708
Increase in unemployment rate (percentage points)[d]	0.8	1.8	3.1
Total loss in gross investment[e]	27	132	294
Total increase in federal debt[f]	41	192	435
Peak increase in federal budget deficit	26	72	123
Peak improvement in U.S. trade balance[g]	17	47	81

a. All recession scenarios assume that the economy is at potential output, assumed to be $5,380 billion, before entering recession in the first quarter of 1990. It is further assumed that potential output grows 2.2 percent a year and that the economy returns after the recession to its potential output growth path at the rate of 3.5 percent a year.

b. GNP losses in the future are calculated from the beginning of recession until the economy returns to full employment.

c. Based on estimated 1990 population of 250 million.

d. The increase in unemployment is based on an estimated current "Okun's Law" relationship of a 1.0 percentage point increase in the unemployment rate for every 2.2 percent decline in real GNP.

e. Ratio of investment loss to GNP loss is assumed to be 25 percent, based on simulations of the Federal Reserve Board econometric model of the U.S. economy, as reported in Barry P. Bosworth, *Tax Incentives and Economic Growth* (Brookings, 1984), p. 123.

f. Assumes a 0.37 elasticity of the budget deficit with respect to changes in real GNP.

g. Assumes that imports have an income elasticity of 2.0.

capita. Significantly, a moderate recession would entail per capita output losses in the short run as large as the projected total growth in output per capita between now and 1995 in the mid-range scenario outlined in the previous chapter.

The estimated output losses also translate into potentially significant declines in employment and private investment, on the one hand, and increases in federal debt (to finance increases in the federal budget deficit), on the other. For example, a moderate recession beginning in 1990 would cut nonresidential investment a total of $132 billion, while permanently raising the federal debt $192 billion. A severe recession would have adverse effects more than twice as bad.

Perhaps the only positive effect of a recession is a temporary improvement in the U.S. trade balance. Thus in the moderate recession scenario outlined in table 3-9, the U.S. trade deficit would narrow in the second year by an estimated $47 billion (in 1990 dollars) compared with a baseline full-employment path of GNP; the corresponding second-year trade improvement in a severe recession scenario is an estimated $81 billion. But each of these two projections assumes that a recession in the United

States does not trigger or is not associated with an economic downturn elsewhere. In a worldwide recession, demand for U.S. exports would also fall, thus limiting any potential improvement in the U.S. trade balance. More important, a recession cannot be a *permanent* cure for the trade deficit. Once the economy has embarked on a recovery, faster growth will again encourage imports and thus move the trade balance back toward its previous position.

What is likely to determine the depth of the next recession? If past experience is any guide, the severity of the next downturn will depend on the shock that triggers it. Thus, for example, any supply shock that pushes up the inflation rate 4 or more percentage points, as did the last two oil shocks, would be likely to produce a contraction as severe as those of 1973–75 and 1981–82. Even in the absence of a supply shock, the result would be similar if policymakers allowed inflation to accelerate over some longer period and then sharply tightened either fiscal or monetary policy to lower inflation. At the other extreme, any recession preceded by an increase in the inflation rate of only 1 or 2 percentage points probably would be short and mild, much like the 1969–70 recession.

But the critical question arises whether policymakers can safely assume that any future economic contraction will be so well behaved. Over the last decade, the U.S. economy has experienced structural changes that some observers claim will deepen the next downturn. Debt obligations of individuals, businesses, and the federal government have increased significantly. Many U.S. financial institutions also are on weak footing. Although none of these developments is likely to trigger a recession, certain of them could deepen the next downturn.

Business and Household Debt

Trends in private sector debt over the last decade have attracted considerable interest and controversy. Perhaps most attention has centered on the rise in the *stock* of debt itself. Figure 3-4 illustrates, for example, that in relation to GNP, total nonfinancial debt in the United States was relatively stable throughout the postwar period until the early 1980s; since then, the debt-GNP ratio has risen markedly. Significantly, all major sectors of the economy—households, businesses, and the government—have increased their debt burdens.

Simple debt-GNP ratios can be misleading, however, because they mix a "stock" measure of debt with a "flow" measure of the ability to service it (GNP). It is more revealing to distinguish between the two

Figure 3-4. *Ratio of Credit Market Debt to GNP (nominal) for Households, Businesses, and Government, 1950–87*

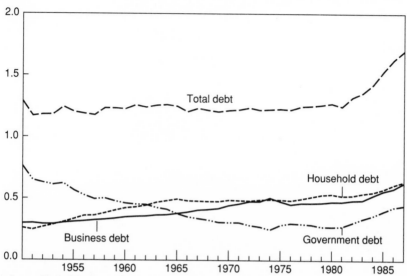

Sources: Board of Governors of the Federal Reserve System, *Balance Sheets for the U.S. Economy, 1948–87* (Washington, D.C., April 1988), pp. 11–15, 16–20, 21–25 and *Flow of Funds Accounts: Financial Assets and Liabilities Year-End, 1963–86*, pp. 3–4; and *Economic Report of the President, February 1988*, p. 260.

kinds of risks debt poses—insolvency and illiquidity—and thus to look to measures that do not confuse the two concepts.

The risks of insolvency, for example, depend on the relationship between a borrower's debt obligations and total assets. A company's total debt may rise as a percentage of its income, but if it has more assets against which to borrow, its risk of insolvency may not have changed. Figure 3-5 illustrates that if assets are measured at their historical cost, debt-to-asset ratios in both the corporate and household sectors have steadily increased, a trend consistent with the debt-GNP ratios. However, in the corporate sector, both debts and assets also can be assessed at their *market values*. Measured that way, as in figure 3-6, corporate debt has shown no upward trend over the past fifteen years, although the debt-to-asset ratio based on market values is currently well above its level during the 1960s. The key reason for the differences in the book- and market-value measures of corporate indebtedness, of course, is the substantial rise in stock prices in the 1980s.[19]

19. A market-value-based debt-to-asset ratio for the household sector cannot be

Figure 3-5. *Nonfinancial Business and Household Total Liabilities to Total Assets Ratio, 1948–87*
Ratio

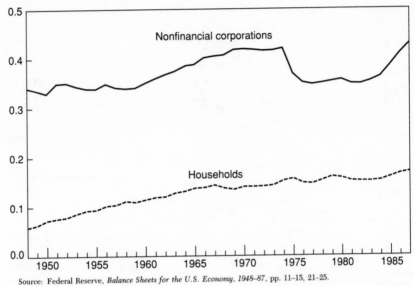

Source: Federal Reserve, *Balance Sheets for the U.S. Economy, 1948–87*, pp. 11–15, 21–25.

From a macroeconomic perspective, however, the risks of insolvency are probably not as important as the risks of illiquidity, or the inability of borrowers to service their debts as they come due. Even solvent borrowers who have temporary difficulty paying interest on their debts will be forced to reduce spending and, in the case of business borrowers, conceivably to lay off workers. As these effects multiply, they can contract spending throughout the economy. Where firms are forced into bankruptcy, cash flows to their suppliers and workers may also be interrupted, perhaps triggering liquidity problems elsewhere in the economy.

Figure 3-7 depicts two measures of illiquidity risks, one for nonfinancial business and one for households. For businesses, interest obligations as a share of cash flow, including after-tax income, interest and depreciation, have risen steeply throughout the postwar period, especially over the past ten years. A similar ratio for households, interest as a share of

computed because market values for household assets are unavailable. However, because the upward trend in the debt-to-asset ratios based on historical cost for both the corporate and household sectors are similar, it is likely that the debt burden of the household sector measured at market value has been advancing, if at all, less rapidly than figure 3-5 suggests.

Figure 3-6. *Ratio of Nonfinancial Corporate Sector Debt to Equity, Market Value, 1961–87*

Ratio

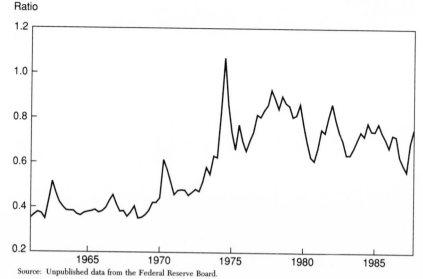

disposable income, has also risen over the past four decades, but at a less dramatic rate.[20]

Why the debt burdens of businesses and households have risen during the 1980s is puzzling. The income tax code has long favored debt finance by both sectors of the economy, allowing corporations to deduct interest but not dividends and permitting individuals to deduct interest paid on mortgages or consumer loans. But until the major tax reforms enacted in 1986, few changes in the tax laws affected financing decisions, and yet interest burdens for both business and household debt continued to climb. Meanwhile, although rising leverage may force corporate managers "back to the wall," thus causing them to become more efficient (see chapter 6), it is not clear why corporations decided to repurchase so much of their own equity (thus pushing up debt-to-asset ratios measured at historical cost) in this decade and not earlier.

Whatever the underlying causes of rising private sector debt burdens,

<hr />

20. Household debt has increased at an even more rapid pace in Japan and Germany, to the point where personal debt-to-income ratios are now between 70 and 90 percent of the U.S. ratio, compared with 30–60 percent in 1969. See Dorothy B. Christelow, "Converging Household Debt Ratios of Four Industrial Countries," *Federal Reserve Bank of New York Quarterly Review*, vol. 12 (Winter 1987–88), p. 35.

Figure 3-7. *Interest Burden of Nonfinancial Business*
and Households, 1947–86[a]

Percent

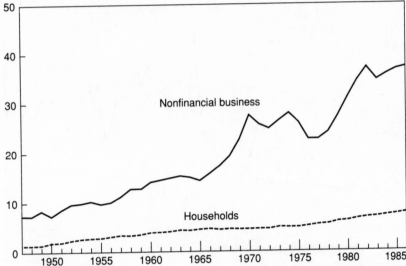

Sources: U.S. Department of Commerce, Bureau of Economic Analysis, *National Income and Product Accounts of the United States, 1929–82* (Washington, D.C., 1986), pp. 63–70, 89–98, 392–93; and *Survey of Current Business*, vol. 68 (June 1988), pp. 5, 7.
a. Nonfinancial business measure is the ratio of interest paid to total cash flow. Interest burden of households is the ratio of household interest to disposable income.

a critical question for macroeconomic policymakers is whether the higher levels of interest in relation to personal income or corporate cash flow pose any special economic risks. One view is that the increase in leverage will affect only the *nature* of the next recession, but not its *severity*.[21] Unlike previous recessions, which hit residential investment especially hard, the next recession, it is argued, will be especially hard on the business sector, as falling corporate profits cause highly leveraged companies to cut back spending more quickly, or even worse, force many companies to go bankrupt. Put another way, higher leverage simply redistributes the adverse effects of any shock to the economy, but does not magnify the total effect of that shock.

The experience of the 1980s seems quite consistent with this view. Figure 3-8 illustrates that after falling for nearly two decades, the annual number of business failures—both small and large—has exploded in the

---

21. See comments and discussion of Lawrence H. Summers on Ben S. Bernanke and John Y. Campbell, "Is There a Corporate Debt Crisis?" *BPEA, 1:1988*, pp. 130–36.

Figure 3-8. *Number of Business Failures, 1945–87*

Number of failures (thousands)

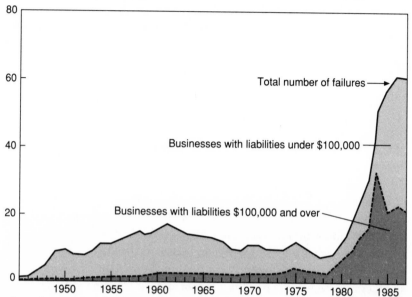

Source: *Economic Report of the President, February 1988,* p. 357.

1980s, and yet the economy has continued to display strong growth. Significantly, total failures each year have nearly tripled during the current expansion, a pattern that clearly suggests that a rising bankruptcy rate need not drag down the overall economy. If so, then an important impact of rising leverage is that it may raise the multiplier effect of changes in monetary policy, that is, the change in real GNP due to any given change in the money supply.[22] Given higher debt-to-asset ratios in the corporate sector, the investment plans of companies should be more sensitive to small movements in interest rates—which should have correspondingly greater effects on available cash flow (after interest)—than in previous decades. Monetary authorities should thus take account of any change in the multiplier that higher leverage may cause.

22. Numerous recent theoretical papers have suggested that balance sheet constraints— reflecting the influence of debt—can increase the variability of consumption, investment, and output. These results are consistent with the view that rising debt ratios can increase the money multiplier. For a guide to this literature, see Mark Gertler, "Financial Structure and Aggregate Economic Activity: An Overview," Working Paper 2559 (Cambridge, Mass.: National Bureau of Economic Research, April 1988), pp. 33–37.

An alternative view is that greater debt burdens may worsen a downturn by creating more uncertainty about the impact of policy changes. Much is likely to depend on the severity of the shock that triggers the recession. Naturally policymakers will be particularly concerned about the chain-reaction effects of corporate bankruptcies, including the damaging effects on consumer and business confidence, at a time when many businesses, especially large firms, are failing. But the uncertainties surrounding these effects are also likely to be greater, and thus the room for policy error grows, the larger the shock that triggers a recession. For example, the monetary authorities may provide a given degree of stimulus to rescue the economy from a downturn only to find that a wave of bankruptcies has so shattered confidence that real activity does not respond as would have been expected. In that event, the recession could be deeper and last longer than it would if the private sector had not been so leveraged.

Which view is correct? The evidence, unfortunately, is mixed, depending upon whether corporate or household debt is the focus.

Using a sample of 643 major corporations, Ben Bernanke and John Campbell have recently simulated the effects on major corporations of another recession as deep as the 1973–75 and 1981–82 downturns.[23] Table 3-10 summarizes the results, illustrating actual interest coverage ratios (interest expense divided by total cash flow) for 1973–75 and 1980–86 and then hypothetical ratios for a repetition of the 1973–75 and 1981–82 recessions beginning in 1986. The interest coverage ratio is a useful proxy for the likelihood of bankruptcy. In particular, a coverage ratio above 1.0 indicates that a corporation has insufficient cash flow (operating income before depreciation, taxes, and interest) to meet its interest obligations; and a ratio that reaches infinity (or is even negative) indicates that a firm's cash flow is zero or negative—essentially close to or in bankruptcy. Table 3-10 reports not only the average coverage ratios for the full sample, but also their distribution, giving special attention to the ratios of the corporations in the 90th and 95th percentiles (or those whose interest coverage ratios are in the top 10 and 5 percent of the distribution, respectively).

The results are disquieting. A rerun of the 1973–75 recession would raise the interest coverage ratio only a bit above the actual levels of 1973-75 in all percentile groups. But another downturn like 1981–82 would

23. Bernanke and Campbell, "Is There A Corporate Debt Crisis?" pp. 83–125.

Table 3-10. *Interest Coverage Ratios for a Sample of Corporations, Actual, 1973–75 and 1980–86, and Projected for Two Possible Recessions Beginning in 1986*[a]

Item	Average for full sample	Percentile		
		50	90	95
Actual levels				
1973	0.12	0.14	0.38	0.50
1974	0.13	0.18	0.53	0.90
1975	0.15	0.19	0.47	0.76
1980	0.18	0.20	0.56	0.95
1981	0.21	0.22	0.66	1.28
1982	0.22	0.24	1.18	∞
1983	0.18	0.20	0.99	∞
1984	0.18	0.19	0.81	∞
1985	0.18	0.21	1.67	∞
1986	0.20	0.22	1.65	∞
1973–75 recession simulation				
1986	0.17	0.18	0.54	1.63
Recession year 1	0.28	0.21	0.58	0.95
Recession year 2	0.26	0.21	0.60	1.11
1981–82 recession simulation				
1986	0.17	0.18	0.59	1.90
Recession year 1	0.19	0.19	0.68	20.60
Recession year 2	0.20	0.21	∞	∞

Source: Ben S. Bernanke and John Y. Campbell, "Is There a Corporate Debt Crisis?" *BPEA, 1:1988*, pp. 106, 120.
a. Interest coverage ratio is defined as the ratio of interest expense divided by total cash flow (operating income before depreciation, taxes, and interest).

have a much greater impact. By the third year, interest payments could not be serviced out of cash flow by the top 10 percent of the corporations in the sample, twice as many as between 1982 and 1986. Put another way, the simulations suggest that another recession comparable to that of 1981–82 could easily double the current number of corporate bankruptcies.

The debt picture in the household sector is noticeably brighter. While the overall ratio of interest payments to income for households has been rising, consumer installment debt in particular has been increasingly concentrated in upper-income households, those best able to weather recession. As shown in table 3-11, low- and middle-income households accounted for a lower share of total installment debt payments in 1986 than in 1983. In addition, the median ratio of payments to income of the poorest households actually declined during this period, although it rose

Table 3-11. *Distribution of Consumer Installment Debt, 1983, 1986*

Income class of household (1986 dollars)	Median ratio of payments to income		Share of total payments	
	1983	1986	1983	1986
Less than 10,000	12.2	8.8	5.2	4.2
10,000–19,999	7.6	8.6	14.5	12.4
20,000–34,999	7.1	7.2	31.4	28.3
35,000–49,999	6.0	6.5	23.4	24.6
50,000 or more	4.2	4.9	25.5	30.5

Source: Robert B. Avery and others, "Changes in Consumer Installment Debt: Evidence from the 1983 and 1986 Surveys of Consumer Finances," *Federal Reserve Bulletin*, vol. 73 (October 1987), p. 764.

modestly in each other household income class. Significantly, over 80 percent of families that have consumer installment debt also have financial assets or home equity sufficient to liquidate their debts in emergencies.[24]

Whatever the likely short-run macroeconomic effects of rising debt ratios, uncertainties about their longer-run consequences are disturbing. If the negative effects of future recessions are concentrated in the corporate sector, many firms may experience greater variation in profitability than they have in earlier years. Consequent increases in the cost of capital for many businesses could lower investment and thus economic growth. We will not know the significance of this effect, if any, until after the next recession, when the financial markets have had time to absorb its impact on corporate profits.

Financial System Fragility

Despite the long-running economic expansion since 1982, the U.S. financial system has been weaker in this decade than at any time since the end of World War II. As shown in figure 3-9, the annual number of bank failures has climbed steadily since 1980, reaching a high of 184 in 1987, a post-Depression record. Even healthy banks are weaker than they once were. Profitability for the banking industry as a whole has steadily declined since the postwar peak year of 1979, when the industry earned over 14 percent on shareholders' equity.[25] In 1987 banks' return on equity plummeted to just 1.9 percent largely on account of record

24. Robert B. Avery and others, "Changes in Consumer Installment Debt: Evidence from the 1983 and 1986 Surveys of Consumer Finances," *Federal Reserve Bulletin*, vol. 73 (October 1987), p. 761.

25. U.S. Bureau of the Census, *Statistical Abstract of the United States, 1986* (Washington, D.C.: Department of Commerce, 1985), p. 495.

Figure 3-9. *Bank Failures, 1934–87*

Number of failures

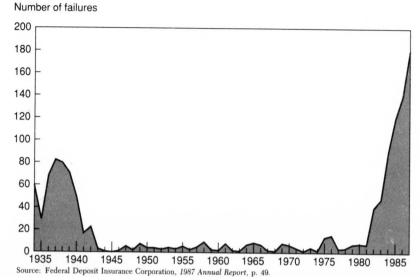

Source: Federal Deposit Insurance Corporation, *1987 Annual Report*, p. 49.

write-offs of loans to developing countries.[26] But even apart from the LDC debt write-offs, the banking industry has experienced severe difficulties. During 1985–87, commercial banks charged off over $45 billion in almost exclusively domestic debt, far exceeding the $28 billion in total charge-offs for the decades between 1950 and 1980.[27]

The financial problems in the savings and loan industry have been even worse. A sizable and growing proportion of thrifts has been losing money and remains in business even while insolvent. In 1987 unprofitable thrifts, one-third of all savings and loans in the United States, lost a total of $13.4 billion, causing the industry as a whole to lose a record $6.8 billion.[28] More troubling, as of April 1988, 504 savings and loans—or 12

26. See Mary M. McLaughlin and Martin H. Wolfson, "The Profitability of Insured Commercial Banks in 1987," *Federal Reserve Bulletin*, vol. 74 (July 1988), p. 405. Through January 1988, U.S. banks had provided $21 billion in reserves against their LDC loans, or about 20 percent of the $108 billion outstanding. Additional reserves of $28 billion would be required if these loans were valued at their trading prices in the secondary market (late 1987). By comparison, total capital in the U.S. banking system at the end of 1987 was $129 billion. See U.S. General Accounting Office, *International Banking: Supervision of Overseas Lending Is Inadequate*, GAO/NSIA D-88-87 (Washington, D.C., May 1988), pp. 16–30.

27. Lowell L. Bryan, *Breaking Up the Bank: Rethinking an Industry under Siege* (Dow Jones-Irwin, 1988), p. 44.

28. Jim McTague, "Bank Board Says Insured Thrifts Lost Record $6.8 Billion in 1987," *American Banker*, March 25, 1988, p. 3.

percent of the nationwide total—were insolvent under generally accepted accounting principles (GAAP). In the first quarter of 1988 alone, those thrifts lost $4.6 billion, pushing the industry as a whole into the red by $3.8 billion.[29]

Although some analysts fear that the failure of one or more big banks could trigger a nationwide deposit run and thus precipitate a recession, such an outcome is highly unlikely. Since it was instituted in the 1930s, federal deposit insurance has eliminated the incentive for insured depositors (those with account balances under the current $100,000 statutory ceiling) to withdraw their funds from troubled depositories. In addition, by arranging mergers of weak banks with healthy ones or by providing other assistance, federal regulators in effect have protected and bolstered the confidence of uninsured depositors (those with accounts above the $100,000 statutory insurance ceiling). These mechanisms should continue to insure the nation against a systemwide banking collapse.

Of course, many more bank failures in the event of a recession could severely deplete the resources of the Federal Deposit Insurance Corporation, which is projected to lose money in 1988 for the first time in the agency's history.[30] But the FDIC's counterpart for thrift institutions, the Federal Savings and Loan Insurance Corporation, has been in precarious financial condition throughout most of the 1980s without precipitating a run on the nation's savings and loans. The reason is that in a true emergency the Federal Reserve would discharge its lender-of-last-resort responsibilities, just as it did after the October 1987 stock market crash. Moreover, there is a widespread expectation that, if necessary to stop a run, Congress would permit the deposit insurers to borrow freely from the Treasury.[31]

29. Robert E. Taylor, "Insured Thrifts Post a Deficit of $3.78 Billion: First Quarter Loss to Boost Pressure for Liquidation or Merger of Some S&Ls," *Wall Street Journal,* June 22, 1988.

30. FDIC chairman William Seidman has predicted that his agency's net worth could decline as much as 10 percent in 1988. See Robert M. Garsson, "FSLIC Action May Be Needed in '88: Riegle: Senator Echoes Proxmire in Urging Swifter Response," *American Banker,* May 26, 1988, p. 12. That decline could be significantly greater in the wake of the FDIC's assistance to North Carolina National Bank in its takeover of First Republic Bank of Texas.

31. Under current law, the FDIC has a line of credit with the Treasury Department of $3 billion. The FSLIC's borrowing limit is $750 million. However, in 1987 Congress passed a nonbinding resolution stating that all federal deposit insurers were backed by the full "faith and credit" of the U.S. government.

More worrisome than a run on the banks is whether a marked increase in bank and thrift insolvencies, especially among larger institutions, would so erode confidence in the American economy as to exacerbate any downturn already under way. As in Texas, where many banks and savings and loans have been in trouble, depository institutions could become less willing to lend, thus inhibiting investment. In addition, both domestic and foreign investors might be shaken by a bank failure and thus require higher yields to justify continued investments in the United States. On previous occasions when interest differentials widened in response to a crisis—the bankruptcy of Penn Central (1970) and the failures of Franklin National Bank (1974) and Continental Illinois Bank (1984)—the effect was temporary, but nevertheless it imposed real costs by reducing earnings and capital spending.[32] Clearly, as long as the weaknesses in the financial system persist, the American economy remains susceptible to similar episodic, but brief, spikes in interest rates in the event of another recession.

A still more serious problem is that a downturn would considerably raise the ultimate taxpayer cost of restoring health to the banking industry. During the summer of 1988, the chairman of the Federal Home Loan Bank Board raised his agency's previous estimate of the cost of closing or forcing the merger of insolvent thrift institutions from $22.7 billion to $30.5 billion, far more than the $20 billion available to the FSLIC through 1990.[33] The ultimate cost is certainly higher. In 1986, the average cost to the FSLIC of assisting the merger of insolvent thrifts with healthy institutions or closing insolvent thrifts was 34 percent of the assets of the troubled institutions. Since the 504 thrifts insolvent under generally accepted accounting principles as of the first quarter of 1988 had $180 billion in assets, the total resolution cost could be at least 60 billion ($180 billion x 0.34).[34] The cost of cleaning up insolvent commercial banks,

---

32. See Andrew S. Carron, "Financial Crises: Recent Experience in U.S. and International Markets," *BPEA*, 2:1982, pp. 395–418; and John J. Merrick, Jr., and Anthony Saunders, "Bank Regulation and Monetary Policy," *Journal of Money, Credit and Banking*, vol. 17 (November 1985), pt. 2, pp. 691–717.

33. Jim McTague, "Wall Ups Estimate by $20 Billion for Rescue of Insolvent Thrifts," *American Banker*, July 8, 1988, p. 1; and Kathleen Day, "$1.2 Billion in Aid Set for S&Ls: Bank Board Action Aimed at Failing Southwest Thrifts," *Washington Post*, August 31, 1988.

34. Federal Home Loan Bank Board, news release, FHLBB 88-117, Washington, D.C., June 21, 1988; and calculations based on Federal Home Loan Bank Board data. Other

mostly in Texas, is also likely to be substantial, although the ultimate total is difficult to estimate.

A recession would not only add to these costs by pushing more depositories near insolvency, but could sow the seeds of future problems by weakening the financial conditions of many others. Once a depository institution approaches or reaches insolvency, but is nevertheless permitted to keep operating, it is likely to lose even more money.[35] The well-known "moral hazard" effect of deposit insurance blunts incentives for managers of depository institutions to hold down risk, especially if they have little or no capital and hence little or nothing to lose.[36] In addition, to attract funds to meet current obligations, insolvent banks and thrifts must pay higher interest rates for their funds. The only way these institutions can compensate for their higher funding costs is to extend riskier loans at higher interest rates. Accordingly, any downturn that increases the number of insolvent or near-insolvent depository institutions will enlarge the number of banks and thrifts that will be tempted to take extraordinary risks, which the deposit insurers and ultimately the taxpayers may bear.

The Federal Budget Deficit and Future Policy Paralysis

The rise in the federal budget deficit over the last seven years has been one of the most important economic developments of the 1980s. Large federal deficits were useful to the economy earlier in the decade, when real output was considerably below its potential level. Fiscal stimulus encouraged private demand and thus helped raise output. But now that output has come close to potential, continuing structural deficits (those at standardized unemployment rates) could actually worsen a future recession by paralyzing both fiscal and monetary policy.

Consider a recession that begins some time in 1989, when the structural

---

respected private analysts have put the ultimate cost in a similar range. See Robert M. Garsson, "FSLIC Will Need Taxpayer Help, Senate Warned," *American Banker*, May 20, 1988, p. 1; and Lowell L. Bryan, "Pay the Price Now for S&L Laxity," *Wall Street Journal*, July 6, 1988.

35. The General Accounting Office found that of the 222 GAAP insolvent thrifts in December 1982, 109 had either ceased to exist or had capital-to-asset ratios below minus 3 percent four years later. Only 25 had capital above 3 percent and were earning a profit. U.S. General Accounting Office, *Thrift Industry: Forbearance for Troubled Institutions 1982–86*, GAO/GGD-87-78BR (Washington, D.C., May 1987), pp. 23–25.

36. See Edward J. Kane, *The Gathering Crisis in Federal Deposit Insurance* (MIT Press, 1985).

federal deficit is projected to represent roughly 3 percent of potential GNP. With such a high deficit, the administration or the Congress could be extremely reluctant to counter a downturn with the usual policy measures—either lower taxes or higher expenditures—for fear of pushing the structural deficit even higher and thus making future deficit reduction even more difficult.[37] In addition, fiscal stimulus when the structural deficit is already high could very well convince investors (private or official) that the budget deficit problem in the United States will never be solved and might even grow worse, provoking them to mount a dollar strike and thus exacerbating the initial downturn. For all these reasons, fiscal policy measures might simply not be used to counteract an economic downturn, or at a minimum, might be used too late. In either case, the economic contraction might be worsened and would be difficult to reverse.

To be sure, the Federal Reserve might fill any void left by fiscal inaction. But the monetary authorities, too, might hesitate. Although, as discussed earlier, a recession would temporarily reduce the current account deficit and in this way strengthen the dollar, the initial impact of an economic downturn in the United States might lower investors' confidence in U.S. investments and thus weaken the dollar. In this environment, the monetary authorities would be reluctant to expand monetary growth for fear of driving the dollar down even further and thus risking future inflation.

There is no way to predict that both fiscal and monetary policy would be affected by a recession in the way just described. But certainly as long as the structural federal budget deficit remains well above its historical norm for comparable periods of high employment, the risk that future policy paralysis could deepen a recession cannot be dismissed.

Policy Suggestions

Governments cannot always avert recession. Nevertheless, intelligent policies can both reduce the likelihood of recession and soften its effects should one take place.

Sustained Deficit Reduction

Orderly reduction of the federal budget deficit can accomplish both goals. By demonstrating to both private investors and central banks that

---

37. As it is, a recession would increase the *actual* deficit, as shown in table 3-9.

a falling U.S. trade deficit and a declining inflow of foreign funds are not inconsistent with stable or declining interest rates, deficit reduction should lower the risk that a sudden fall in the dollar would produce a runup in interest rates. And deficit reduction *now* will better enable the federal government to cushion the nation against a potentially severe recession in the future because it will give policymakers more elbow room to use stimulative fiscal policy, as well as growth-oriented monetary policy, to restore purchasing power in the event of another downturn.

Gradual, but consistent, reduction of the federal budget deficit will also have salutary long-term consequences. By reducing the strain on credit markets caused by government borrowing, it will lower real interest rates and thus encourage private capital formation, enhancing productivity growth. A lower deficit will also reduce U.S. dependence on foreign capital to finance the current shortfall between national saving and investment. With less foreign borrowing, Americans would later be able to consume more of their own output here at home, rather than shipping it abroad to service debts owed to foreign creditors.

Cushions against a Future Oil Shock

Given that abrupt increases in the price of oil have triggered or worsened the last three recessions, it is only appropriate that the nation have policies in place to protect against another severe supply interruption and price jump. Two strategies have been suggested or adopted.

The first approach seeks to reduce the demand for imported oil, thereby to increase excess production capacity within the OPEC nations and make it more difficult for them to act in concert to restrict supply. Some advocates of this approach favor a tariff on imported oil, not only to reduce domestic oil consumption, but to push up the price received by domestic oil producers and encourage greater domestic oil production. A major drawback is that a tariff would redistribute substantial sums to oil producers and produce additional oil at a very high marginal consumer cost.[38] In addition, by raising the price of all oil products and not just

38. For example, a $5 a barrel tariff would permit U.S. oil producers to reap additional revenues (and profits) of about $18 billion a year and would increase consumer prices by about $30 billion a year. At a crude oil price of $16 a barrel, a $5 tariff would permit crude prices to increase approximately 30 percent. If, optimistically, the price elasticity of domestic oil supply is 0.2, then oil production could be expected to rise 6 percent, or about 600,000 barrels a day. At this rate, the tariff would generate additional oil at a marginal consumer cost of about $140 a barrel, or almost ten times the pretariff price.

those, such as gasoline, that are purchased by ultimate consumers, a crude oil tariff would have an adverse affect on the manufacturing sector. For these reasons, others have advocated purely "demand-side" measures, such as a gasoline tax, to reduce oil imports. A gasoline tax, however, would concentrate demand reduction on the segment of oil use (transportation) that is less responsive to price changes than is the demand for other petroleum products (for which natural gas or even coal may serve as a substitute).[39]

As devices for raising revenue or conserving energy, either an oil tariff or a gasoline tax (or any other type of "energy tax") may or may not be desirable, depending on the weight one gives to the factors just described. But the case for using either to prevent another oil supply interruption is weak. Clearly, neither measure can prevent a reduction in supply due to war or revolution, such as occurred in 1978–79. In addition, the United States consumes only about 35 percent of the oil consumed by all free world countries. Thus, any steps the United States takes to reduce its own demand for oil imports will have a muted effect on total world oil demand and thus on excess production capacity within the OPEC countries. It is therefore far from clear that by permanently lowering its demand for OPEC oil the United States can keep OPEC producers from agreeing on a joint production cutback.

The best way for the United States to cushion itself against another supply interruption is to accelerate and expand the storage of oil in the Strategic Petroleum Reserve (SPR). By the end of 1988, the SPR should contain about 550 million barrels. Total government-controlled stocks in the twenty-one industrialized nations, including the United States, that belong to the International Energy Agency (IEA) now exceed 935 million barrels, about six times the level ten years ago.[40] At this level, oil stocks among these nations could be drawn down at the rate of 3-5 million barrels a day during an oil disruption lasting six months. By comparison, the average six-month supply disruption during the 1973–74 Arab oil embargo was approximately 1.5 million barrels a day; during the 1978–

39. Douglas R. Bohi, *Analyzing Demand Behavior: A Study of Energy Elasticities* (Johns Hopkins University Press for Resources for the Future, 1981), pp. 159–60.

40. Prepared statement of William F. Martin, Deputy Secretary of the U.S. Department of Energy, before the Senate Committee on Energy and Natural Resources, May 12, 1988, p. 35. The IEA was formed in 1974 to help coordinate international oil supplies in the event of another supply interruption.

79 oil shock triggered by the Iranian revolution, it was a little over 2 million barrels a day.[41]

Nevertheless, nagging questions about the adequacy of current storage levels persist. Recent analyses suggest that despite the great strides over the past decade, optimal storage levels for all IEA countries combined are twice what they are now.[42] For *individual countries* such as the United States, however, optimal storage levels are likely to be even higher because of the "free rider" problem in the event of a future oil crisis. Because the oil market is worldwide, the benefits of oil stockpile releases by any one country accrue to all other countries. Accordingly, to protect its own interests, the United States should not count on other countries either to build appropriate oil stockpiles or to release oil from them in an emergency, despite the informal and formal procedures that the IEA members have adopted to coordinate energy supply management.

Even if the United States were to set as its objective a doubling of the SPR—a low figure given the free rider problem—current fill rates are too slow. In its fiscal 1989 budget the administration sought authority for adding to the SPR by at most 36 million barrels a year, at which rate the SPR would not double for another fifteen years.[43] The United States should consider at least doubling that fill rate (especially now that oil prices are relatively low), financing the program with revenue from a gasoline tax (or an oil tariff). For example, the additional cost of raising the annual fill rate from 36 million to 72 million barrels would be approximately $600 million, less than 10 percent of the revenues from a 10 cent a gallon gasoline tax. The remaining revenues from the tax would help reduce the federal budget deficit.

Strengthening the Banking System

As noted, the current weaknesses in the financial system could exacerbate a future recession by causing investors to lose confidence in

41. Ibid.

42. For a listing of these studies, see John P. Weyant, "Coordinated Stock Drawdowns: Pros and Cons," in George Horwich and David Leo Weimer, eds., *Responding to International Oil Crises* (Washington, D.C.: American Enterprise Institute, 1988), pp. 196–97.

43. Specifically, the administration proposed to continue the SPR fill rate at 50,000 barrels a day or 18 million barrels a year, as well as to transfer another 50,000 barrels a day from the Naval Petroleum Reserve (whose release rate is one-thirtieth as fast as that from the SPR) to the SPR. *Budget of the United States Government, Fiscal Year 1989*, pp. 1–9.

the U.S. economy. Even absent a recession, continuing problems among financial institutions expose depositors and ultimately taxpayers to higher costs in the future for merging or closing more insolvent banks and thrifts.

Two measures would significantly reduce these risks. First, additional capital must be brought into the depository system to increase the stake of shareholders in the institutions they own and to provide a better cushion for the deposit insurers. A major step in the right direction has been taken by the introduction of the new risk-based capital standards agreed upon by commercial bank regulators from the United States, Japan, and Europe.[44] The new standards will compel those banks that are now weakly capitalized—and thus the most susceptible to failure in the event of a recession—to increase their capital cushion substantially or to reduce in size.[45]

The new capital requirements should not be limited to commercial banks. Similar, if not identical, requirements should also be imposed on thrifts. Equally important, the accounting systems for both banks and thrifts should be identical, so that capital for both types of institutions is measured the same way. For the present, both institutions should use generally accepted accounting principles. Over the longer run, regulators and the public would be better served by an accounting system that measures assets held by banks and thrifts at something close to their market value.[46]

Many institutions that are already insolvent or nearly so, however,

44. Under the new system all banks will be required by 1992 to have "primary" capital, or shareholders' equity and retained earnings, equal to 4 percent of "risk-adjusted assets," and to have "secondary capital," which includes subordinated debt and loan loss reserves, double that amount. The new capital system is "risk-based" because banks will be required to provide higher proportions of capital (as a percentage of assets) for risky assets such as commercial loans than for those assets posing less risk, such as government bonds. In addition, for the first time, banks will have to set aside capital against their off-balance sheet commitments, such as standby letters of credit.

45. Money center banks alone may have to raise $15 billion in additional capital by 1992, or otherwise shrink in size. See John M. Berry, "Central Banks Pushed Minimum Capital Rules: 12-Nation Pact Designed to Protect World System," *Washington Post*, July 13, 1988.

46. For assets that are traded on the markets, such as federal and municipal securities and the growing volumes of asset-backed instruments, this can be readily done. For loans that are not traded, regulators should at least be able to require the institutions to adjust their values for fluctuations in interest rates (that is, require the reporting of both assets and liabilities on the basis of present discounted values). See Kane, *Gathering Crisis in Deposit Insurance*.

will not be able to raise additional capital, at least under present management. Accordingly, a second critical component of any policy to ensure a sound financial sector must be the closure or forced merger of the many troubled commercial banks and thrifts. Otherwise, the ultimate costs of resolving these difficulties are likely only to mount.

But this policy almost surely will require additional resources. As already noted, the FSLIC may be short by $40 billion, perhaps even more, to deal fully with the problems at insolvent thrifts. Meanwhile, the FDIC's reserves by the end of 1988 are likely to be no more than $15 billion at best; the true figure, after taking into account the final cost of resolving all currently troubled banks, especially those in Texas, may be much lower. Accordingly, even if the two insurance funds were merged—a widely discussed option—their total resources almost certainly would not be sufficient to deal with all troubled depositories.

Healthy banks and thrifts will suffer as long as problem institutions remain open. As noted earlier, to stay liquid, troubled banks and thrifts must offer depositors premium rates on deposits, bidding up the rates on the deposits that healthy depositories offer as well. Thus, even well-run institutions may be forced to take greater risks to compensate for higher funding costs, or otherwise to suffer an erosion in the "spread" between deposit and lending rates. Accordingly, even if they were forced to bear some part of the cost for resolving problems at troubled institutions, healthy banks and thrifts could be better off if their insolvent competitors were no longer in business.

In the end, policymakers will have to decide whether to require surviving banks and thrifts to shoulder all the costs or to shift part of the cost to taxpayers. One "solution" that almost surely will not work is to saddle the thrift industry with all of the additional costs. As part of the recapitalization of the FSLIC in 1987, savings and loans already pay deposit insurance premiums more than twice as large as those that commercial banks pay to the FDIC. Adding to their burden will only widen thrifts' competitive disparity with commercial banks, further weakening the thrift industry and raising the ultimate resolution cost.

Reducing Private Sector Leverage

Several policy options have been offered to reduce the economic risks posed by the increase in leverage in the private sector.

One approach is to discourage borrowing directly. By allowing corporations to deduct their interest payments but not their dividends, the income tax code encourages corporations to assume more debt than they would if the tax treatment for interest and dividend payments were neutral. This bias toward leverage could be corrected by allowing corporations to deduct both interest and dividends and by taxing both payments when they are received as income by individuals. Meanwhile, the income tax law has also long favored debt accumulation by households through the mortgage interest deduction. The Tax Reform Act of 1986 has phased out the deduction for interest on consumer debt and limited the deductibility of home equity mortgage interest to mortgage debt no greater than the purchase price of a home and the cost of subsequent improvements. Nevertheless, households could be discouraged from borrowing if the mortgage interest deduction were scaled back further, perhaps by reducing the current $1 million ceiling on mortgage debt eligible for the interest deduction.

Any approach that takes away longstanding tax benefits, however, will encounter stiff political opposition. For that reason, a potentially more attractive alternative is to discourage borrowing by encouraging *saving*. Unfortunately, previous efforts to do so through the tax system appear to have had little or no success. From 1981 through 1986, the tax law permitted individuals to deduct up to $2,000 annually for contributions to Individual Retirement Accounts (IRAs). Yet the personal saving rate (saving as a share of disposable personal income) fell over this period from 7.3 percent to just 4.2 percent, the lowest level since the end of World War II. Summers and Carroll have pointed to scattered evidence suggesting that the IRA deduction nevertheless raised the saving rate over what it otherwise would have been.[47] In addition, both authors have found that greater tax incentives for private saving in Canada help explain why the saving rate has increased in that country while declining in the United States.[48] Nevertheless, the weight of the evidence casts strong

---

47. Lawrence Summers and Chris Carroll, "Why Is U.S. National Saving So Low?" *BPEA*, 2:1987, pp. 607–35. The authors note that most IRA contributors had relatively little wealth or capital income and that more than 60 percent contributed less than the statutory maximum amount. Both patterns suggest that a part of the funds placed in IRA accounts represented incremental saving, rather than transfers of accumulated assets.

48. Chris Carroll and Lawrence H. Summers, "Why Have Private Savings Rates in the United States and Canada Diverged?" *Journal of Monetary Economics*, vol. 20 (September 1987), pp. 249–79.

doubt on the effectiveness of tax incentives to encourage household saving.[49]

Although the prospects for affecting total private sector borrowing through the tax system are slim, there is little doubt that the *financial impact* of debt can be mitigated through lower interest rates. As already noted, the best mechanism for reducing interest rates without running a risk of inflation is to reduce the federal budget deficit while permitting faster monetary growth. The Congressional Budget Office has simulated the effects of cutting the federal deficit using several large-scale econometric models and has compared its findings with those of many published studies.[50] Taken together, the findings broadly suggest that for each reduction in the fiscal deficit of 1 percent of potential GNP, interest rates, both nominal and real, could easily fall 50 basis points. Given a projected federal fiscal deficit for 1989 of roughly 3 percent of potential GNP, interest rates could drop by 1.5 percentage points if the deficit were eliminated.[51] Over time, such a reduction could considerably ease any financial burdens that firms and households now face in servicing their debts.

Conclusion

The outlook for the economy is qualified optimism. If the economy suffers no dramatic shocks, growth can continue even as the federal budget deficit is steadily reduced. The same is true even if no further deficit reduction measures are taken, although the risks of a financial shock—specifically a dollar strike coupled with another collapse of stock prices—then go up. At this writing, the risks that other kinds of shocks, including food or energy price increases, will soon trigger a recession appear relatively small.

The growth of corporate debt over the past decade could deepen the next recession if one should nevertheless occur, although it is also possible

49. See Harvey Galper and Charles Byce, "Individual Retirement Accounts: Facts And Issues," *Tax Notes,* June 2, 1986, pp. 917–21.

50. See Jacob S. Dreyer, "Fiscal Targets, Monetary Goals and Interest Rates," paper presented to the National Association of Business Economists, New Orleans, Lousiana, October 5, 1987.

51. Martin Feldstein has argued that if financial markets believed a multiyear deficit plan would actually be implemented, then interest rates could drop *immediately* by as much as 2 percentage points. Feldstein, "Halving the Pain of Budget Balance," *Wall Street Journal,* May 25, 1988.

that higher leverage will simply cause the negative effects of a future downturn to be distributed differently than in previous downturns. Weaknesses among depository institutions could worsen a recession, but the more worrisome concern is that another economic contraction would impose greater strains on many financial institutions and ultimately raise the social cost of forcing the insolvent ones to close or merge with healthier partners. What could most influence the depth of the next recession is the progress that is made beforehand in reducing the federal budget deficit. If the economy enters a recession before sizable cuts are made in the deficit, political reluctance to stimulate the economy through fiscal policy measures may, in combination with fears by the monetary authorities of creating money too rapidly, prolong the downturn.

Certain policy steps can mitigate both the likelihood of another recession and its severity. Gradual reduction of the federal budget deficit—at or around the pace implied by the Gramm-Rudman-Hollings legislation—will minimize the likelihood that a dollar strike could set off a big increase in interest rates. In addition, by permitting interest rates to fall, deficit reduction will also lower private debt service burdens. A more rapid and substantial increase in the Strategic Petroleum Reserve, perhaps financed by an increase in the gasoline tax, will help provide insurance against another oil price shock. Shoring up the capital base of our nation's depository institutions—while quickly closing down those that are no longer solvent—will strengthen the financial system and reduce the long-run cost of dealing with the insolvency problem. None of the steps will guarantee that the economy will be free from a future recession. But they would considerably raise the chances that the U.S. economy can continue to grow at or near its potential rate without significant interruption.

CHAPTER FOUR

Incomes, Families, and Living Standards

Frank Levy

BY ONE standard, the 1988 presidential campaign broke the rules. Experts said that when inflation and unemployment were low, the economy would not be a political issue. In 1988 inflation and unemployment were low, but the economy was a subject of vigorous political debate nonetheless.

Although some candidates touched a feeling among working class voters that they were losing ground,[1] unease extended beyond blue collar workers. According to opinion polls, a plurality of all parents were worried about their children's economic future.[2] And the children seemed attuned to the fear. In the fall of 1987, 80 percent of all male college freshmen and 72 percent of all female college freshmen felt that making a "great deal of money" was an essential or very important goal in their lives. Both numbers were about thirty percentage points higher than they had been in the early 1970s.[3]

In this chapter I argue that the voters' economic concerns have a basis

I wish to thank Richard Michel for comments on earlier drafts; Charlie Brown for statistical advice; Chuck Byce and Chrissy de Fontenay for extensive programming assistance; and Pat Purcell, Caroline Ratcliffe, Amy Salsbury, and Lorelei Stewart for research assistance.

1. Examples include Richard Gephardt's commercial featuring the "$48,000 K-Car," Jesse Jackson's speeches on the victims of "economic violence," and Pat Robertson's speech to South Carolina textile workers in which he argues that their industry was destroyed by international bankers.

2. *USA Today*, January 25, 1988.

3. The 1987 data are contained in Alexander W. Astin, Kenneth C. Green, William S. Korn, and Marilynn Shalit, *The American Freshman: National Norms for Fall 1987* (Cooperative Institutional Research Program of the American Council on Education and the University of California at Los Angeles, Graduate School of Education, December 1987). Figures for the early 1970s come from the same publication for earlier years.

in fact. Low inflation and low unemployment are important dimensions of a healthy economy, but a third, less visible dimension centers on the wages that jobs pay and the rate at which those wages grow. This third dimension is shaped by the growth of labor productivity and by the supply and demand for different kinds of labor. Together, these forces determine whether incomes rise or fall both for the labor force on average and for specific groups of workers.

At first glance, rising incomes look like a bonus: If future generations could earn as much as today's middle class, it would be quite good enough. But post-World War II America has relied on steadily rising incomes to ease the frictions that arise in any society: frictions among regions and among income classes, friction between generations and friction between workers in rising and declining industries. When incomes grow slowly, as they have in recent years, many of these frictions come to the surface and account for some of the economic unease that, despite low inflation and unemployment, permeated the 1988 presidential campaign.

Defining Living Standards

Do we live better today than we did ten years ago? This question is central to my inquiry, but I can only give approximate answers. The answers are limited by the data available and the value judgments that are made.

The data problem begins with the measurement of income. The standard source of detailed income statistics is the U.S. census. In annual publications, the census presents income statistics ranging from the distribution of family incomes to the distribution of individual incomes of men aged 25–34, with exactly twelve years of education. But the census obtains this information through individual interviews, and in these interviews the census defines income as pretax money receipts.[4] The definition has the virtue of simplicity, which increases the chance of citizen cooperation, but it ignores the fact that about 15 percent of all income now comes in forms other than money: employer-provided health insurance and pension contributions, government-provided food stamps and medicare, and so on. The national dollars spent on each of these

---

4. More precisely, the census interviews one respondent in each household who is asked to provide information about each household member.

items are known, but the amounts of these items received by specific workers and families are not known.[5]

Beyond the difficulties of measuring income lies a second issue: Having more income and "living better" are not identical concepts. Consider two families. In the first, the husband earns $45,000 while the wife stays home with the family's children. In the second, the husband and wife both work with a joint income of $50,000, and their children are in daycare. The second family has the greater income, but if one wanted to know which family was "living better," one would want to correct both families' incomes for work expenses that, for the two-earner family, include daycare. One might also find that while the two-earner family has more money, it is shorter on time since the wife continues to do most of the housework in addition to working at her paid job.[6] The inability to make such adjustments to a large set of data clouds the question of "living better."

The relationship between income and living better arises at a deeper level when one considers family size. Economists usually measure the national living standard by using average income per capita (that is, total national income divided by the total population). If one thinks of income per capita in terms of individual families, it implies that a mother and father lower their standard of living when they move from one child to two (with no corresponding increase in income), a judgment that is far from obvious.[7] The point is important because while income per capita has grown steadily in the last decade, very low U.S. birth rates have been one important determinant of that growth.

Finally, individuals, and indeed whole countries, can for a time live beyond their incomes by borrowing. In chapter 2, Robert Lawrence

5. One might also argue that the census income data should be reduced for taxes paid. That adjustment would be appropriate if we were measuring only private consumption and savings, but taxes finance government services—social security, national defense, local schools, and roads. These items also affect an individual's well-being even if people do not benefit equally from every dollar spent and even if people often argue violently over the appropriate level of that spending. For this reason, the income statistics reported here are not adjusted for taxes paid. *Survey of Current Business*, vol. 68 (June 1988), tables 2.1, 3.11.

6. For a discussion of this point, see Suzanne M. Bianchi and Daphne Spain, *American Women in Transition* (New York: Russell Sage Foundation, 1986), pp. 231–33, and the references cited there.

7. Income per capita falls because the family's income is now being divided among four persons rather than three.

describes how, for the past seven years, the United States as a whole has spent more than it produced by borrowing from foreign nations. This form of living better cannot last, and eventually living standards have to be brought back into line with national income and production, reduced by the amount needed to pay the accumulated interest. To the extent that people perceive the nation's debtor status, it helps explain the poll results, cited earlier, which show Americans feeling uneasy about their children's economic future.

These examples suggest that as one examines past and future U.S. living standards, no single statistic serves to summarize trends. Rather, one must use multiple statistics, including workers' earnings, family incomes, and income per capita to construct an accurate picture. The resulting picture will be too complex for a ninety-second television news story, but with a little more space the recent history and probable near-term future of American living standards can be told clearly and unambiguously.

I begin the story by reviewing general trends in workers' earnings, trends primarily shaped by macroeconomic events, including oil price shocks and the growth of productivity. I then look at the earnings of specific groups of workers—male and female workers of different ages and educations—and use these experiences to examine the proposition that the economy no longer produces middle-class jobs.

I turn from workers' earnings to look at two more general measures of living standards: income per capita and family income. These two measures depend on workers' earnings,[8] but they also depend on demographic trends, including the number of families headed by single women, the number of families with two earners, and the birth rate in the population. These demographic trends are important in explaining why, in recent years, income per capita has grown more rapidly than earnings per worker and why family income inequality is increasing, particularly among families with children.

I conclude the chapter by exploring whether the current generation of young workers will live as well as their parents have lived. To construct a first answer to this question, I use the macroeconomic scenarios developed in chapter 2 by Lawrence to project the earnings of today's

---

8. They are affected by other income trends such as the rate of increase of social security benefits.

men, aged 30, over a twenty-year period, and I compare the projected earnings of these young men with the earnings of their fathers.

Economic Growth and Workers' Earnings

In any study of living standards, the starting point is the trend in workers' earnings.[9] In census statistics, about four-fifths of all tabulated income represents wages, salaries, and self-employment income paid to workers, and so these earnings are a major indicator of the nation's purchasing power.[10] A look at these earnings since World War II reveals a clear pattern: strong growth through 1973 and much slower growth thereafter.

How do we experience our earnings growth? At the end of a bad week at work, we often feel as if we were pushing up a crowded flight of stairs, elbowing past competitors along the way. In this picture, pay increases reflect nothing but an individual's merit. The truth is more complex. Merit determines advancement in relation to other workers, but real earnings gains reflect both relative advancement and the pace at which average incomes rise.[11]

In a healthy economy, rising labor productivity—the rising output of each worker—generates the additional output necessary to pay higher real earnings, and so most workers can see their paychecks grow in absolute terms.[12] The push for advancement still occurs, but it takes place on an up escalator rather than a flight of stairs. Some people will move up faster than others, but most people will make absolute gains as the whole earnings scale rises.

One can see this phenomenon by tracking over time the average

9. In this chapter, workers are defined as persons who receive wages, salary, or self-employment income during the year, including corporate executives, assembly line personnel, schoolteachers, architects, and others.

10. Other sources of income reported in the census include interest, dividends, rent, and transfers (for example, social security payments, unemployment insurance payments, and so on). Income not reported by the census includes capital gains and such nonmoney income as employer-paid fringe benefits, food stamps, medicare, and medicaid. Because the census asks respondents for pretax money incomes, their estimates of money income include a degree of double counting: one's social security taxes get counted in one's (pretax) income and in someone else's social security check.

11. Real earnings gains refer to increases in earnings adjusted for changes in inflation, that is, changes in purchasing power.

12. More precisely, increases in output for each worker will be divided among higher wages, higher profits, and lower prices.

Table 4-1. *The Stagnation of Workers' Incomes after 1973*

Year in which men were age 50	Men's average income at age 50 (full-time workers only, 1987 dollars)[a]		Percent growth in the income scale over the previous decade	
	Census	Adjusted	Census	Adjusted
1946	$15,257	$15,529	. . .	. . .
1956	$18,558	$19,208	21.6	23.7
1966	$23,971	$25,168	29.2	31.0
1973[b]	$30,578	$32,701	b	b
1976	$30,179	$32,752	25.9	30.1
1986	$32,960	$36,228	9.2	10.6

Source: Income statistics from U.S. Bureau of the Census, *Current Population Reports*, series P-60, various issues (Washington, D.C.: Department of Commerce). Income for adjustments from U.S. Department of Commerce, Bureau of Economic Analysis, national income and product accounts.

a. "Average Income of men at 50, Full Time Workers Only" refers to the median income of male, year-round, full-time workers, ages 45–54. *Economic Report of the President, February 1988, table B-4.* Conversion to 1987 dollars made using the personal consumption expenditure index.

b. As noted in the text, the process of deep stagnation began at the end of 1973 with the first OPEC oil price shock. The growth rate of incomes between 1973 and 1986 on a per decade basis was 6.0 percent (census) and 8.3 percent (adjusted).

annual income of men, aged 45–54, who worked year-round and full time, a statistic dominated by men's wages and salaries (table 4-1).[13] Focusing on men who work year-round and full time makes it possible to isolate the effects of underlying income trends while eliminating fluctuations caused by changes in unemployment. And because the oldest baby boomers have not yet turned 45, the incomes of men, aged 45–55, have not been overwhelmed by big increases in cohort size.[14] Still, this benchmark does have one problem: census income data exclude the value of fringe benefits, which in recent years, have become a rising share of compensation. For this reason, table 4-1 contains two columns,

13. Ideally, a benchmark would include only wages, salaries, and self-employment income—that is, earnings. Analysts are forced to use a total income statistic (which includes interest payments and so on) because the census did not publish earnings statistics by age in the 1950s and 1960s. Nonetheless, for middle-aged men who work full time, income is a good approximation for earnings.

14. Even in a healthy economy, baby boomers would not have moved up the ladder as fast as their older brothers and sisters because their large numbers increased competition for jobs. See Richard A. Easterlin, *Birth and Fortune: The Impact of Numbers on Personal Welfare* (Basic Books, 1980); and James P. Smith and Finis Welch, "No Time to be Young: The Economic Prospects for Large Cohorts in the United States," *Population and Development Review*, vol. 7 (March 1981), pp. 71–83. See also the discussion in appendix A of this chapter.

one for income published by the census and the other for income figures with approximate adjustments for fringe benefits.[15]

From the end of World War II through 1973 labor productivity grew at an average rate of 3 percent a year (slightly lower at the end of the period), and, as shown in table 4-1, the extra output provided the margin for higher wages.[16] In 1946, for example, the average 50-year-old man working full time had an income of $15,257 (in 1987 dollars). This benchmark rose steadily so that by 1973, the year that ended with the first OPEC oil price increase, the average 50-year-old man who worked full time had income of $30,578.

Relatively little of the earnings gain reflected men's movement out of "bad" jobs into "good" jobs. There was some change in men's occupational structure, particularly in the movement of labor out of low-wage agriculture. But the gains reported in table 4-1 reflected rising earnings in all occupations. For example, in 1969, a 40-year-old man working as a machine operator earned $20,000 (in 1987 dollars), as much as a typical manager had earned in 1949. But after 1973, income growth slowed dramatically for men and women in all occupations.

At the end of 1973, the fourfold increase in the price of oil led immediately to both recession and inflation and by 1975, the census benchmark had fallen by about 3 percent.[17] More important, 1973 marked the beginning of the sharp slowdown in the growth of productivity discussed by Martin Neil Baily and Margaret M. Blair in chapter 6.[18] The income loss from the 1973–74 oil price shock followed by slow-growing productivity meant that the income benchmark did not regain its 1973 level until 1979.[19] Then the Iranian revolution and the Iran-Iraq

15. These corrections are made by inflating census estimates of median individual income by the ratio of "other labor income" (which includes employers' contributions for private fringe benefits) to "wage and salary income," in which both figures are taken from the national income and product accounts. U.S. Bureau of Economic Analysis, *The National Income and Product Accounts of the United States, 1929–82* (Washington, D.C.: Department of Commerce, 1986), table 2-1; and *Survey of Current Business*, various issues.

16. *Economic Report of the President, February 1988*, p. 300.

17. Average earnings for all 50-year-old men (as distinct from full-time workers) fell more sharply because unemployment rose sharply in the 1974–75 recession. U.S. Bureau of the Census, CPS microdata files.

18. As Martin Neil Baily and Margaret M. Blair explain, the increase in oil prices marked the beginning of this productivity slowdown, but it was only one of many factors causing the slowdown. See chap. 6.

19. U.S. Bureau of the Census, "Money Income of Households, Families, and Persons

war triggered the second major OPEC increase in oil prices, and the cycle began again. Between the years 1973 and 1986, the census benchmark grew at a rate of only about 6 percent each decade compared with 20 percent to 29 percent a decade during the 1950s and 1960s. Total compensation increased faster than wages and salaries as employers paid higher social security taxes and health insurance premiums. But when the benchmark is adjusted for these benefits, it grew by 8.3 percent a decade between 1973 and 1986, less than one-third of its earlier growth rate.[20]

The post-1973 slowdown in the growth of workers' incomes was important because fast-growing earnings had become an integral part of American life. Consider, for example, the rapid growth of the middle class after World War II. If the term is taken literally, a growing middle class suggests a distribution of family incomes that is becoming more equal. Family income equality did grow a little in the 1950s and 1960s. But the real nature of the growing middle class was rising incomes.[21] In 1947 the average family had an income (in 1987 dollars) of about $14,830. By 1973 this figure had almost doubled, and the average family had an income of $28,890. Inequality among family incomes had not declined radically but a growing proportion of families could afford a middle-class lifestyle—a single-family home, one or two cars, a washing machine and dryer—and it was in this sense that the middle class grew.[22] After 1973, family incomes stagnated (following workers' individual incomes), and articles describing the "vanishing middle class" became increasingly common.[23]

---

in the United States: 1986," *Current Population Reports*, series P-60, no. 159 (Washington, D.C.: Department of Commerce, 1988), p. 107, table 30.

20. The impact of slower wage growth on men's income was often reinforced by higher unemployment in the post-1973 period.

21. In 1947 the middle three-fifths of families received 53.0 percent of all family income. In 1969 (the post-World War II year of greatest equality), that share was 54.8 percent but by 1986 it had fallen to 53.2 percent. See U.S. Bureau of the Census, "Money Income of Households, Families and Persons in the United States, 1986," p. 39, table 12.

22. Ibid., table 10. This same growth of earnings caused the proportion of the population below the poverty line to fall from about 22.4 percent in 1959 to 11.1 percent in 1973. By 1986, the share of the population below the poverty line was 13.6 percent. U.S. Bureau of the Census, "Poverty in the United States: 1986," *Current Population Reports*, series P-60, no. 160 (Washington, D.C.: Department of Commerce, 1986), table 1.

23. See, for example, Bob Kuttner, "The Declining Middle," *Atlantic Monthly*, vol. 252 (July 1983), pp. 60–72; Bruce Steinberg, "The Mass Market is Splitting Apart," *Fortune*,

Rising incomes were also important in cushioning industrial shifts. Today the movement of employment from goods production to service production is discussed as if it is the movement from good jobs to bad jobs. But the transition to services has been occurring for at least fifty years and it has usually been considered benign.[24] In the late 1950s, fully one-half of all hours of employment were already in the service sector and even at that time, workers who had not gone to college typically earned 20 percent less in the service sector than similar workers earned in manufacturing and construction.[25] But when earnings were growing rapidly, a worker could lose a "good" job and take a pay cut but still hope to grow back to his earlier standard of living. After earnings stagnated, getting a "good job" seemed like the only way to advance, and the shortage of good jobs, particularly for younger, less educated men, became a source of real concern.

Rising wages helped to establish the idea that each generation would live much better than the previous one. Consider, for example, a father in his mid-forties and his eighteen-year-old son who is preparing to leave home. As the son leaves, he looks at his father's salary and what it would buy and keeps the memory as a personal yardstick. In the 1950s and 1960s, the young man would have measured up quickly. By the time the son was 30 years old, he would have been earning about 15 percent more than his father had earned twelve years earlier.[26] The young man would have known early in life that he would live at least as well as he had seen his parents live. Today, the situation is less certain. The average man, aged 30, who works full time earns about $24,000, about $5,000 less (in 1987 dollars) than his father would have earned twelve years

---

November 28, 1983, pp. 76–82; and Lester C. Thurow, "The Disappearance of the Middle Class," *New York Times*, February 5, 1984. For a somewhat different view on this subject, see Robert J. Samuelson, "Middle-Class Media Myth," *National Journal*, December 31, 1983, pp. 2673–78; and Frank Levy, *Dollars and Dreams: The Changing American Income Distribution* (W.W. Norton, 1988), chaps. 2 and 8.

24. For example, in 1940, the distinguished economist Colin Clark described "the most important concomitant of economic progress, namely, the movement of the working population from agriculture to manufacture and from manufacture to commerce and services." *The Conditions of Economic Progress* (London: Macmillan and Co., 1940), p. 176.

25. See, for example, Victor R. Fuchs, *The Service Economy* (New York: National Bureau of Economic Research, 1968), chap. 6, table 47.

26. As indicated by the rising income levels of table 4-1, the father's income would have also increased over the twelve years.

ago.[27] The young man may still outearn his father, but the outcome is not a foregone conclusion. The resulting uncertainty helps to explain the parental anxiety for their children's future reported earlier in this chapter. It also helps to explain the first signs of economic conflict across generations, including the charge that benefits for the elderly are inequitably large.[28]

In all of these examples, rising labor productivity and earnings played a subtle role. Before 1973, workers took the fast growth of their earnings as their due and failed to give credit to a rapidly growing wage scale. It was only when income growth slowed that Americans began to understand how fast-rising earnings had become an integral part of American life. Among other things, those earnings helped to reduce the frictions that arise in any society.

Workers' Incomes and Middle-Class Jobs

The statistics of table 4-1 tell a clear story, but they are not the numbers that appear in public debate. What is debated publicly, and with some heat, is the proposition that the economy no longer creates "middle-class jobs," a term that has at least two definitions. A middle-class job can be one that pays enough to support a middle-class living standard, which today includes a single-family house, one or two cars, and so on. In this first definition, rising earnings mean more middle-class jobs even if earnings are becoming less equal.[29] Alternatively, a middle-class job can be a job with earnings in the middle of the earnings distribution. In this second definition, rising earnings can still mean fewer middle-class jobs if earnings inequality is growing.

Those analysts who see a decline in middle-class jobs usually find the cause in the growth of employment in the service sector. Between 1970 and 1985, the proportion of all employment in the service sector (on a

27. Later in this chapter, I show that the father-son comparison looks more optimistic for fathers and sons who went to college than for fathers and sons who went only to high school.

28. See, for example, Phillip Longman, *Born to Pay: The New Politics of Aging in America* (Houghton Mifflin, 1987), and the activities of Americans for Generational Equity with which Longman is associated.

29. This would be true if the earnings of low-wage jobs were increasing, but the earnings of higher-wage jobs were increasing faster. Rising earnings could also mean more middle-class jobs if the number of high-earnings and low-earnings jobs was growing faster than the number of "average jobs."

basis that is equivalent to full-time work) has risen from 65 percent to 72 percent.[30] Some of this increase reflects the rapid growth of women's participation in the labor force.[31] But in the early and mid-1980s, the shift also reflected a decline in manufacturing employment driven by the 1980 and 1981–82 recessions and the overvalued dollar of 1983–87.[32] Economists have established that workers of a given age and education typically earn 15 percent to 20 percent less in the service sector than similar workers earn in goods-producing industries (manufacturing, construction, and mining).[33] Given this difference in earnings, a big enough shift of labor between sectors might account for a declining number of jobs that purchase a middle-class standard of living. At the same time, some observers assert that service sector earnings—the earnings of hamburger flippers and investment bankers—are inherently less equal than incomes from goods production.[34] If this assertion were true, a growing share of labor in the service sector could lead to a growing inequality of earnings and a smaller "middle class" of jobs.

But the fact that a theory is plausible does not make it true, and many economists argue that middle-class jobs are not vanishing at all. They say that manufacturing job losses have been concentrated in low wage textiles rather than high-wage steel and autos and that the bulk of newly created jobs are high-status, white collar jobs that traditionally pay well.[35]

30. Proportions derived from "persons engaged in production by industry" as shown in the national income and product accounts. See Bureau of Economic Analysis, *National Income and Product Accounts of the United States, 1929–82*, table 6-10; and *Survey of Current Business*, vol. 66 (July 1986), p. 68, table 6.10.

31. Both traditional women's occupations (teachers, sales personnel, clerical personnel), and newer women's occupations (including lawyers, doctors, MBAs) are largely concentrated in industries in the service sectors. Data on this point appear later in this section.

32. A more precise description would add a third factor—the relatively strong growth of manufacturing productivity in the 1980s, which meant that the slow growth of demand for U.S. manufactured goods resulted in sharp reductions in the demand for manufacturing employment.

33. See, for example, Fuchs, *Service Economy*, for sectoral wage differences that existed in the 1950s and 1960s. Tabulations of the March 1980 CPS microdata file show that in 1979, a woman, aged 30, with a high school diploma, who worked full time earned about $17,200 a year (in 1987 dollars) if she worked in goods-producing industries and $14,700 if she worked in the service sector. Men's earnings data showed similar differences across sectors.

34. See, for example, Kuttner, "Declining Middle," and Richard M. Cyert, "Easing Labor's Transition Trauma," *New York Times*, July 22, 1984.

35. See, for example, *Economic Report of the President, February 1988*, pp. 60–61; Marvin H. Kosters and Murray N. Ross, "A Shrinking Middle Class?" *The Public Interest*,

Which view is correct? Is the number of middle-class jobs shrinking or stable or growing? The most widely cited study in this debate is "The Great American Job Machine," a paper prepared by Barry Bluestone and Bennett Harrison for the Joint Economic Committee of Congress. In the paper, Bluestone and Harrison examined changes over time in the distribution of annual earnings for all workers and determined that 58 percent of the net new jobs created between 1979 and 1984 paid less than $7,012 a year in 1984 (or $7,712 in 1987 dollars). They concluded that the shift to a service economy was causing a rapid decline in the economy's ability to generate middle-class jobs.[36]

To obtain this result Bluestone and Harrison examined changes over time in the distribution of annual earnings for all workers. But this distribution depends on many different variables—not just the structure of jobs—and so it can change for many different reasons. For example, annual earnings reflect both the wages that jobs pay and the hours people work. If, over time, working women tend to work more hours each year (as they have), their annual earnings will increase even if their jobs and wages remain unchanged. In addition, the distribution combines earnings statistics for all workers—men, women, adults, and teenagers. Accordingly, movements in the distribution can reflect demography—for example, more working teenagers—as easily as changes in the job structure. Finally, the distribution can be influenced by the macroeconomic factors— the oil price shocks and low productivity growth described earlier— which affect earnings in all occupations. The existence of these problems does not mean that Bluestone and Harrison are wrong. Rather, it means that to settle the "middle class job" debate, the earnings distribution must be analyzed so that the changing experience of different kinds of workers is revealed.

To focus the discussion, I restrict attention to the experience of men and women workers between the ages of 25 and 55. The presence or

---

no. 90 (Winter 1988), pp. 3–27; Robert J. Samuelson, "The American Job Machine," *Newsweek,* February 23, 1987, p. 57; Warren T. Brookes, "Low-Pay Jobs: The Big Lie," *Wall Street Journal,* March 25, 1987; and Janet L. Norwood, "The Job Machine Has Not Broken Down," *New York Times,* February 22, 1987. An earlier piece that was not written as part of this debate but bears on it is Neal H. Rosenthal, "The Shrinking Middle Class: Myth or Reality?" *Monthly Labor Review,* vol. 108 (March 1985), pp. 3–10.

36. Barry Bluestone and Bennett Harrison, "The Great American Job Machine: The Proliferation of Low-Wage Employment in the U.S. Economy," a study prepared for the Joint Economic Committee of the U.S. Congress, Washington, D.C., December 1986.

Figure 4-1. *Composition of Prime-Age Workers by Age, Sex, and Education, 1973, 1986*

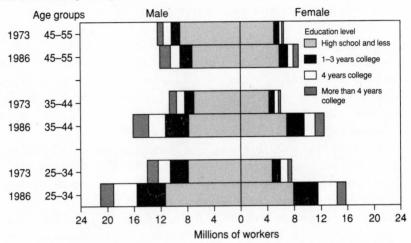

Source: Author's calculations based on U.S. Bureau of the Census, Current Population Survey (CPS) microdata files.

absence of middle-class jobs is most important as it affects these prime age workers. Figure 4-1 displays the age and educational composition of this group for 1973 and 1986. The year 1973 marks the onset of the earnings stagnation described earlier. The latest available census wage data are from 1986. Between the two years, a greater proportion of women and younger, better educated workers entered the labor force (the baby boom's coming of age).

Figure 4-2 compares the 1973 and 1986 earnings distributions for these prime-age working men and women. Because earnings have grown slowly since 1973, the 1973 and 1986 earnings distribution overlap to a substantial degree, which makes side-by-side comparisons meaningful.

The distributions in figure 4-2 correct Bluestone and Harrison's work in several ways suggested by their critics.[37] Nonetheless, the distributions

37. For example, the distributions in figure 4-2 focus on workers, aged 25–55, to avoid the low earnings of students and semiretired persons. In addition, conversions are made to 1987 dollars using the personal consumption expenditure index rather than the consumer price index, which overstated inflation during the 1970s. Finally, the distributions in figure 4-2 are displayed in $10,000 increments (in 1987 dollars) rather than the "low-medium-high" classifications used by Bluestone and Harrison. As Kosters and Ross show, Bluestone and Harrison's conclusions are potentially sensitive to these corrections including, in particular, the precise choice of the cutoffs between low, medium, and high earnings. See Kosters and Ross, "Shrinking Middle Class?"

Figure 4-2. *Earnings Distribution of Men and Women, 1973, 1986*

Men and women, aged 25–55, who worked more than one hour a year

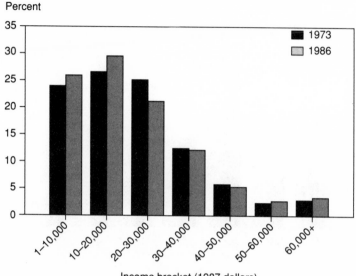

Percent

Income bracket (1987 dollars)

Source: Author's calculations based on CPS microdata files.

support a common interpretation of their work: since 1973 the proportion of adult workers with earnings in the $20,000–$50,000 range has declined while the proportions with earnings lower than $20,000 and higher than $50,000 have both increased.

In figures 4-3 and 4-4, I break apart the aggregate earnings distribution to look at men and women separately, and a more complicated picture emerges. The picture for men (figure 4-3) again shows a declining proportion of workers in the $20,000–$50,000 range.[38] If I arbitrarily say that a worker must earn at least $20,000 a year to support a middle-class living standard, then figure 4-2 is consistent with both definitions of fewer middle-class jobs: A declining proportion of prime age men earn more than $20,000 a year, and the distribution of these men's earnings shows greater inequality (and a "smaller middle"). Keep in mind, however,

38. In some sense the picture for men has deteriorated more sharply than figure 4-3 suggests because that figure omits the growing proportion of men who report no earnings during the course of a year. According to microdata files from U.S. Bureau of the Census, Current Population Survey, the proportion of men, aged 25–34, reporting no earnings rose from about 1 percent in 1973 to 6 percent in 1986.

Figure 4-3. *Earnings Distribution of Prime-Age Men, 1973, 1986*
Men, aged 25–55, who worked more than one hour a year

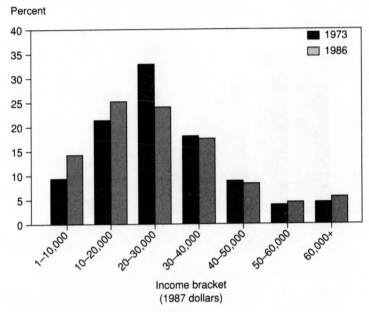

Percent

Income bracket
(1987 dollars)

Source: Author's calculations based on CPS microdata files.

that a shift from good jobs to bad jobs is only one possible explanation for this movement.

The picture for women (figure 4-4) is quite different: a declining proportion of women with earnings below $10,000 and a *growing* proportion of women earning $20,000 or more. These data indicate that the ability of women to earn a middle-class income is increasing.

Why have these changes occurred? To begin to answer the question, recall that changes in annual earnings can come from changes in hourly earnings (that is, wage rates) and from changes in hours worked.[39] One can examine the movements of wage rates by looking at changes in the

39. I use the terms "wage rate" and "wages" to refer to a rate of compensation for each hour even though the worker may view his or her salary on a monthly or annual basis. Changes in wage rates can come from a changing job structure, but they can also come from changing demography. For example, during the 1970s, the largest baby-boom cohorts entered the work force and the group of all men, aged 25–55, came to include relatively more 30-year-olds and relatively fewer 50-year-olds. Thirty-year-olds earn, on average, less than 50-year-olds and so the changing age patterns would have meant a changing wage rate pattern as well.

Figure 4-4. *Earnings Distribution of Prime-Age Women, 1973, 1986*
Women, aged 25–55, who worked at least one hour a year

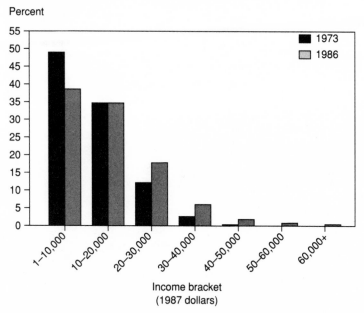

Percent

Income bracket
(1987 dollars)

Source: Author's calculations based on CPS microdata files.

annual earnings of year-round, full-time workers. These are men and women who work at least thirty-five hours a week and fifty weeks a year, and changes in their annual earnings primarily reflect changes in wage rates. Table 4-2 reports 1973 and 1986 average annual earnings for men and women who are year-round, full-time workers. For clarity, the data are restricted to workers of either of two levels of education: exactly twelve years of high school or exactly four years of college.

No group's wages grew rapidly after 1973,[40] but with this slow growth, two clear patterns emerge. First, women's earnings grew faster than men's. Second, young, less educated workers fared worse than other groups.[41] For example, among older full-time workers, aged 35–44, with

40. Recall from table 4-1 that when the economy was strong, wages were growing at about 25 percent a decade, which would have meant a 33 percent increase in the thirteen years between 1973 and 1986.

41. The reader may note that for the period 1973 to 1986, the earnings of men, aged 45–54, show a modest increase in table 4-1 and no increase in table 4-2. Table 4-1 reports average earnings for all male, full-time workers, aged 45–54, grouped together. This group

Table 4-2. *Men's and Women's Average Annual Earnings,*
by Age and Education, 1973, 1986
Year-round, full-time workers

Age and education[a]	Mean annual earnings (1987 dollars)		Percent change in annual earnings
	1973	*1986*	
Men, 25–34			
4 yrs. high school	26,364	22,226	−16
4 yrs. college	32,038	31,745	−1
Men, 35–44			
4 yrs. high school	29,739	27,739	−7
4 yrs. college	43,333	40,194	−7
Men, 45–55			
4 yrs. high school	30,623	29,894	−2
4 yrs. college	45,757	45,974	—
Women, 25–34			
4 yrs. high school	15,171	15,701	3
4 yrs. college	20,751	23,332	12
Women, 35–44			
4 yrs. high school	16,021	17,762	11
4 yrs. college	23,205	26,214	13
Women, 45–55			
4 yrs. high school	16,240	17,400	7
4 yrs. college	23,096	25,560	11

Source: Author's tabulation based on U.S. Bureau of the Census, Current Population Survey (CPS) microdata files. Adjustments to 1987 dollars made based on the personal consumption expenditure index, *Economic Report of the President*, February 1988, table B-3.
a. Four years of college refers to persons with exactly four years of college and excludes people with postgraduate education.

four years of college, women's annual earnings grew by 13 percent while men's annual earnings declined by 7 percent. And among workers of other ages and educational levels, women's earnings typically grew modestly while men's earnings declined. At the same time, the earnings of women, aged 25–34, with only a high school education grew by only 3 percent, well below the 7 percent to 12 percent gains for other groups of women. And the earnings of men with a high school education, aged 25–34, fell by 16 percent, by far the biggest decline in the table.[42]

___

contained a greater proportion of college educated men in 1986 than in 1973. This change in composition meant that average earnings in the group increased even though high school and college educated workers, taken separately, showed no earnings increase.

42. While table 4-2 looks only at workers with four years of high school and four years of college, similar statistics for other groups show that among men or women of a given age, the wages of workers who did not finish high school did not grow as fast as the wages

Table 4-3. *Men and Women Who Worked at Least One Hour during the Year, Mean Annual Earnings, by Age and Education, 1973, 1986*

Age and education[a]	Mean annual earnings (1987 dollars)		Percent change in annual earnings
	1973	1986	
Men, 25–34			
4 yrs. high school	24,644	19,387	− 21
4 yrs. college	28,569	28,792	1
Men, 35–44			
4 yrs. high school	28,461	24,992	− 12
4 yrs. college	42,266	37,728	− 11
Men, 45–55			
4 yrs. high school	29,353	27,027	− 8
4 yrs. college	44,332	42,696	− 4
Women, 25–34			
4 yrs. high school	9,599	11,182	16
4 yrs. college	14,561	18,924	30
Women, 35–44			
4 yrs. high school	10,697	12,570	18
4 yrs. college	14,564	20,050	38
Women, 45–55			
4 yrs. high school	11,967	13,199	10
4 yrs. college	18,439	19,503	6

Source: Mean earnings tabulated from CPS microdata files. Adjustments to 1987 dollars made based on the personal consumption expenditure index, *Economic Report of the President, February 1988*, table B-3.

a. Four years of college refers to persons with exactly four years of college and excludes people with postgraduate education.

Do these data imply anything about the shift of labor from good jobs to bad jobs? By the early 1970s, a substantial majority of men and women with at least a year of college were already employed in the service sector. Yet these groups' earnings did relatively better than the earnings of their less educated peers (table 4-2). This suggests that a story of good jobs and bad jobs (that is, goods production jobs and jobs in the service sector) does not apply equally to all workers. Rather, the story applies to some groups of workers within a context of stagnant wages shaped by macroeconomic forces.

Table 4-3 reports average earnings for all men and women, aged 25–

---

of workers who did finish high school. The wages of workers who had one to three years of college grew faster than the wages of high school workers but slower than the wages of college graduates, and so on. Frank Levy and Richard C. Michel, "Individual Earnings by Sex, Education, and Age: Recent U.S. Trends," paper prepared for the Joint Economic Committee of the U.S. Congress, Washington, D.C., 1988.

55, who worked at least one hour during the year, the same group of workers used in figures 4-1, 4-2, 4-3, and 4-4. These data combine part-time workers with full-time workers and reflect both changes in wage rates and changes in hours worked. A comparison of tables 4-2 and 4-3 shows that a group's hourly wages and its annual hours of work typically reinforced each other by moving in the same direction. For example, the earnings of high school men, aged 25–34, who worked full time declined by 16 percent—a surrogate for the change in their wages. But the earnings of high school men, aged 25–34, who worked at all declined by 21 percent, indicating that average hours worked declined as well.[43] Conversely, women, aged 25–34, with four years of college had a 12 percent earnings gain among full-time workers but a 30 percent earnings gain among all workers, which suggests that the group's average annual hours of work increased.

In sum, wage growth after 1973 was slow, but some groups did better than others. The performance of different groups can be explained by changes in supply and demand for different kinds of labor.

Supply and demand analysis tells us that if the demand for different kinds of labor remains stable, the groups that grow the fastest should have the slowest-growing (or fastest-declining) wages. But exactly the opposite pattern has occurred: The groups whose numbers grew the fastest were also the groups with the biggest gains in average earnings.

Consider, for example, men and women, aged 35–44, with four years of college. Within this group, the number of working women increased much faster than the number of working men, but women typically showed gains in both wages and hours worked while men showed declines in both.[44] The increase in both women's wages and women's hours of work is reflected in the upward shift of earnings in figure 4-4.

43. Put differently, if average hours for each worker had not declined, one would expect average earnings for all workers to have fallen by 16 percent just as they did for full-time workers.

44. These results are reported in table 4-11 in appendix C, in which hours of work are inferred in the following way. Consider women, aged 25–34, with four years of college. Among members of this group who worked full time, annual earnings increased by 12 percent (table 4-2). I use this 12 percent figure in table 4-11 as a surrogate for the increase in wages. Among members of the group who worked at all (full time or part time), annual earnings increased by 30 percent (table 4-3). Annual earnings are the product of hourly wages and hours worked each year. If wages increased by 12 percent, an annual earnings increase of 30 percent implies that average hours worked each year increased by 16 percent.

Similarly, among both young men and young women, aged 25–34, the number with college educations grew significantly faster than the number with twelve years of education, but it was the high school workers whose earnings fared worse. The clearest case involves younger, high school educated men. In the late 1950s, a thirty-year-old man with four years of college had income 30 percent higher than a thirty-year-old man with four years of high school. During the 1960s and early 1970s, the number of new college graduates grew rapidly and the college-high school income gap for these men closed to 25 percent in 1969 and 15 percent in 1973.[45] The trend was sufficiently strong to suggest that the market for college educated workers might be saturated and that college was no longer a good economic investment.[46] The college-high school income gap for young men remained between 15 percent and 20 percent for the rest of the 1970s. It then began to open, and by 1986 it had widened to 49 percent.[47] College men's earnings generally had not risen (table 4-3), but high school men's earnings had declined. The declining earnings of high school educated men—particularly younger ones—are largely responsible for the decline in the proportion of men earning $20,000 to $30,000 and the increasing proportion of men earning less than $20,000 shown in figure 4-3.[48]

These patterns suggest that the experience of different groups of workers was not driven by changes in labor supply but rather by changes in the demand for labor. In particular, while a good jobs-bad jobs story cannot explain the weak trend in overall wage growth, it can help to explain why some groups of workers did better than this trend while others did worse.

In the early 1970s, a significant percentage of less educated men were employed in the goods-producing industries. About 50 percent of men

45. U.S. Bureau of the Census, "Income in 1969 of Families and Persons in the United States," *Current Population Reports*, series P-60, no. 75 (Washington, D.C.: Department of Commerce, 1970), and "Money Income in 1973 of Families and Persons in the United States," *Current Population Reports*, series P-60, no. 97 (Washington, D.C.: Department of Commerce, 1975), p. 77, table 36.

46. See, for example, Richard B. Freeman, *The Overeducated American* (Academic Press, 1976).

47. CPS microdata files.

48. For more detail on this point, see Levy and Michel, "Individual Earnings." If average earnings were adjusted for men who report no earnings at all (under the assumption that they are involuntarily out of the labor force), the high school-college earnings gap for men, aged 30, would stand at 55 percent.

Table 4-4. *Distribution of Employed Men and Women,*
by Industrial Sector, 1973
Percent

Education	Durable manufacturing	Nondurable goods, mining, and construction industries	Service industries	Agri- culture
All employed men, 25–55[a]				
Less than high school	23	30	40	7
4 yrs. high school	22	24	50	4
1–3 yrs. college	18	19	61	2
4 yrs. college	16	15	67	2
4+ yrs. college	9	8	82	1
All employed women, 25–55[a]				
Less than high school	15	22	54	9
4 yrs. high school	11	12	74	3
1–3 yrs. college	6	14	79	1
4 yrs. college	2	6	91	1
4+ yrs. college	1	2	96	1

Source: Author's tabulations based on the March 1974 CPS microdata file.
a. Figures add to 100 percent.

with a high school education or less were in manufacturing, mining, and construction while 30 percent of men who had at least one year of college were so employed (table 4-4). Women of all educational levels were more highly concentrated in the service sector, but here too, less educated women were relatively more likely to be in goods production—particularly in textiles and other nondurable manufacturing.

An individual's choice of industry was at least partially motivated by salary. Among less educated men and women of all ages, those employed in goods production in 1973 typically earned 10 percent to 15 percent more a year than those employed in the service sector. The gap reflected the harsh nature of many goods production jobs (for example, heavy assembly line work), greater unionization, and the relatively large firm size that characterize many goods-producing firms.[49] This earnings gap

49. Estimate of this gap comes from the author's tabulations of the March 1974 CPS microdata files. The gap's existence implies that certain industries generate rents to labor that are not competed away, a conclusion accepted by many authors. For a discussion of such rents, see William T. Dickens and Lawrence F. Katz, "Interindustry Wage Differences and Theories of Wage Determination," Working Paper 2271 (Cambridge, Mass.: National

across industries suggests that a greater number of less educated men (and perhaps women), who were working in services at lower earnings, would have chosen to work in goods-producing industries if jobs had been available.

In fact, vacancies in the production of goods would not grow appreciably over the next thirteen years. Goods-producing industries are sensitive to economic downturns, and the years after 1973 saw sharp downturns: 1973–75 and 1980–82. In addition, the post-1982 recovery was accompanied by the overvaluation of the dollar, which undercut foreign demand for U.S. manufactured exports. The slow growth of manufacturing output, coupled with a revival of manufacturing productivity, meant that manufacturing employment in 1986 was below its level in 1979.[50]

When a sector of the economy is under pressure, the greatest adjustments are typically concentrated on young workers. In manufacturing, the use of seniority-based layoffs affected young workers both because they were the first to be let go and because they entered the labor market too late to get the jobs in the first place.

Compare the 1973 and 1986 distribution of men and women, aged 25–34, by their industry of employment. Among young men who had a high school education or less, the proportion in goods producing industries fell from about 50 percent in 1973 to 42 percent in 1986 with the sharpest decline in durable manufacturing (see table 4-12 in appendix C to this chapter). The percentage of these men working in the service sector increased modestly, but the greater increase was among men who reported no work during the year. Persons who report no earnings are not included in the average earnings figures of tables 4-2 through 4-4 but one can speculate that the increase in no-work status indicated a situation in which the decline in manufacturing employment made young, less educated men a kind of "glut on the market." They had to scramble for

---

Bureau of Economic Research, June 1987); and Lawrence F. Katz and Lawrence H. Summers, "Can Inter-Industry Wage Differentials Justify Strategic Trade Policy?" (Harvard University and National Bureau of Economic Research, April 1988).

50. As discussed in chap. 6, manufacturing productivity has been increasing in recent years but overall productivity growth remains weak because of slow productivity growth in the service sector. On the relationship between goods producing industries and recessions, see Robert Z. Lawrence, *Can America Compete?* (Brookings, 1984). Katz and Summers, "Can Inter-Industry Wage Differentials," argue that, for whatever reason, industries with high wage premiums (that is, economic rents) are often export-producing industries or those that would have been hurt by the high dollar.

work in the service sector, a scramble that put additional pressure on
the group's wages and hours worked. The data also show that less
educated women were less likely to work in goods-producing industries
in 1986 than they had been in 1973.

The sharp shift away from goods-producing industries was restricted
to less educated workers. A minority of college educated young men and
women worked in goods-producing industries in 1973, but such workers
were slightly more likely to work in goods production in 1986. This result
is striking since the number of college educated workers grew much
faster over the period than those with only a high school education (table
4-11 in appendix C to this chapter).

In sum, there has been a movement from good to bad jobs primarily
for one group in the labor force: younger, less educated men. The weak
growth of manufacturing employment appears responsible for the fact
that these individuals and, to a lesser extent, young less educated women,
have lost ground vis-à-vis the general trend of slow wage growth. But
the trend was determined by macroeconomic forces, including low
productivity growth and the lost income of two oil price shocks, rather
than by employment shifts among sectors. For example, table 4-3 showed
that the average earnings of men, aged 25–34, with four years of college
stagnated between 1973 and 1986. But these men had not shifted heavily
into the service sector. To the contrary, they were slightly more
concentrated in goods production by the end of the period. The fact that
their earnings stopped growing (and in fact had declined) reflected
conditions in the overall economy rather than any move from "good jobs"
to "bad jobs."

Indeed, the story of the vanishing middle-class jobs really has three
plots. First, the post-1973 slow growth of earnings, a trend caused by
macroeconomic factors, affected earnings in almost all jobs. When earnings
were growing rapidly, a machine operator would earn more today (in
real terms) than a manager earned a decade earlier. Conversely, when
earnings grow slowly or decline, good white collar jobs—for example,
computer programmers—can pay their occupiers too little to purchase
what is defined as a middle class living standard, for example, enough to
carry a mortgage on a single-family home (which today typically requires
two paychecks). In this sense, slow-growing earnings have limited the
number of middle-class jobs, and this helps to account for the wide
audience the middle-class jobs debate has attracted.

Second, vanishing middle-class jobs reflect a shift of employment from good jobs to bad jobs, primarily for younger, less educated men and, to a lesser extent, younger, less educated women. This trend helps to explain both the growing inequality in all men's earnings and the growing proportion of high school educated men who earn under $20,000 a year. In 1973, 64 percent of male high school graduates, aged 25–34, reported earning more than $20,000 (in 1987 dollars). In 1986, only 40 percent reported earnings that high.[51] For these men, the issue is not whether the economy is producing good jobs, but the education one needs to get those jobs. Precisely because these men have been hurt by shrinking manufacturing employment, an improvement in the U.S. international trade position (with a corresponding increase in manufacturing exports) may help their situation.

Finally, the story of the vanishing middle-class jobs is more a story about men than women. Women's earnings are systematically below those of men, but the proportion of women earning more than $20,000 rose from 16 percent in 1973 to 27 percent in 1986.[52] Part of this increase reflects increased hours of work, but part reflects rising wages (table 4-2). Among younger women, as among younger men, there is evidence of growing inequality between more and less educated workers. But on the whole, women's position in the labor market has improved moderately over this period both in absolute terms and relative to men.

Living Standards of Families and Children

In the long view of U.S. economic history, the period from 1947 to 1973 was unusual for both relative tranquility and sustained income growth.[53] But most people form expectations based on their experience rather than on history books. By the early 1970s, Americans had come to view steadily rising living standards as almost a law of nature with all the benefits described earlier: a steadily expanding middle class, the knowledge that each generation would do better than the previous one,

51. Author's calculations based on the CPS microdata files.

52. Ibid.

53. This happy condition was not restricted to the United States. Angus Maddison, in his recent survey of economic growth, calls the period 1947–73 a "golden age" for all industrialized countries. See Angus Maddison, "Growth and Slowdown in Advanced Capitalist Economies," *Journal of Economic Literature*, vol. 25 (June 1987), pp. 649–98. See also chap. 6 in this volume.

and so on. In this context, the post-1973 stagnation of workers' incomes could have come as an enormous shock to the country.

There was a shock,[54] but it was smaller than might have been expected. An examination of the data suggests one reason. Income per capita, the most widely used measure of living standards, was growing strongly even though income for each worker (that is, earnings) was not. The census reports that between 1973 and 1986, the real median income of all full-time women workers rose a modest 10 percent while the median income of full-time male workers declined by 2 percent. But despite this slow growth, income per capita (average income for each man, woman and child in the population) rose from $9,926 to $12,150 (in 1987 dollars), a brisk 22 percent over the same period.[55] How could income per capita grow for a period well after 1973 if workers' earnings grew slowly?

The apparent contradiction can be resolved by understanding the great changes that have taken place in U.S. families and households. These changes were driven by two major trends, both of them under way for several decades.

First, female participation in the labor force increased enormously. Among women, aged 20 and over, labor force participation rose slowly, from 35 percent in the 1950s to 40 percent in the late 1960s, but then it surged to 57 percent today.[56] From a macroeconomic perspective, the increase meant that a growing proportion of adults were at work; total earnings in the economy could rise sharply even though the typical worker did not see great gains. From an individual perspective, more working women meant more husband-wife families had two paychecks instead of one, a shift that boosted income per capita (that is, for each man, woman, and child) in families even though men's and women's earnings were growing slowly.

Second, a sharp decline in the birth rate, partly related to women's

54. For example, the taxpayers' revolt of the late 1970s reflected, in part, the tension between stagnant incomes and growing government expenditures.

55. The actual income figures for working women are $15,553 (1973) and $17,147 (1986). For men, the figures are $27,490 (1973) and $26,926 (1986) with all figures in 1987 dollars. See U.S. Bureau of the Census, "Money Income of Households, Families, and Persons in the United States: 1986," tables 28, 29. Conversion to 1987 dollars was made using the personal consumption expenditure index. Over the same period, the Department of Commerce measure of disposable income per capita, a measure that corrects for both taxes paid and such noncash income as fringe benefits, food stamps, and medicare, also rose by 21 percent.

56. *Economic Report of the President, February 1988*, p. 290, table B-37.

Table 4-5. *Households and the Labor Force, 1973, 1987*

Item	1973	1987
Average number of persons in a household[a]	3.01	2.66
Percentage of the U.S. population in the civilian labor force[b]	42%	50%

Source: U.S. Bureau of the Census, "Household and Family Characteristics," *Current Population Reports*, series P-20, no. 258 (March 1973) and no. 424 (March 1987) (Washington, D.C.: Department of Commerce, 1973, 1988); and *Economic Report of the President, February 1988*, tables B-31, B-32.
a. Includes both families and unrelated individuals.
b. Population includes persons of all ages, not only persons 16 and above.

participation in the labor force, occurred. The decline began in the mid-1960s (the end of the baby boom) and continued through the late 1970s when it stabilized at about 5 percent below the birth rate necessary to replace the current population.[57] Low birth rates were reflected in fewer children in each family (which, other things equal, also boosted income per capita) as well as in the way that young people postponed marriage and families in the first place. In 1970 half of all women were married by the age of 21 and half of all men were married by the age of 23. By 1986 both groups married two years later, resulting in a growing number of persons who lived as unrelated individuals.[58] In short, rising female participation in the labor force, together with low birth rates, meant that a growing proportion of the whole population was at work. In the early 1970s, 42 percent of the entire population was in the labor force. By 1987 more working women and fewer children meant that percentage had risen to 50 percent (table 4-5). With more people at work, income per capita could keep rising even though income for each worker was stagnant.[59]

57. More precisely, it is the total fertility rate that is 5 percent below replacement. The total fertility rate measures the total number of children born to a woman over her childbearing years, and this statistic determines population growth. The birth rate in a given year reflects both fertility and the timing of births. If, for example, women decide to have their children later in life the birth rate will temporarily fall even though total fertility was unchanged. See U.S. Bureau of the Census, *Statistical Abstract of the United States, 1988* (Washington, D.C.: Department of Commerce, 1987), p. 59.

58. U.S. Bureau of the Census, "Marital Status and Living Arrangements, March 1986" *Current Population Reports*, series P-20, no. 418 (Washington, D.C.: Department of Commerce, 1987), table B.

59. In chapter 2, Lawrence shows how since 1982, the United States has also increased living standards by borrowing from abroad. This is because higher borrowing has allowed

A final change in household structure deserves particular attention: the growing number of families headed by single women. Between 1973 and 1987, the number of husband-wife families under 65 grew by 2.8 million families (7.1 percent), but the number of female-headed families under 65 grew by 3.6 million (66.4 percent) (see table 4-13 in appendix C to this chapter).[60]

Both the rise in labor force participation by women and the decline in the birth rate began well before the oil price shocks and the productivity slowdown, but they still help offset the post-1973 stagnation. The ability of household changes to offset future stagnation in incomes and earning is more limited. Almost two-thirds of young husband-wife families begin marriage with two paychecks, and adding another paycheck is not an option. The birth rate, while very low, has stabilized in recent years. A continued reduction in family size cannot be expected. In the long run, then, income per capita can grow no faster than income for each worker.

The same family changes that helped to increase income per capita after 1973 also helped to reshape the family income distribution. This reshaping is less than one might suppose and is best understood in historical context.

By absolute standards, the U.S. family income distribution has never been very equal. In the post-World War II period, 1969 was the year of greatest family income equality. But even in that year, the richest one-fifth of families had 40.6 percent of all family income while the poorest one-fifth had 5.6 percent, a ratio of $7.25 in the top fifth to $1.00 in the bottom. After 1969 family income inequality increased moderately during the 1970s and more sharply in the 1980s so that in 1986, the richest one-fifth of families received 43.7 percent of all income while the poorest one-fifth received 4.6 percent, a ratio of $9.50 to $1.00.[61]

Americans to consume—both privately and through government expenditure—more than they earn. In addition, foreign borrowing and the resulting high value of the dollar led to cheap imports, which restrained inflation from reducing real earnings.

60. In husband-wife families, the person listed as family head was under 65.

61. At the same time, one should not assume that the richest one-fifth of families included only millionaires. The income for this group in 1986 was about $50,000. In contrast, the poorest one-fifth of families had incomes below $13,886. See U.S. Bureau of the Census, "Money Income of Households, Families and Persons in the United States: 1986," p. 39, table 12. Available evidence suggests the family income distribution was significantly less equal before World War II than it has been in recent decades. For further discussion, see Levy, *Dollars and Dreams.*

Figure 4-5. *Distribution of Families by Income, 1973, 1986*

Percent

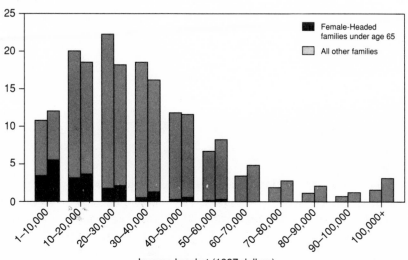

Income bracket (1987 dollars)

Source: Author's calculations based on CPS microdata files.

The growing inequality of family incomes was driven in part by less equal earnings (for example, figure 4-3) but also by changing family demographics. In 1986 the income of the average two-earner family was $28,300 (in 1987 dollars), about three times as large as the income of the average female-headed family ($12,000). This variation is larger than the variation among earnings of, for example, working men of different ages and educations (table 4-3). Given this variation, it is not surprising that recent shifts in the family income distribution have been driven largely by changes in family structure.

Figure 4-5 displays the family income distributions for 1973 and 1986 (with all incomes expressed in 1987 dollars), and summary statistics are contained in table 4-6. These two distributions are separated by thirteen years, but they still overlap substantially, a fact that underlines the slow growth of family incomes over the period.[62] What has happened to middle-class families over this period? As in the case of middle-class jobs, the question has two meanings. If a middle-class family is defined as one that can afford a middle-class standard of living, the slow growth of family

62. The same point arose with respect to the overlap of earnings distributions in figures 4-2, 4-3, and 4-4.

Table 4-6. *Summary of the 1973 and 1986 Family Income Distributions*

Family income class (1987 dollars)	Percent of all families in income class		Percent of all children in income class[a]	
	1973	1986	1973	1986
Below $20,000[a]	31	31	27	33
$20–$50,000	53	47	57	46
Over $50,000	16	22	16	21
Total	100	100	100	100
(over $80,000)[b]	(4)	(6)	(3)	(5)

Source: Author's tabulations based on the March 1974 and March 1987 CPS microdata files.
a. Children grouped by their family's income.
b. Over $80,000 contained in over $50,000 category.

incomes means the middle class has increased at a very slow rate. When median family income is adjusted for inflation, it grew by 6 percent between 1973 ($28,890) and 1986 ($30,670) or about 5 percent a decade. By contrast, between 1947 and 1973, median family income grew from $14,830 to $28,890 or by 36 percent a decade.[63] Compared with the earlier decades family incomes and, by implication, the middle class have grown slowly since 1973, particularly in light of the shift to two-earner families.[64]

A second definition of a middle-class family includes changes in income inequality and the extent to which families are moving from the middle of the income distribution to the top and the bottom. Then the changing structure of American families becomes important.

When one looks at families, regardless of structure, it appears that the middle of the income distribution has declined, but not in the way portrayed in popular discussion (figure 4-5). The proportion of families with high incomes (over $50,000) has grown; the proportion of families in the middle ($20,000–$50,000) has declined; but the proportion of

63. U.S. Bureau of the Census, "Money Income of Households, Families, and Persons in the United States: 1986," table 10.

64. A recent report by the U.S. Congressional Budget Office (CBO) argues that family incomes did not stagnate but actually rose by 20 percent between 1970 and 1986. The CBO report differs from other analyses primarily because it defines families to include unrelated individuals, and it adjusts family incomes for changing family size. It is the decline in family size (including the increased number of unrelated individuals), rather than rising real family incomes, that leads to the report's conclusion. In this sense, the CBO report is similar to the analysis of income per capita presented earlier in this section. See U.S. Congressional Budget Office, *Trends in Family Income: 1970–1986* (Washington, D.C., 1988).

Table 4-7. *Characteristics of Families with Incomes Less Than $20,000, 1973, 1986*

Income in 1987 dollars

Type of family	1973	1986
	Percent of all families with incomes less than $20,000	
Husband-wife, less than 65	48	43
Female head, less than 65	23	31
Head, 65 or over	29	26
Total	100	100
	Chances that a family has income less than $20,000	
Husband-wife, less than 65	19	19
Female head, less than 65	70	67
Head, 65 or over	64	46
All families	31	31

Source: Author's tabulations based on March 1974 and March 1987 CPS microdata files.

families at the bottom (less than $20,000) has remained constant. These figures say that a number of families are being left behind. But the figures also say that a decline in the middle of the distribution is because more families are gaining than are losing ground.

While the proportion of families in each income range has not moved dramatically, the types of families in each income range have changed more quickly in ways that clarify the role of family structure. At the lower end of the distribution, the proportion of families with incomes below $20,000 has remained constant. But the composition of this group has shifted toward the growing number of families headed by single women (table 4-7). By contrast, families over 65, who used to be concentrated in the lower end of the distribution, have sharply improved their position.[65]

At the upper end of the distribution, the proportion of families with incomes over $50,000 has grown, largely reflecting the increasing number of two-earner families. Among two-earner families, average income has not changed dramatically. In both 1973 and 1986, one-quarter of such families had incomes over $50,000 (in 1987 dollars). But two-earner

65. On the improving status of the elderly, see *Economic Report of the President, February 1985*, chap. 5.

families have become a growing share of all families, and the share of all families with incomes above $50,000 has grown correspondingly.[66]

In an accounting sense, then, the data say that if the number of female-headed families had not increased, family income inequality would be lower and the proportion of families with incomes under $20,000 would be lower as well. In practice, this would mean reducing the out-of-wedlock birth rate (about one American child in five is now born to an unwed mother) and reducing the rate of divorce while encouraging the rate of remarriage.

There are only vague ideas on how to accomplish such changes.[67] But if the increase in female-headed families cannot be fully explained, one implication of the increase is clear: a growing inequality in the status of children. Recall that from the mid-1960s to the late 1970s, U.S. birth rates fell steadily. In this context, the percentage of children in female-headed households grew rapidly both because the number of children in female-headed households was growing and because the number of children in two-parent families was declining. By 1987, 22 percent of all children were in families headed by women (another 3 percent lived with neither parent), and most of these families had relatively low incomes (table 4-8).

The effect of these shifts can be seen in table 4-6 and figure 4-6, which compare the 1973 and 1986 income distributions of children and classify children by the incomes of their families. Since 1973, the proportion of all children in families with incomes below $10,000 has increased from 10 percent to 16 percent and fully one third of the nation's children now live in families with incomes below $20,000. At the same time, the proportion of children in families with incomes above $50,000 has also increased, partly reflecting the growing number of two-earner families.

---

66. Author's calculations based on CPS microdata files.

67. There is, for example, enormous disagreement on the causes of the growing number of out-of-wedlock births. Charles Murray argues that this trend reflects the incentives of too liberal welfare policies while the general economy plays almost no role. In contrast, William Julius Wilson dismisses the role played by welfare policy, arguing instead that the growing number of out-of-wedlock births among blacks reflects the declining number of manufacturing jobs in central cities and the resulting joblessness among less educated black men. See Charles Murray, *Losing Ground: American Social Policy, 1950–1980* (Basic Books, 1984); and William Julius Wilson, *The Truly Disadvantaged: The Inner City, the Underclass, and Public Policy* (University of Chicago Press, 1987). To the extent that Wilson is correct, increased marriage rates, while desirable on many grounds, will not automatically boost income.

Table 4-8. *The Living Arrangements of Children, 1973, 1987*

People with whom children reside	Percent of children	
	1973 (67.9 million children)	*1987* (62.9 million children)
Both parents	82	71
Widowed or divorced mother	6	10
Single mother or mother with absent spouse	6	12
Father only	1	3
Neither parent	3	3
Total	98[a]	99[a]

Source: U.S. Bureau of the Census, "Marital Status and Living Arrangements," *Current Population Reports*, series P-20, no. 255 (March 1973) and no. 423 (March 1987) (Washington, D.C.: Department of Commerce, 1973, 1988), tables 4, 5.

a. Percentages do not add to 100 because the numbers for children who live with a mother or father who is the head of a subfamily have been left out.

In sum, the standard picture of a shrinking middle class with growing concentrations at the top and bottom is not a good description of all families taken together, but it is not a bad description of all families who have children. Researchers have not established definitive links between a child's family income, the kind of education the child receives, and the child's ultimate performance as an adult worker. But for persons concerned about the nation's long-run rate of productivity growth, the fact that one-sixth of all children now live in families with incomes under $10,000 is not an encouraging sign.[68]

The Future

The analysis, to this point, has focused on past trends in incomes and living standards. It is useful now to look to the near-term future by examining future earnings, family incomes, and income inequality.

Earlier sections described how workers' earnings were determined by the growth of labor productivity, modified by the supply and demand for different kinds of labor. These forces projected over the next decade, reveal four general points:

—The rate of future productivity growth is not known, but if post-1980 experience is a guide, output each hour should increase between 1.25 percent and 1.9 percent a year.

68. For a fuller discussion, see chap. 7 in this volume.

Figure 4-6. *Distribution of Children by Family Income, 1973, 1986*

Percent

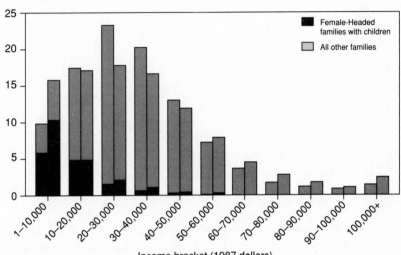

Income bracket (1987 dollars)

Source: Author's calculations based on CPS microdata files.

—The labor force is moving from a period of very rapid growth to very slow growth. Between 1976 and 1986 the number of workers, aged 20–34, grew by 11 million. Between 1986 and 1996, the number of workers in their twenties will decline by 5 million. This should improve the demand for workers at all levels, including, in particular, less educated men and women.[69]

—A lowered trade deficit, other things equal, should also increase, manufacturing employment and the demand for less educated men.[70]

—Offsetting these trends to an unknown degree is the possibility that educational requirements are rising throughout the occupational structure in ways that may reduce demand for less educated labor (see chapter 7).

Productivity growth will determine the general earnings level, while the other three forces will help to determine the distribution of earnings among men and women of different ages and educational levels. While

69. Social Security Administration, *Economic Projections for OASDHI Cost and Insurance Estimates: 1987*, Actuarial Study 101 (Baltimore, Md.: Department of Health and Human Services, May 1988), pp. 34–35, table A-1.

70. When the midrange macroeconomic scenario of chap. 2 is combined with an assumed 3 percent a year growth in manufacturing productivity, manufacturing employment in 1992 will rise to its level before the 1980–82 recession.

Figure 4-7. *Father-Son Income Comparisons for College Graduates, 1961–2006*

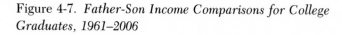

1987 dollars

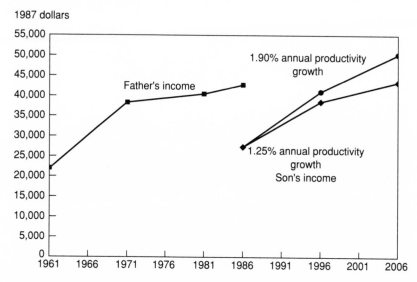

one cannot summarize these forces in a single measure, some representative calculations can address the following question: Will young men today earn more than their fathers earned?[71]

Consider a man who was 25 in 1961, the year in which he had a son. By 1986 (the year of the latest available census data), the man would have been 55 and his son would have been 30. If one assumes the father had the average earnings of men of his age and education, the father's income history may be constructed by referring to past census reports. The same source reveals the son's 1986 income, which can be projected into the future by use of simple estimating equations based on assumed productivity growth, and changes in the unemployment rate or, for high school educated men, changes in the availability of manufacturing jobs.[72]

Figure 4-7 displays this father-son comparison for a father and son who both have exactly four years of college. The comparison is reasonably optimistic. Despite the earnings deterioration of recent years, the son, aged 30, earned $26,000 in 1986, about $4,000 more than his father, at

---

71. I restrict this example to fathers and sons because it requires calculations back as far as the early 1960s, when most adult women did not participate in the labor force. This makes the comparable mother-daughter comparison difficult to interpret.

72. Equations and assumptions are contained in appendix A in this chapter.

Figure 4-8. *Father-Son Income Comparisons for High School Graduates, 1961–2006*

1987 dollars

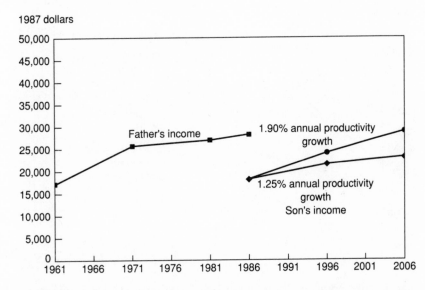

the same age, had earned in 1961 (all figures are expressed in 1987 dollars). At the same time, the father had the advantage of working almost half his career (after age 30) when productivity was growing at 2 percent to 3 percent a year. If the son's career spans a period when productivity grows by only 1.25 percent a year, the son's earnings at 50 will reach $43,300 or $1,700 more than his father earned in 1986. But if productivity during the son's career increases by 1.9 percent a year, the son's earnings at 50 will top off at $51,200, about $10,000 more than his father earned in 1986 (the father's best year).

Figure 4-8 displays a similar comparison for fathers and sons who had a high school education. While the future projections assume the closing of the trade deficit and the associated increase in labor demand, today's 30-year-old will just about equal his father's earnings even if productivity grows at 1.9 percent a year. This result reflects the fact that the son starts from a relatively low level of income (that is, the earnings of high school men, aged 30, in 1986, which fell sharply since the early 1970s), and subsequent income changes simply reflect movements in the economy. Because the labor force is now growing so slowly, it may be that new cohorts of high school graduates start at sharply higher wage rates

Table 4-9. *Chances That a Man Will Be Making Less at Age 40 than at Age 30*

Worker	Annual rate of productivity growth (percent)		
	0.0	1.25	1.9
Man with 12 yrs. of high school	43	31	24
Man with 4 yrs. of college	30	19	14

Sources: Author's calculations as described in appendix B to this chapter.

and so face much different futures.[73] Nonetheless, the projections emphasize that the position of a young, less educated man or women is more precarious today than it was a generation ago.

I argued earlier that rapidly rising productivity and earnings provided a cushion against the loss of "good jobs" and the other transitions that are part of any economy. The equations that underlie figures 4-7 and 4-8 can make this argument explicit. The income paths shown in figures 4-7 and 4-8 say that high school men and college men will both, on average, see growing earnings as they pass from 30 to 40. But in practice, some men will do better than this average while others will do worse. In particular, it is useful to estimate the chances that a man will be making less at 40 than he did at 30—a mark of downward mobility—and how this chance depends on the general rate of productivity growth. Rough estimates are contained in table 4-9.

If productivity did not grow at all, a worker's gain in earnings as he passed from 30 to 40 would depend entirely on his additional seniority and experience. In that situation, a high school man would have a 43 percent probability of losing ground over the decade while a college man would have a probability of 30 percent. As the rate of productivity growth increases, both probabilities fall sharply but even with productivity growing at 1.9 percent a year, a fairly optimistic near-term forecast, a high school man still has a one-in-four chance of losing ground while a college man has a chance of one-in-seven. Productivity growth rates in the 3 percent range—similar to those in the 1950s and early 1960s—are required to minimize the chances of losing ground for this age group.

73. A related question is how much tighter labor markets would affect the wages of current workers (as distinct from future workers). See appendix A for a short discussion of this issue.

The projections in figures 4-7 and 4-8 also embody a similar but more general point. The optimistic scenarios in these figures show sons doing as well as or slightly better than their fathers. This is a reasonable outcome, but it represents far less of the growth and upward mobility that was present in earlier decades. It follows that the virtues of rapid growth—the rapidly expanding middle class, the cushion for industrial change, the early certainty that each generation will live better than the previous one—will be in short supply.

The projection of workers' incomes poses problems, but the projection of the family income distribution is far more complex. In looking to the future, it is important to restate two points made earlier. First, the family and household changes that permitted income per capita to grow faster than income per worker are now largely exhausted. If labor productivity grows slowly, income per capita will also grow slowly, more slowly than in most of the U.S. post-World War II experience.

Second, movements in the inequality of family income will continue to be heavily influenced by demographic factors—the balance of female-headed families and two-earner families. Given recent trends in divorce and out-of-wedlock births, a gloomy forecast seems inevitable. But it is worth reviewing one theory of marriage and family structure that reaches a more optimistic conclusion.[74]

The theory—decidedly nonfeminist—begins by assuming that the primary initiative for marriage lies with men who typically want to marry women two to three years younger than themselves. Beginning in the late 1960s (when the first baby-boom cohorts were turning 21) each new cohort of adults was larger than the preceding one. In any year, the number of 23-year-old women was substantially larger than the number of 25-year-old men, and so men felt less risk in delaying marriage while they explored their options. The risk of divorce for men was also reduced because of the large number of available partners.[75] Now the last of the baby boom has passed into its twenties, and the situation is reversing.

74. Jib Fowles, "Coming Soon: More Men Than Women," *New York Times,* June 5, 1988.

75. This general theory parallels William Julius Wilson's explanation for the rapid growth of female-headed families among blacks. Wilson argues that the demographic ratio of women to "marriageable" men is further increased among blacks because black men have high rates of unemployment, incarceration, and homicide. See Wilson, *Truly Disadvantaged.*

Men, aged 25, will now see relatively few women, aged 23, and the men will feel great pressure to establish and maintain stable relationships.[76]

Even if this theory is correct, its effects will be concentrated among families that will form in the future. The current distribution of families will continue to work their way through the system. With them come the large percentage of children in families with very low incomes. As emphasized in other chapters in this book, the challenge for the coming decade is to bring national spending into line with national output while not savaging investment. In a real sense, these children—a large part of the future U.S. labor force—are one of the most important investments of all.

Conclusion

I conclude this chapter by summarizing the significant points.

—In terms of workers' incomes, the post-World War II years divide into two parts. In the years 1946–73, workers' incomes grew briskly. Since 1973, workers' incomes have grown much more slowly. This slow growth owes far more to macroeconomic forces than a shift from "good" jobs to "bad" jobs.

—No group of workers has made big income gains since the early 1970s, but average earnings for women of most ages and education have grown while average earnings for most men have declined. Among both men and women, the earnings of younger, less educated workers have done much worse than earnings of other groups. For these groups, the slow growth of "good" jobs in manufacturing does seem to be important.

—Despite the slow growth in workers' incomes, income per capita— the usual measure of living standards—has continued to increase largely because of changes in family and household structure. Women's increasing participation in the labor force and low birth rates have meant more two-earner families and fewer children in each family, both of which help to increase income per capita (that is, income for each man, woman, and child).

—The same demographic changes are reshaping the family income

76. In a related argument, Richard Easterlin, *Birth and Fortune*, argues that the end of the baby boom will mean that future new workers will experience relatively higher wages (because of their smaller cohort size), and they will respond to their relatively improved economic condition by having higher fertility rates.

distribution. The proportion of families with incomes between $20,000 and $50,000 has declined, with the proportion of families with incomes below $20,000 remaining constant and the proportion of families with income over $50,000 increasing. Much of this change represents the income gap between the growing number of female-headed families and the growing number of two-earner families.

—Within the family income distribution, the incomes of families with children are becoming significantly less equal. One-sixth of all children now live in families with incomes under $10,000 a year.

—It is reasonable to forecast that today's young college educated worker will earn more than his college educated father by a modest amount. But the future of today's young high school educated worker is less certain unless the country returns to very rapid economic growth. The kind of upward mobility implied by these projections is significantly less than the kind of mobility that was taken for granted in the 1950s and 1960s.

Appendix A: The Projection of Workers' Incomes

In this appendix, I describe the model used to estimate the projected workers' incomes displayed in figures 4-7 and 4-8. Average 1986 incomes for men, aged 30, with four years of high school and four years of college are observed directly from the U.S. Census Current Population Survey. The problem is to forecast what these men will be earning when they are 40 (in 1996) and 50 (in 2006). Data for this estimation are limited to the published average incomes of men, classified by age and education, taken from the Current Population Survey beginning in 1958.

The estimation can take two, somewhat different, forms. Consider estimating the incomes of college educated men who will be 40 years old in 1996. One technique involves a pure cross-section model that uses variables including productivity growth, the unemployment rate, cohort size, and so on to estimate the average income of college educated men, aged 40, in a single year. The resulting equation is combined with macroeconomic projections to directly estimate income at age 40 in 1996.

The second model estimates income *growth* of college educated men between 30 and 40, as a function of the same kinds of variables. The estimate results in an income-growth factor—say 28 percent—and this is applied to a group's actual income at age 30 to estimate its income at age 40.[77]

While the second technique seems less direct, it is more accurate because of the manner in which labor markets adjust to change. Evidence suggests that when labor markets are in transition, a disproportionate share of the adjustment falls on entry-level workers. This is consistent with the earnings data in table 4-3, which show that as manufacturing employment weakened in the early 1980s, the earnings of high school educated men, aged 25–34, fell much more sharply than the earnings of older high school men who were partially protected by job seniority.

Consider one result of this adjustment process. In 1973 the earnings of high school men, aged 35–44, were 15 percent higher than high school men, aged 25–34. By 1986 the corresponding gap had opened from 14 percent to 29 percent. The growing gap suggests that the passage of time will not automatically move today's young workers to the earnings levels of today's older workers. Rather, it suggests that today's young workers are on their own "track." The track will be influenced by macroeconomic forces, but it is not necessarily the same track followed by workers who entered the labor market in earlier years.

To estimate what today's workers, aged 30, will be earning in ten years, one cannot simply project forward the earnings of today's workers at age 40. Rather, one must begin with what today's workers, aged 30, actually earn and estimate how much that will grow.[78]

Equation (1) estimates the income growth between the ages of 30 and

77. A third, more complete technique combines both kinds of estimation in a pooled cross-section, time-series model. This technique requires panel data (a series of repeated observations on the same individuals over time) that were not available.

78. The cross-section and growth models mirror, to a certain extent, the disagreement among Easterlin and Smith and Welch on the future earnings of baby-boom cohorts. Easterlin argues that a member of a big baby-boom cohort experiences relatively low entry-level wages and slow wage growth throughout his or her life—that is, he or she is on a "track." Smith and Welch argue that while members of the baby-boom cohort may begin their careers at low wages, they quickly become substitutes for older workers, and so the long-run effect on their wages is fairly modest—that is, they catch up to a significant extent. Recent economic arguments about hysteresis in labor markets implicitly side with the Easterlin view. See Easterlin, *Birth and Fortune*, Smith and Welch, "No Time to Be Young," and Olivier J. Blanchard and Lawrence H. Summers, "Hysteresis and the European Unemployment Problem," in Stanley Fischer, ed., *NBER Macroeconomics Annual 1986* (MIT Press, 1986), pp. 15–78.

40 for a set of grouped data for men with one to three years of college
and four years of college:

1) $\text{Ln} \dfrac{(\text{Income } e, a + 10, t + 10)}{(\text{Income } e, a, t)} = f(\text{ch-prod, ch-unemp, ed})$

Income e, a, t = median income of all men with e years of
education who are in age group a (for ex-
ample, 25–34 years old), in year t (for example, 1965).

Income e, $a + 10$, $t + 10$ = median income of all men with e years of
education who are in age group $a + 10$ (for
example, 35–44 years old) in year $t + 10$ (for
example, 1975).

ch-prod = the total growth of nonfarm business productivity between year t and year $t + 10$.

ch-unemp = the change in the unemployment rate between year $t + 10$ and year t.

ed = 1 if observation referred to men with 1–3
years of college.

= 0 if observation referred to men with 4 years
of college.

A similar equation was estimated for men's income growth as they
passed from 40 to 50. Parallel equations were estimated for the income
growth of men who had one to three years or four years of high school.
For men who did not go beyond high school, the change in the
unemployment rate between years $t + 10$ and t was replaced by the
change in the ratio of manufacturing employment to the number of such
men, aged 25–55. This variable is designed to measure the availability
of manufacturing jobs for less educated men.[79]

Regression results are summarized in table 4-10.

Appendix B: Estimating the Number of Downwardly Mobile

This appendix details the procedure used to estimate the illustrative
probabilities that a man will earn less at age 40 than at age 30. I begin

79. Various cohort size variables were also tested in these equations but they proved
generally insignificant. This implies that cohort size has its biggest effect on entry-level
earnings and and has relatively less affect on subsequent earnings growth.

Table 4-10. *Estimated Equations of Income Growth for Men*

Conditions	Men passing from 30 to 40		Men passing from 40 to 50	
	Men with 1–3 yrs. high school or 4 yrs. high school	Men with 1–3 yrs. college or 4 yrs. college	Men with 1–3 yrs. high school or 4 yrs. high school	Men with 1–3 yrs. college or 4 yrs. college
Change in productivity	.9977 (5.8295)[a]	1.0495 (4.7194)	.9845 (5.4508)	1.1866 (5.3576)
Change in unemployment rate	. . .	.0142 (2.1984)	. . .	.0058 (.9053)
Change in availability of manufacturing jobs	.7126 (5.3596)	. . .	.5610 (3.9982)	. . .
Education[b]	−.1031 (−7.3144)	−.0898 (−4.9101)	−.0777 (−5.2219)	−.0422 (−2.3166)
Constant	−.9859 (−5.1684)	−.8327 (−3.1708)	−1.0678 (−5.3039)	−1.2225 (−4.6742)
Number of obs.	32	32	32	32
Corrected R^2	.923	.824	.891	.778

a. t-statistics in parentheses.
b. Education is a (0,1) variable, which is 1 if dependent variable is from the lower of the two educational groups in the regression.

by representing the log earnings at age 30 and at age 40 as standard earnings-generating functions:

1 a) $\ln(Y30) = B'X + e_{30}$
  b) $\ln(Y40) = C'Z + e_{40}$

where X and Z are vectors of personal characteristics,
e_{30} and e_{40} are normally distributed with mean zero and, for simplicity, equal variances, σ_e^2.

Suppose that the man's earnings between 30 and 40 are expected to grow by a factor, G (for example 1.37 or 37 percent). Since the man's personal characteristics will be unchanged between the two years, one can write as follows:

2 a) $E(\ln(Y30)) = u$
  b) $E(\ln(Y40)) = u + \ln(G)$

where u is the expected value of the natural log of earnings at age 30.

Given (1) and (2), the probability that a man will earn less at age 40 than at age 30 is equivalent to the probability that $(e_{30}-e_{40})$ is less than $\ln(G)$—that is, that the stochastic variation in earnings is sufficiently negative to offset the average growth.

Since e_{30} and e_{40} are both normally distributed, their difference is also normally distributed with mean 0 and variance equal to

$$3) \qquad\qquad \sigma^2 = 2 \times \sigma_e^2 - 2\,\text{cov}\,(e_{30}e_{40})$$

For the computations in this chapter, estimates of σ_e^2, $\text{cov}(e_{30},\ e_{40})$ and σ^2 were adapted from Lillard and Willis with an estimated variance estimate (3) of .1535. Estimates of the growth factor, G, were taken from the equations in table 4-10, in appendix A.[80]

80. In their work, based on the Panel Study of Income Dynamics, Lillard and Willis estimate a variance for the natural log of men's earnings of .307 which I assume applies to men's earnings at ages 30 and 40. They also demonstrate that the correlation of a man's earnings in year t and year $t + x$ approaches .75 after about five years, suggesting that the covariance between an individual's earnings in year t and $t + 10$ is about .229. See Lee A. Lillard and Robert J. Willis, "Dynamic Aspects of Earning Mobility," *Econometrica*, vol. 46 (September 1978), pp. 985–1012.

Appendix C: Additional Tables

Table 4-11. *Changes in Group Size, Wage Rates, and Annual Hours of Work for Men and Women Workers, Aged 25–55, 1973–86*

	Number of workers (millions)		Percent change in group size	Percent change in wages	Percent change in annual hours worked
	1973	1986			
Men, 25–34					
4 yrs. high school	5.3	8.4	58	−16	−6
4 yrs. college	1.8	3.3	83	−1	2
Men, 35–44					
4 yrs. high school	3.9	5.4	38	−7	−5
4 yrs. college	1.1	2.5	127	−7	−4
Men, 45–55					
4 yrs. high school	4.3	4.4	2	−2	−6
4 yrs. college	1.1	1.4	27	. . .	−4
Women, 25–34					
4 yrs. high school	3.5	6.5	85	3	13
4 yrs. college	1.1	2.9	164	12	16
Women, 35–44					
4 yrs. high school	2.8	5.5	96	11	6
4 yrs. college	.5	1.7	240	12	23
Women, 45–55					
4 yrs. high school	3.0	4.2	40	7	3
4 yrs. college	.4	.8	100	11	5

Source: Author's tabulations based on March 1974 and March 1987 CPS microdata files. Computations for percent changes in wages and hours are described in text.

Table 4-12. *Distribution of Men and Women, Aged 25–34, across Industrial Sectors, 1973 versus 1986*
Percent

Age and education	Durable manufac-turing	Other goods-produc-ing industries	Service industries	Agri-culture	Persons who did not work[a]
All Men, 25–34[b]					
Less than high school 1973	24	28	35	7	6
1986	14	29	33	8	13
4 yrs. high school 1973	24	24	46	3	3
1986	15	26	50	4	5
1–3 yrs. college 1973	17	18	57	2	6
1986	13	18	63	2	4
4 yrs. college 1973	12	14	68	2	4
1986	13	13	70	2	2
4+ yrs. college 1973	09	07	79	1	4
1986	09	08	77	1	5
Women, 25–34, who work at least 1 hour[b]					
Less than high school 1973	17	25	52	6	. . .
1986	11	18	68	3	. . .
4 yrs. high school 1973	12	14	72	2	. . .
1986	8	11	80	1	. . .
1–3 yrs. college 1973	8	8	83	1	. . .
1986	5	6	88	1	. . .
4 yrs. college 1973	2	5	92	1	. . .
1986	5	7	87	1	. . .
4+ yrs. college 1973	2	2	95	1	. . .
1986	5	4	90	1	. . .

Source: Author's tabulations based on March 1974 and March 1986 CPS microdata files.
a. Refers to persons who did not work at all during the year including unemployed, disabled, and persons who are out of the labor force voluntarily.
b. Figures add to 100 percent, and the no-work category for women is omitted.

Table 4-13. *Comparison of Household Structure, 1973, 1987*

Type of family	Number of families (thousands)		Average family size (persons in each family)	
	1973	1987	1973	1987
Families with head 65 or over	7,590	10,229	. . .	. . .
Families with head less than 65				
Husband-Wife (percent with working wife)	40,215 (46)	43,078 (62)	3.54[a]	3.25[a]
Female head	5,437	9,045	3.22[a]	2.98[a]
Male head (no wife present)	1,131	2,137	2.83[a]	2.67[a]
All families	54,373	64,491	3.48	3.19

	Number of unrelated individuals (thousands)	
	1973	1987
Men and women, 65 or over	6,292	9,184
Men, less than 65	6,099	12,383
Women, less than 65	5,869	10,112
Total unrelated individuals	18,260	31,679

Sources: U.S. Bureau of the Census, "Household and Family Characteristics" (March 1973) and (March 1987), "Money Income of Households, Families, and Persons in the United States: 1986," *Current Population Reports*, series P-60, no. 159 (Washington, D.C.: Department of Commerce, 1988), p. 70, and "Money Income in 1973 of Families and Persons in the United States," *Current Population Reports*, series P-60, no. 97 (Washington, D.C: Department of Commerce, 1975), p. 49.

a. Figure includes families in which the head is 65 or over.

CHAPTER FIVE

The Regional Shift of U.S. Economic Activity

Robert W. Crandall

IN ONE fashion or another, the other chapters in this volume address likely prospects for American living standards on a nationwide basis. During the last decade, however, economic performance has diverged widely across different regions of the U.S. economy. This chapter takes a detailed look at past and projected regional shifts in U.S. economic activity and their implications for the distribution of income and average U.S. living standards.

The chapter documents the long-term population shift from the North and East to the South and West, a process that has accelerated since 1970. To some, this gravitation is part of a general trend in the deindustrialization and deunionization of the U.S. economy, with firms moving to take advantage of nonunion, low-wage workers in the South and West.[1] Others fear that the loss of high-paying industrial jobs in the North and East to lower-paying industrial jobs in the South and West contributes to the decline of the middle class in the United States.[2] The evidence surveyed in this chapter fails to support these fears. The population shift away from the Rust Belt toward the Sun Belt does not seem to be due to lower real wages paid in the states in the South and West. Better weather and a better business climate appear more likely to account for the success of the Sun Belt in generating new jobs.

1. Barry Bluestone and Bennett Harrison, *The Deindustrialization of America: Plant Closings, Community Abandonment, and the Dismantling of Basic Industry* (Basic Books, 1982).

2. Barry Bluestone and Bennett Harrison, *The Great American Job Machine: The Proliferation of Low Wage Employment in the U.S. Economy,* prepared for the U.S. Joint Economic Committee (Washington, D.C., December 1986). For a different view, see Robert Z. Lawrence, "Sectoral Shifts and the Size of the Middle Class," *Brookings Review,* vol. 3 (Fall 1984), pp. 3–11.

Surprisingly, the regional shift in industrial activity has had little effect on wage differences in manufacturing between regions. Outside manufacturing, regional disparities in per capita *incomes* did narrow significantly between 1970 and 1980, as the gap between the Rust Belt and Sun Belt in worker education, skills, and experience shrank. In the 1980s, however, the narrowing in regional disparities halted, and unemployment became more volatile because of turbulence in the energy and agricultural sectors.

The Shift to the Sun Belt and Its Effects on Income Levels

During the last half of the nineteenth century nearly two-thirds of the U.S. population lived in the Northeast and Midwest regions of the country. These regions were the most industrialized and offered the greatest economic opportunities to the average American worker. Just before the turn of the new century, the population began to shift gradually to the South and particularly to the West. This shift was gradual until the mid-1960s, evoking no alarm among observers of the American economy. In the past two decades, however, the shift has accelerated as the older industrialized areas in the Great Lakes states, upstate New York, and western Pennsylvania have lost their preeminent position in U.S. manufacturing.

Table 5-1 illustrates the strength of these population shifts. The older, Rust Belt regions—including the states from Maine to New Jersey and from New Jersey to the Dakotas—lost nearly 7 percent of their share of the U.S. population to the Sun Belt during 1970–86, a rate of decline that was more than double the 1950–70 rate.[3]

The shift of population from the North and East to the South and West is obviously associated with a corresponding shift in economic activity. For decades the southern and western regional economies have grown much more rapidly than the older northern and eastern industrial regions. Table 5-2 shows that real personal income has grown more rapidly in the South and West than in the rest of the country during every decade since 1940. Surprisingly, there appears to be little evidence of a reversal in this trend despite the recent collapse of the energy sector in the Southwest.

---

3. The Rust Belt, as defined in this chapter, includes all of the states in the New England, Middle Atlantic, East North Central, and West North Central census regions. The Sun Belt comprises the rest—including the South Atlantic, East South Central, West South Central, Mountain, and Pacific census regions.

Table 5-1. *Share of Population, Rust Belt versus Sun Belt,
Selected Years, 1900–86*

Year	Sun Belt[a] Percent of U.S. population	Rust Belt[b] Percent of U.S. population	Rust Belt[b] Rate of loss (average annual percentage change)[c]
1900	37.8	62.2	. . .
1940	42.4	57.6	− 0.2
1950	44.5	55.5	− 0.4
1960	46.3	53.7	− 0.3
1970	48.0	52.0	− 0.3
1980	52.3	47.7	− 0.9
1986	54.7	45.3	− 0.9

Sources: U.S. Bureau of the Census, *Census of Population, 1980, Number of Inhabitants,* series PC80-1-A1, U.S. Summary (Washington, D.C.: Department of Commerce, 1983), table 8, and *Statistical Abstract of the United States, 1988* (Washington, D.C.: Department of Commerce, 1987), p. 18, no. 21.
    a. South Atlantic, East South Central, West South Central, Mountain, and Pacific.
    b. New England, Middle Atlantic, East North Central, and West North Central.
    c. Change from year reported in row above.

The more rapid growth of the Sun Belt has not eradicated all differences in per capita income (figure 5-1), but the regional differences in this measure of well-being have certainly narrowed dramatically since the 1930s. From 1930 until about 1980, per capita income steadily evened out across the states. Since 1980, however, that trend has stopped and even reversed. Two factors are responsible for this change in direction: a sharp upswing in economic growth in the New England and Middle Atlantic regions, and the oil-related slowdown in the Southwest. If the New England and southwestern states are excluded, the Sun Belt–Rust Belt gap in per capita incomes remains very close to its 1980 level.

The recent recovery in New England and in the Middle Atlantic states does not mean that the Northeast is attracting *goods-producing* industries back from the South. In fact, manufacturing in the Rust Belt continues to slide. The spurt of growth in the New England states instead is due to an acceleration in the growth of their nonmanufacturing sectors. Despite that acceleration, there is no evidence of major change in the mix of sectors in the Sun Belt or the Rust Belt. The Sun Belt has enlarged its share of earnings across all principal industries although its relative increase in manufacturing is somewhat greater than its increase in the other sectors. Between 1970 and 1987 the Sun Belt's share of total U.S. private nonfarm earnings rose from 42.6 to 51.1 percent, its share of

Table 5-2. *Annual Growth in Real Personal Income, Rust Belt versus Sun Belt, 1940–87*
Percent

Period	United States	Rust Belt	Sun Belt	Difference, Rust Belt less Sun Belt
1940–50	4.7	3.9	6.3	−2.4
1950–60	3.3	2.8	4.1	−1.3
1960–70	4.7	4.1	5.4	−1.3
1970–77	3.2	2.2	4.3	−2.1
1977–87	2.5	1.8	3.2	−1.4

Sources: *Survey of Current Business*, vol. 62 (August 1982), table 1; vol. 67 (August 1987), table 1; vol. 68 (April 1988), table 2; and *Economic Report of the President, February 1988*, table B-3 (for price deflator).
  a. Real personal income is computed as personal income ÷ personal consumption expenditures deflator.

private nonfarm earnings excluding mining and agriculture rose from 42.1 to 50.7 percent, its share of goods production (manufacturing, mining, agriculture, and construction) rose from 39.4 to 49.4 percent, and its share of manufacturing alone rose from 35.5 to 45.3 percent.[4]

Because much of the current concern over the loss of U.S. competitiveness and of economic opportunities for middle-class Americans centers on what economists call "goods production," that group of activities nevertheless merits special attention. When earnings data are arrayed by region (table 5-3), it can been seen that all of the Rust Belt's loss in earnings from goods production has been in the Middle Atlantic and East North Central states. These states have been dominant in such heavy industries as steel, motor vehicles, and machinery in past decades. The clear winners in the Sun Belt, meanwhile, have been the South Atlantic, Mountain, and Pacific states. More modest increases have been shown by the South Central states.

Table 5-3 shows also that there has not been a sharp rebound in the Rust Belt's share of income from goods production since the dollar began to weaken in 1985. The mild upturn in the New England and Middle Atlantic states was fueled by construction, not manufacturing.[5] Nor is there sunshine everywhere in the Sun Belt. Shrinking earnings in the

4. Author's calculations using data from the Bureau of Economic Analysis, Regional Management Division, Quarterly Personal Income by Major Source and Earnings by Industry, 1969–1987, data base. (Hereafter BEA income and earnings data base.) The calculations use total earnings—labor income plus proprietors' income—for each sector. These data differ from personal income because they exclude dividends, interest, rental income, and transfer income and include employers' contributions for social insurance.
    5. Ibid.

Figure 5-1. *Trends in per Capita Income, Rust Belt versus Sun Belt, 1958–86*

Percentage of U. S. average

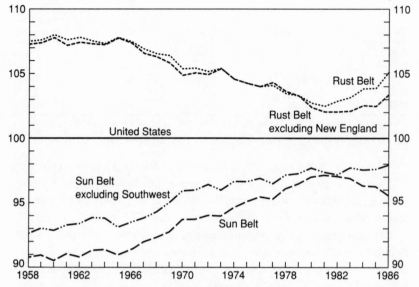

Source: U.S. Bureau of the Census, *Statistical Abstract of the United States* (Washington, D.C.: Department of Commerce), various issues.

West South Central states since 1985, reflecting the collapse of energy-related production, have offset the continuing increases in the southeastern and western states. As a result, the shift in goods production to the Sun Belt seems to have abated since 1985, although this may be a temporary pause given the long-term shift in manufacturing to the South and West.

The Shifting Manufacturing Base

Most interest in regional economic change focuses on the manufacturing sector because manufacturing firms obviously are more mobile than mining or agriculture; and services, though mobile, are diverse and less easily analyzed. Data collected by the Bureau of the Census on the net output of manufacturing industries also show a steady decline in the Rust Belt's share of manufacturing over the entire post-World War II period. Since 1967 this decline has been 10 percentage points—from 64 percent of U.S. output to 54 percent in 1985, the most recent year for which

Table 5-3. *Share of Total U.S. Earnings from Manufacturing, Mining, Construction, and Agriculture, Rust Belt versus Sun Belt, Selected Years, 1970–87*[a]

Percent

Region	1970	1975	1980	1985	1987
New England	6.8	6.1	6.1	6.8	7.1
Middle Atlantic	20.9	18.4	16.2	15.6	15.7
East North Central	26.3	25.2	23.1	21.5	21.2
West North Central	6.6	6.8	6.8	6.5	6.6
All Rust Belt	60.6	56.5	52.2	50.4	50.6
South Atlantic	12.1	12.6	12.9	14.0	14.8
East South Central	5.0	5.6	5.5	5.4	5.5
West South Central	7.3	9.0	10.9	10.8	9.2
Mountain	2.7	3.5	4.3	4.4	4.1
Pacific	12.3	12.9	14.2	15.0	15.8
All Sun Belt	39.4	43.6	47.8	49.6	49.4

Source: Author's calculations using data from Bureau of Economic Analysis, Regional Economic Management Division, Quarterly Personal Income by Major Source and Earnings by Industry, 1969–87, data base (April 1988). (Hereafter BEA income and earnings data base.)

a. The outputs of manufacturing, mining, construction, and agriculture are economic "goods"; data here are aggregated "goods production."

data are available. Contrary to recent suggestions, though, the United States is not becoming a bicoastal industrial economy; between 1967 and 1985 the share of manufacturing accounted for by coastal states actually declined (from 48 to 44 percent).[6]

One might think that the Sun Belt is growing because the Rust Belt has been cursed with such troubled industries as heavy machinery, steel, and automobiles. But a glance at the 1967–85 growth rates for the twenty basic manufacturing industries demonstrates that there must be other causes. As shown in table 5-4 national growth rates differ across industries, but those traditionally dominated by the North and East—machinery, transportation equipment, electrical machinery, and metals—have done no worse than those that are principally sited in the South and West—textiles, lumber, and petroleum products. Had the Rust Belt maintained its 1967 share of each manufacturing industry, in 1985 it would have

6. Author's calculations using data from U.S. Bureau of the Census, *1985 Annual Survey of Manufactures, Geographic Area Statistics*, series M85 (AS)-5 (Washington, D.C.: Department of Commerce, 1987), table 1. "The Bi-Coastal Economy: Regional Patterns of Economic Growth During the Reagan Administration," Staff Study by the Democratic Staff of the Joint Economic Committee, rev. ed., 99 Cong., 2 sess. (Washington, D.C., July 1986).

Table 5-4. *Annual Changes in Real Output in Twenty Basic Manufacturing Industries, Rust Belt versus Sun Belt, 1967–85*[a]
Average annual percentage change

Industry	Rust Belt	Sun Belt	United States
Food products	3.1	4.4	3.7
Tobacco products	−11.1	1.8	1.4
Textiles	0.2	3.2	2.4
Apparel	0.2	4.1	2.0
Lumber	1.8	2.1	2.1
Furniture	2.1	2.9	2.5
Paper	3.1	4.3	3.6
Printing	1.3	4.1	2.2
Chemicals	3.6	4.9	4.2
Petroleum products	−0.5	−2.2	−1.8
Rubber and plastics	5.4	8.5	6.1
Leather products	−2.5	0.0	−1.9
Stone, clay, and glass	0.1	2.7	1.2
Metals	−2.8	−0.9	−2.3
Metal fabricating	1.3	3.5	2.0
Machinery	3.6	8.4	4.9
Electrical machinery	3.2	8.1	5.2
Transportation equipment	1.9	4.7	3.0
Instruments	5.0	12.2	6.6
Miscellaneous	0.1	2.6	0.8

Sources: Author's calculations using data from U.S. Bureau of the Census, *1985 Annual Survey of Manufactures, Geographic Area Statistics,* series M85(AS)-5 (Washington, D.C.: Department of Commerce, 1987), table 2, and *Census of Manufactures, 1967,* vol. 2, pts. 1–3 (Washington, D.C.: Department of Commerce, 1971), table 2, for each two-digit SIC group.
a. "Basic" is defined here as two-digit Standard Industrial Classification categories, 20 through 39.

increased its share of U.S. manufacturing slightly, from 64.2 to 65.8 percent. Instead, it lost 10 percentage points during these eighteen years.

A further look at table 5-4 provides some insight into the extent of the shift of manufacturing industries to the Sun Belt. The growth in real value added between 1967 and 1985 is greater in the Sun Belt than in the Rust Belt for every basic manufacturing industry except petroleum products. (The North is blessed by not having large reserves of oil, it appears!) Clearly, it is not that the Rust Belt is the home of declining manufacturing industries, but that the Rust Belt is losing its appeal as a manufacturing center *in general.*

Not surprisingly, table 5-5 demonstrates a similar pattern in regional employment. The northern and eastern regions have steadily lost jobs in manufacturing since 1967, while the southern and western regions have

Table 5-5. *Employment in Manufacturing, Rust Belt versus Sun Belt, Selected Years, 1967–88*
Thousands of workers

Region	1967	1977	1985	1988(2)[a]
New England	1,566	1,407	1,470	1,357
Middle Atlantic	4,325	3,569	3,104	2,923
East North Central	5,155	4,896	4,213	4,122
West North Central	1,226	1,327	1,315	1,332
Total Rust Belt	12,272	11,199	10,102	9,734
South Atlantic	2,569	2,878	3,079	3,159
East South Central	1,132	1,368	1,322	1,378
West South Central	1,106	1,469	1,566	1,482
Mountain	322	477	612	610
Pacific	2,068	2,229	2,617	2,683
Total Sun Belt	7,197	8,421	9,196	9,312
Total United States	19,469	19,620	19,298	19,046

Sources: U.S. Bureau of Labor Statistics, *Employment and Earnings and Monthly Report on the Labor Force*, vol. 14 (Washington, D.C.: Department of Labor, March 1968), table B-7, and *Employment and Earnings*, vols. 25, 33, 35 (Washington, D.C.: Department of Labor, March 1978, 1986, 1988), table B-8.
a. Not seasonally adjusted.

steadily gained them. By February of 1988, the Sun Belt had virtually caught up with the Rust Belt in total manufacturing employment.

The growth rates for the value added in manufacturing further confirm the relative industrial decline of northern and eastern states. Table 5-6 reports these data, adjusted for differences in industrial structure, over the 1967–77 and 1977–85 periods. For both periods the Rust Belt (except for New England and the West North Central region in 1977–85) performed less successfully than the rest of the country. These results are similar to those obtained by Fuchs for 1929–54,[7] suggesting that the northeastern regions' unattractiveness as a manufacturing location is not a new phenomenon. The exceptions are New England, whose manufacturing industries rebounded between 1977 and 1985, although they are now receding again, and the South Central states, which show a decided slowdown in 1977–85.

Given that manufacturing has been shifting southward and westward since 1929 if not earlier, is there any reason to believe that a reversal is now in progress? The most recent census data displayed above extend

---

7. Victor R. Fuchs, *Changes in the Location of Manufacturing in the United States since 1929* (Yale University Press, 1962), chaps. 1, 3.

Table 5-6. *Adjusted Increases in Manufacturing Value Added,*
Rust Belt versus Sun Belt, 1929–85[a]

Percent

Region	1929–54	1967–77	1977–85
Rust Belt			
New England	−20.0	−24.3	15.2
Middle Atlantic	−19.3	−45.4	−17.4
East North Central	−7.2	−17.5	−22.1
West North Central	1.2	25.3	5.7
Sun Belt			
South Atlantic	33.4	30.2	32.0
East South Central	38.3	36.7	−1.3
West South Central	41.9	81.4	1.8
Mountain	30.4	110.4	56.9
Pacific	34.8	33.8	20.8

Sources: Victor R. Fuchs, *Changes in the Location of Manufacturing in the United States since 1929* (Yale University Press, 1962), table 1:9; and author's calculations using data from U.S. Bureau of the Census, *Census of Manufactures*, various issues.

a. Adjusted for differences in industrial structure. These rates are equal to the region's growth less the growth that the region would have experienced had all of its basic (two-digit) Standard Industrial Classification manufacturing industries grown at the average national rate.

only through 1985, the last year for which an *Annual Survey of Manufactures* is available. Since 1985, however, the dollar has fallen dramatically. To what extent has the dollar's depreciation boosted the fortunes of Rust Belt states?

Branson and Love have estimated how exchange rates have affected the growth of manufacturing in various states and census regions. They have found that the two North Central regions and the two South Central regions were most susceptible to the 1980–85 rise in exchange rates. In these regions, the appreciation of the dollar cut back jobs in manufacturing 7.7–11.2 percent in 1985.[8] In contrast, the dollar's run-up had little effect on the New England and Middle Atlantic states.

It is still too soon to determine if the fall in the dollar since 1985 has had symmetrical effects on employment in these census regions, but we can examine recent employment data for some early indications. Through February 1988 employment in manufacturing nationwide was still 1.3 percent below its 1985 level. In the Rust Belt, as a whole, manufacturing employment was 3.8 percent lower than in 1985, with jobs down 7.7 percent in New England and 5.8 percent in the Middle Atlantic states.

8. William H. Branson and James P. Love, "The Real Exchange Rate and Employment in U.S. Manufacturing: State and Regional Results," Working Paper 2435 (Cambridge, Mass.: National Bureau of Economic Research, November 1987), table R-2.

Manufacturing jobs rose modestly in much of the Sun Belt (1.2 percent) but continued to decline in the energy-intensive West South Central (down 5.3 percent) and Mountain (down 0.4 percent) regions.[9]

The reason for the superior performance of the southeastern region during the 1985–88 period may be found in differences in the growth in production across industries. Since 1985 nondurable goods production (textiles, paper, chemicals) has grown more rapidly than durables production (machinery, electrical machinery, transportation equipment).[10] Many of these nondurables industries are concentrated in the Southeast.

Despite the relatively poor performance of Rust Belt manufacturing since 1985, it would be a mistake to conclude that the continuing shift of manufacturing to the Southeast and West has led to a decline in private-sector jobs in the Northeast. Employment in nonmanufacturing sectors has grown rapidly since 1985 in both areas (Rust Belt: 4.3 percent; Sun Belt: 5.8 percent), and the regional disparities in the growth of total nonfarm employment are much less pronounced than those in the manufacturing sector alone (−3.8 percent versus 1.2 percent). In short, the Rust Belt lags behind the Sun Belt only slightly in the recent growth of total nonfarm employment, but much more severely in manufacturing employment.

Causes of the Shift in Manufacturing

In his study Fuchs noted that he could assign perhaps a third of the 1929–54 shift in manufacturing to the attraction of lower-cost labor, a third to the "pull" of natural resources, and the remainder to a variety of demand-related and unexplained forces.[11] This accounting is consistent with later studies that attribute only a small share of the shift to the availability of lower-cost, nonunion labor in the South.[12] The analysis here of the 1967–85 data agrees with these studies. There does appear

9. U.S. Bureau of Labor Statistics, *Employment and Earnings*, vols. 33, 35 (Washington, D.C.: Department of Labor, March 1986, 1988), table B-8.

10. *Economic Indicators*, prepared for the Joint Economic Committee by the Council of Economic Advisers, 100 Cong., 2 sess. (Washington, D.C., June 1988), p. 17.

11. Fuchs, *Changes in the Location of Manufacturing*.

12. See, for example, Thomas R. Plaut and Joseph E. Pluta, "Business Climate, Taxes and Expenditures, and State Industrial Growth in the United States," *Southern Economic Journal*, vol. 50 (July 1983), pp. 99–119; and Dennis W. Carlton, "The Location and Employment Choices of New Firms: An Econometric Model with Discrete and Continuous Endogenous Variables," *Review of Economics and Statistics*, vol. 65 (August 1983), pp. 440–49.

Table 5-7. *Average Manufacturing Wage, Rust Belt versus Sun Belt,*
1967, 1977, 1985

	1967		1977		1985	
Region	Dollars per hour	Share of East North Central wage	Dollars per hour	Share of East North Central wage	Dollars per hour	Share of East North Central wage
Rust Belt						
New England	2.75	0.83	5.24	0.75	9.35	0.81
Middle Atlantic	2.94	0.89	5.90	0.85	9.86	0.85
East North Central	3.30	1.0	6.96	1.0	11.58	1.0
West North Central	2.95	0.89	6.00	0.86	10.20	0.88
Sun Belt						
South Atlantic	2.36	0.72	4.82	0.69	8.33	0.72
East South Central	2.40	0.73	5.00	0.72	8.59	0.74
West South Central	2.65	0.80	5.48	0.79	9.69	0.84
Mountain	2.98	0.90	5.80	0.83	9.88	0.85
Pacific	3.28	0.99	6.11	0.88	10.41	0.90

Source: Author's calculations using data from U.S. Bureau of the Census, *1985 Annual Survey of Manufactures,*
Geographic Area Statistics, table 1.

to be a mild relationship of shifting industrial location to wage differences
since 1967, but no immediately discernible effect of unionization per se.[13]

If the attractiveness of southern and western regions as plant sites
rested on their lower real wage rates for given human skills, one might
expect to see a narrowing of reported wage rate differences over time.
As firms moved to apparently lower-wage areas, they would bid up the
wages in these areas and depress wages in the regions that they abandoned
or that were declining. But in fact, manufacturing wage differentials
between regions have not generally narrowed much over the past two
decades (table 5-7). Some studies suggest that real wages in the South
are no lower than in the North after accounting for the differences in
human capital (education, skills, talents).[14]

Nor can unionization explain as much as in earlier generations. Unions'

13. An analysis of the shift of two-digit Standard Industrial Classification (SIC) manufacturing industries from the Rust Belt to the Sun Belt between 1967 and 1985 shows that
the proportional shift is only mildly correlated with the difference in wage rates between
the regions but is not correlated with the degree of industry unionization.

14. There is substantial literature on this topic that is inconclusive at this juncture.
Sahling and Smith find that *nominal* wages are generally higher in northern states, but
that these higher wages do not offset a higher cost of living in these regions. See Leonard
G. Sahling and Sharon P. Smith, "Notes: Regional Wage Differentials: Has the South Risen
Again?" *Review of Economics and Statistics,* vol. 65 (February 1983), pp. 131–35. Gerking
and Weirick find that there are no regional differences in real wages after accounting for
differences in human capital, years employed by the current employer, and local living

share of all employees in the entire nonagricultural private sector has fallen dramatically in the past thirty years, from 33 percent in 1958 to 18 percent in 1986. The drop in the manufacturing sector alone is perhaps even more dramatic: from 52 percent to 24 percent.[15] With unions representing only a quarter of all manufacturing workers in 1986, the average manufacturer's decision about where to build plants could not be much affected by regional differences in unionization. Japanese auto companies and U.S. steel minimills may be so motivated, but they account for a very small share of U.S. manufacturing employment.

The universality of the shift of industrial production also argues against raw materials being the attraction in the South and West. Lower real transportation costs and the declining materials-intensity of GNP argue against this explanation, which Fuchs found important in an earlier period. As materials handling, transportation, and logistical problems have receded so have the apparent benefits of large scale. Most industries now are more dispersed across the country than in 1967, and the average size of manufacturing establishments (measured by the number of employees) has fallen slightly.[16] This smaller average scale suggests that existing manufacturing firms have more flexibility in choosing plant sites and that new, small-scale manufacturers are becoming more prevalent.

What then may be at the root of the continuing shift of industry to sunnier climes? The business climate may simply be better in these

conditions. Shelby D. Gerking and William N. Weirick, "Notes: Compensating Differences and Interregional Wage Differentials," *Review of Economics and Statistics*, vol. 65 (August 1983), pp. 483–87. More recently, Farber and Newman found that the South suffered a decline in real wages between 1973 and 1979 relative to the West and an *increase* in real wages relative to the Northeast and North Central regions. In each case there was a reduction in the relative return on human capital characteristics in the South during 1973–79. See Stephen C. Farber and Robert J. Newman, "Accounting for South/Non-South Real Wage Differentials and for Changes in Those Differentials over Time," *Review of Economics and Statistics*, vol. 69 (May 1987), pp. 215–23.

15. U.S. Bureau of Labor Statistics, *Handbook of Labor Statistics*, bulletin 2070 (Washington, D.C.: Department of Labor, December 1980), table 162, and *Employment and Earnings*, vol. 35 (January 1988), table 60.

16. Author's calculations using data from U.S. Bureau of the Census, *Census of Manufactures, 1967*, vol. 2, pts. 1–3 (Washington, D.C.: Department of Commerce, 1971), table 2 for SIC groups 20–39, *1985 Annual Survey of Manufactures: Geographic Area Statistics*, table 2, and *Census of Manufactures General Summary: Part 2, Industry Statistics by Employment Size of Establishment* (Washington, D.C.: Department of Commerce), various issues.

areas, attracting workers and entrepreneurs alike. One currently popular theory is that Sun Belt states are more hospitable to new businesses.[17] For example, it is undeniable, as discussed below, that new business starts in these states are far greater than in the older industrial states.

Besides the business climate, better weather itself may account for a sizable part of population and job shift to the South and West.[18] As industry no longer needs to be near Appalachian or midwestern coal, or near Minnesota iron ore, steel and steel fabricating move away from the harsh winters of the Great Lakes. Other industries follow. Unionization and relatively high wages in the North may be partly responsible for the shift of industry southward and westward, but one cannot discount the possibility that many Americans may simply wish to live in a more genial climate. That is to be found in the South and West, not the cruel, cold North.

The Effect of the Shift on Wage Rates

Most of the economics literature on industrial location focuses on the effect of unionization, wage differentials, tax rates, and other factors on site choice but by and large ignores the feedback of changes in location on wage rates. This section reviews the changes in regional manufacturing wage rates since 1967 and their relationship to regional changes in output.

Table 5-7 has already illustrated that regional wage differentials in manufacturing have not changed much since 1967. Because these averages may conceal large changes in the skill levels needed across individual industries, one must look at changes in location and in wage rates for specific industries. The analysis here focuses on eight basic industries—lumber, paper, metals, and the various machinery and metal fabrication industries—that produce important tradable goods.

Table 5-8 arrays the changes between 1967 and 1985 in relative wages and shares of total labor hours for each of the eight industries for five census regions—two low-wage regions and three high-wage regions. The top panel shows the change in each region's percentage of the total hours worked in each industry. It is no surprise that the South Atlantic region enlarged its share of industry labor used from 1.6 to 5.3 percent, while

17. See Plaut and Pluta, "Business Climate, Taxes, and Expenditures."
18. Farber and Newman, "Accounting for South/Non-South Real Wage Differentials," account for these environmental factors in their analysis of regional wage differences. Plaut and Pluta, "Business Climate, Taxes, and Expenditures," find that climate is the most important variable in explaining shifts in manufacturing employment.

Table 5-8. *Changes in Share of Employment and Relative Wages in Heavy Industries, 1967–85*

Industry	Low-wage areas		High-wage areas		
	South Atlantic	East South Central	East North Central	Middle Atlantic	Pacific
	Change in percentage of U.S. labor hours				
Lumber	4.2	−0.2	0.8	−1.8	−4.1
Paper	2.7	2.3	−2.9	−5.0	0.3
Chemicals	3.2	−0.7	−2.7	−4.9	1.4
Metals	3.7	1.8	−3.1	−8.4	1.9
Fabricated metal products	1.6	1.3	−4.8	−5.2	1.9
Machinery	5.0	1.8	−12.0	−4.7	4.2
Electrical machinery	5.3	1.3	−12.1	−8.3	6.4
Transportation equipment	2.5	2.1	−0.6	−3.7	−1.0
	Percentage change in relative wage[a]				
Lumber	3.9	5.1	−3.6	−4.2	−0.7
Paper	3.3	4.9	−2.0	−5.8	2.1
Chemicals	2.9	3.1	−2.2	−2.8	−13.8
Metals	−0.6	−1.9	5.5	0.6	−8.6
Fabricated metal products	8.1	−1.1	4.4	−4.3	−9.9
Machinery	4.3	1.2	2.7	2.2	−3.4
Electrical machinery	5.5	5.9	2.5	−4.1	−4.2
Transportation equipment	−10.9	7.5	6.3	−2.1	−3.5

Source: See table 5-4.
a. Change, 1967–85, in region's wage ÷ U.S. wage × 100.

the share of the East North Central states declined as much as 12.1 percent (in the electrical machinery sector) between 1967 and 1985. Is there evidence that these shifts caused wages to converge?

For the two low-wage regions, relative wages rose in general but not universally in these eight industries. In the East North Central and Middle Atlantic Regions, however, there is no clear relationship between loss of market share and changes in wages. In fact, in the East North Central (Great Lakes) states, wages in metals, fabricated metal products, machinery, electrical machinery, and transportation equipment climbed a lot despite sizable losses of market share. Wages in the West behaved even more strangely. Relative wages in the Pacific region generally fell in those industries enjoying a gain in relative employment. Thus one may not conclude that shifts in manufacturing employment have generally closed the gap between northern and southern wages.[19]

19. It is likely that there are two related forces operating to create these changes. In those industries in which labor market institutions have created large regional wage

Table 5-9. *Changes in Industry Wage Rates and the Shift of Industry to the Sun Belt, 1967–85*

Industry	Percentage change in hourly earnings	Shift in percent value added to Sun Belt
Food products	235	5.6
Tobacco products	461	5.3
Textiles	228	10.5
Apparel	171	17.0
Lumber	236	1.2
Furniture	219	3.7
Paper	282	5.3
Printing	192	11.0
Chemicals	275	5.9
Petroleum products	264	10.3
Rubber and plastics	205	15.2
Leather products	183	8.3
Stone, clay, and glass	243	11.4
Metals	252	6.9
Metal fabricating	230	8.5
Machinery	229	17.4
Electrical machinery	241	20.4
Transportation equipment	281	11.3
Instruments	231	22.5
Miscellaneous	221	8.7
All manufacturing	240	11.3

Source: See table 5-4.

If regional shifts in employment have failed to even out wage differentials, have they suppressed wages nationally? A currently popular notion is that the search for low-cost labor by industrial firms depresses wages for all workers. Footloose industries arguably bid wages down by threatening to leave or by actually leaving the northeastern states, thereby placing downward pressure on wage rates throughout the country. But the data in table 5-9 contradict this theory. The table illustrates that there is no correlation between U.S. industry wage rates and the shift of industry away from the Rust Belt states.

disparities, employers may be shifting to the lower-wage southern regions. At the same time the overall increase in demand for labor in the South may be raising wages there.

The Narrowing Gap in Regional per Capita Incomes

If the shift in manufacturing has failed to close regional wage differentials in manufacturing industries, why have the regional differences in per capita income narrowed so dramatically over the past fifty years (figure 5-1)? The answer must lie outside of manufacturing which, after all, accounts for less than 20 percent of all jobs.[20]

In a recent paper, Medoff found that the regional imbalances in the U.S. economy had led to larger wage increases in the West and South than in the Rust Belt.[21] Using two occupational categories—maintenance, tool room, and power plant workers and office-clerical workers—he looked at wage increases between 1960 and 1980. Although his regional breakdown was not precisely the same as the census regions used in this chapter, he found that wage increases were higher in the Southeast, Pacific, and Southwest regions than in the Northeast and Middle Atlantic states. The differences, however, were surprisingly small, amounting to as little as 0.2 percent to a maximum of 0.6 percent a year. These differential rates of growth would allow the closing of no more than a 5 to 15 percent wage gap between the Sun Belt and the Rust Belt in twenty years.

The occupational categories used by Medoff are obviously not those that would be dominated by manufacturing firms, so his results may still be consistent with little narrowing of the regional differences in manufacturing wages. The insensitivity of regional wages in individual manufacturing to changes in regional location of firms is also consistent with recent research on interindustry wage differentials. This research concludes that there are large industry-specific rents (returns above the next best use of the labor) being earned by industrial workers in the United States and other countries.[22]

20. U.S. Bureau of Labor Statistics, *Employment and Earnings*, vol. 35 (March 1988), table B-1.

21. James L. Medoff, "U.S. Labor Markets: Imbalance, Wage Growth, and Productivity in the 1970s," *Brookings Papers on Economic Activity*, 1:1983, p. 105.

22. Lawrence F. Katz and Lawrence H. Summers, "Can Inter-Industry Wage Differentials Justify Strategic Trade Policy?" (Harvard University and the National Bureau of Economic Research, April 1988); and William T. Dickens and Lawrence F. Katz, "Inter-Industry Wage Differences and Theories of Wage Determination," Working Paper 2271 (Cambridge, Mass.: National Bureau of Economic Research, June 1987).

Undoubtedly the narrowing of the regional differences in income per capita reflects the dwindling North-South differences in the makeup of the work force. In 1960 the population aged 25 and older had 10.7 median years of schooling in the Northeast, 10.7 in the North Central, 9.6 in the South, and 12.0 in the West. In 1980 the disparity in educational levels had lessened noticeably, to 12.5, 12.5, 12.3, and 12.7.[23] Moreover, the share of prime age workers, age 25 to 44, in the labor force rose more rapidly in the South than in the North. Finally, there was a slow rise in the share of black workers in the North Central and Northeastern regions, while the share of black workers in the South actually fell between 1960 and 1980.[24] All these general demographic trends might be expected to narrow the income differentials between northern and southern regions of the country even if wage differences in manufacturing did not shrink.

Income distribution across various regions of the country is of course also affected by farm income. By the laws of nature, the regional composition of agricultural income is much less subject to change than the regional distribution of manufacturing, construction, or even services. Nevertheless, the recent turbulence in the agricultural sector is worth examining. Nearly 40 percent of agricultural activity is concentrated in the Midwest; therefore, hard times in agriculture add to the woes of the receding midwestern manufacturing base.

Throughout the 1970s real farm incomes were extremely volatile. The net incomes of farm proprietors surged in the early 1970s but fell back in the late 1970s. By the end of the decade, real incomes earned from farming were below their 1970 level, but land prices had soared to 60 percent above their 1970 level.[25] In the early 1980s the real net income of farm proprietors fell precipitously. In 1983 farm proprietors' real incomes were only $12.2 billion, or about one-fifth their 1973-74 level. This decline in income

23. U.S. Bureau of the Census, *Census of Population, 1980, General Social and Economic Characteristics*, United States Summary, series PC 80-1-C1 (Washington, D.C.: Department of Commerce, 1983), table 83.

24. Between 1960 and 1980 the share of the labor force accounted for by black workers fell from 19.2 to 16.6 percent in the South but rose from 7.2 to 8.7 percent in the Northeast and from 6.6 to 7.7 percent in the North Central regions. Ibid., tables 86, 87.

25. Author's calculations using data from U.S. Bureau of the Census, *Statistical Abstract of the United States, 1988* (Washington, D.C.: Department of Commerce, 1987), tables 1066, 1079; and *Economic Report of the President, February 1988*, tables B-96, B-97.

has strongly affected agricultural land values. Between 1972 and 1982 the average nominal value of farm land rose 13 percent a year, but since then the value of an average acre has fallen 8 percent a year. Total assets in farming have fallen 27 percent in nominal terms over the 1982–86 period, forcing many farmers into bankruptcy.[26] Land purchases based on the expectation of inflation have turned sour.

For those farmers who survived, however, a recovery has occurred. Real farm incomes in 1986 were back to their level of the late 1970s, although still substantially below the halcyon days of 1973–74. Land prices continued to fall through 1987. This disinflation may now be ending, but the memories of foreclosures and bankruptcies linger and their effects upon the midwestern economy have not fully receded.

Increasing Volatility of Employment

The instability in farm incomes, oil prices, and general economic activity in the 1980s has been reflected in an increasing dispersion of unemployment rates. Although population and economic activity have continued to move to the South and West, the rate of joblessness has actually risen in the Sun Belt relative to the Rust Belt. In 1977 the weighted average unemployment rate was 7.5 percent in Rust Belt states but only 7.1 percent in Sun Belt states. Ten years later the Rust Belt rate had fallen to 5.7 percent, but the Sun Belt rate had dropped only modestly, to 6.6 percent, in large part because of the collapse in the energy sector.[27]

A statistical analysis shows that between 1969 and 1979 state unemployment rates became more and more similar (see table 5-10). But since the 1982 recession the variance in unemployment has been rising steadily. By 1987 the coefficient of variation in unemployment rates was higher than at any other time in the past twenty years, suggesting that the recent economic expansion has been more uneven than the upturns of the 1970s. The growing dispersion of joblessness can hardly be attributed to the shifting of industrial activity, which has been occurring for decades. The volatility in state unemployment rates in recent years is more a

26. U.S. Bureau of the Census, *Statistical Abstract of the United States, 1986* (1985), table 1136; *1988* (1987), tables 1065, 1067, 1074.

27. Author's calculations using data from U.S. Bureau of the Census, *Statistical Abstract of the United States,* 1978, p. 409, and U.S. Bureau of Labor Statistics, *Geographic Profile of Employment and Unemployment, 1987.*

Table 5-10. *Unemployment across States, Selected Years, 1969–87*
Percent of labor force

Year	Mean	Standard deviation	Coefficient of variation
1969	3.67	1.13	0.31
1971	5.68	1.72	0.30
1973	4.63	1.52	0.33
1975	8.03	2.13	0.27
1977	6.66	1.60	0.24
1979	5.56	1.39	0.25
1981	7.31	1.87	0.26
1983	9.28	2.51	0.27
1985	7.11	1.92	0.27
1987	6.26	2.12	0.34

Sources: Author's calculations using data from U.S. Bureau of the Census, *Statistical Abstract of the United States*, annual issues, 1970–88; and U.S. Bureau of Labor Statistics, *Employment and Earnings*, vol. 35 (April 1988), table D-1.

result of instability in energy and agriculture markets than of migration of industry.

Nevertheless, as industry shifts to the South and West, there is great concern over the effects of plant closures and devastated communities in the Rust Belt. Stereotypical of such problems are the shutdowns of steel-producing plants in western Pennsylvania and eastern Ohio. But the hardships of the steel industry provide little insight into the general phenomenon of plant closure.

Two recent studies have used firm-level data collected by Dun and Bradstreet to examine the role of new starts and plant closures on employment in the industrial sector of the economy. James P. Miller's calculations for 1969–75 found that the rate of job loss due to plant closures was no greater in the northern regions than in the South and West, with the exception of the Pacific region. The greater employment growth in Sun Belt manufacturing during this period is partly attributable to a much greater rate of new starts and to expansion of existing plants in this region.[28]

A later study by Armington and others for 1976–80 confirmed Miller's results. Although confined to thirty-five major metropolitan areas, it

28. James P. Miller, "Manufacturing Relocations in the United States, 1969–75," in Richard B. McKenzie, ed., *Plant Closings: Public or Private Choices?* rev. ed. (Washington, D.C.: Cato Institute, 1984). See also, Richard B. McKenzie, *Fugitive Industry: The Economics and Politics of Deindustrialization* (San Francisco: Pacific Institute for Public Policy Research, 1984), pp. 59–74.

included the entire private industrial sector.[29] The analysis revealed fewer employment losses due to plant closures in the Northeast and North Central regions than in the South and West. Again, employment gains in the Sun Belt were substantially greater than those in the northern regions because new plant formation and expansions of existing plants boosted employment far more in the South and West than in the northern regions.

These two studies strongly suggest that it is a mistake to focus on plant closings as a source of the Rust Belt's difficulties. If the North is to regain industrial jobs lost to other regions, it must pay more attention to attracting new and expanding industrial establishments than to avoiding or preventing closures of existing plants.

Volatility as a Cause for Policy Concern

The evidence in this chapter suggests that although business activity has been slowly and steadily migrating to the South and West, this migration has not caused the nationwide standard of living to decline. Instead, the shifts in location simply have narrowed the gap in incomes between northern residents and those in the Sun Belt.

The principal policy concern posed by business migration is not that some older industrial plants close while others open in different regions, but that the dislocations attending this natural evolution are exacerbated by cyclical swings in economic activity or changes in the value of the dollar. Yet, as just shown, the relative impact of plant closures on employment did not increase in the Rust Belt over the 1970s. Nor were plant closures more important in the Rust Belt than in the Sun Belt. At the same time, however, the variance in unemployment rates across states has risen in the 1980s. Could this be a signal that the plant closure problem has finally begun to have a differential impact across regions and states?

Because there are no recent analyses of data at the firm level for the

---

29. Catherine Armington, Candee Harris, and Marjorie Odle, *Formation and Growth in High Technology Businesses: A Regional Assessment* (Brookings, Business Microdata Project, September 1983), p. 39. Between 1976 and 1980 closures in the Northeast and North Central regions reduced employment 15.8–17.2 percent; in the South, 18.5–19.0; and in the West, 20.0–21.7 percent. Formations and expansions boosted employment in the northern regions 14.2–21.3 percent; in the South, 22.3–34.2 percent; and in the West, 26.8–33.5 percent.

Table 5-11. Percentage Deviation from Trend in the Regional Growth of Personal Income, by Sector of the Economy and Region, 1970–79 and 1980–87

Mean squared deviation from trend × 100

Region	Manufacturing		Mining		Construction		Agriculture		All other	
	1970–79	1980–87	1970–79	1980–87	1970–79	1980–87	1970–79	1980–87	1970–79	1980–87
New England	0.14	0.05	7.17	2.92	0.58	0.32	0.32	1.84	0.02	0.02
Middle Atlantic	0.07	0.06	2.10	0.74	0.53	0.28	0.25	0.21	0.03	0.01
East North Central	0.22	0.03	1.01	0.41	0.30	0.84	0.21	0.38	0.03	0.02
West North Central	0.09	0.11	0.53	0.74	0.18	0.61	0.14	0.62	0.14	0.04
All Rust Belt	0.13	0.13	1.18	0.57	0.29	0.54	0.20	0.36	0.04	0.02
South Atlantic	0.15	0.07	1.50	0.82	0.93	0.51	0.17	0.45	0.05	0.01
East South Central	0.15	0.13	1.67	0.59	0.24	0.47	0.25	0.68	0.05	0.02
West South Central	0.07	0.10	0.49	1.60	0.14	0.27	0.17	0.26	0.02	0.04
Mountain	0.11	0.07	0.33	0.59	0.84	0.31	0.27	0.28	0.04	0.01
Pacific	0.13	0.05	0.75	0.35	0.19	0.48	0.19	0.63	0.01	0.02
All Sun Belt	0.10	0.05	0.51	0.68	0.18	0.23	0.17	0.38	0.02	0.01

Source: BEA income and earnings data base.

1980–87 period, one must seek other explanations of the apparent growth in volatility of economic conditions across states. For this purpose, it is useful to examine Bureau of Economic Analysis data on personal income by state, looking for evidence of increasing volatility by sector of the economy.

Table 5-11 provides estimates for different regions of the average percentage deviation from trend of real income derived from manufacturing, mining, construction, agriculture, and "all other" sectors of the economy. These data show that intraregional volatility in real incomes from manufacturing has *decreased* in the 1980s relative to the 1970s, while volatility in real incomes from construction and agriculture has greatly increased. The picture in mining is rather mixed, where real incomes have grown less volatile in most regions but in the Southwest have increased greatly because of gyrations in oil prices.

These data on the volatility of real incomes point to unstable prices and interest rates, not regional migration, as the reasons for the greater disparity in recent years in economic activity across states. The shift of population to the South and West has not accelerated in the 1980s but seems to have continued at its 1970s rate. The income growth in the South has slowed since oil prices began to fall in 1982. As a result, the Sun Belt's share of nonfarm private income has remained almost constant between the first quarter of 1982 and the fourth quarter of 1987.[30] Thus the rising volatility in incomes in the 1980s is ironically the result of the continuing shift of population to the Sun Belt without a coincident rise in economic activity in that half of the country, particularly in the Southwest.

Had monetary and fiscal policy been more stable, farmers might not have levered their purchases of farm land to a level that triggered a wave of bankruptcies and foreclosures in the 1980s. Texas banks might not have financed the enormous excess supply of commercial real estate in Dallas and Houston. And steel companies might have invested less in iron ore facilities that eventually brought on a wave of bankruptcies in the mid-1980s.

Conclusion

Quite clearly, the regional shift of population and income in the United States is not a recent phenomenon. Throughout the twentieth century,

30. BEA income and earnings data base.

population and income have shifted to the South and West. Although this movement accelerated somewhat in the 1960s and 1970s, it has aroused concern only recently.

Economists have not yet provided a complete explanation for the relative decline of the industrialized northern regions of the United States in recent decades, but clearly the North's decline is not simply limited to a few troubled industries that could be revived by a dose of industrial policy. The northeastern and midwestern regions have witnessed a relative decline in virtually every primary manufacturing industry, not just autos, steel, or machine tools.

Nor is the decline in the Rust Belt's manufacturing industries attributable to the disproportionate effect of large-scale plant closings in that region. Recent studies demonstrate that the loss of employment due to plant closings in the Sun Belt is at least as great as in the older Rust Belt regions. The Sun Belt, however, enjoys significantly greater job growth due to new plants than does the Rust Belt. It is the failure of the northern and northeastern states to attract new plants that is at the root of their decline.

Higher wage rates and greater union activity in the North are not the primary reasons for the gravitation of industry to the South and West. There has been a surprising stability in interregional wage differentials across manufacturing industries. Indeed, some Rust Belt wage premia have actually risen as industry has shifted to the Sun Belt. Better weather and more attractive business climates are the most likely factors responsible for the success of the Sun Belt states in attracting industrial activity.

Despite the relative stability in regional wage differentials in manufacturing, the regional gap in per capita incomes has declined dramatically since 1929, although recently the gap has stabilized. The rise in per capita incomes in the South compared with the rest of the country through 1980 probably reflects the substantial narrowing of regional differences in worker education, skill, and experience levels.

The recent rebound of New England is not attributable to revival of manufacturing in that region. Employment in manufacturing continues to fall in New England as per capita incomes rise relative to the rest of the country. This experience demonstrates that it is not necessary to revive dying manufacturing industries, or even to attract new high-wage manufacturing industries, to provide a rising standard of living for a region's work force.

Of greater concern than the long-term regional shift of population and income is the increasing volatility in regional incomes in the 1980s. The Rust Belt was plainly hurt by the sharp rise of the dollar in the early 1980s. The Farm Belt was damaged severely by the dislocations caused by rapid inflation and disinflation in land prices. Instability in oil prices created boom and bust conditions in the Southwest in the past fifteen years.

If there is a national policy concern in the shifting regional distribution of U.S. economic activity, then, it is in curbing future volatility in prices, exchange rates, and incomes. A steady migration of new ventures to the South and West is not a problem per se if it is anticipated and if it is sufficiently gradual to allow people to adjust. However, the rise and fall of the dollar, oil prices, and prices in general in the late 1970s and early 1980s were so severe as to create large problems for millions of Americans. More stable monetary and fiscal policies might help to avoid many of these problems. If, however, political forces do not permit this stability in macroeconomic policies, one must wonder how a set of microeconomic industrial policies could possibly be stabilizing.

CHAPTER SIX

Productivity and American Management

Martin Neil Baily and Margaret M. Blair

AMERICAN living standards in the long run depend on the growth in productivity. The more goods and services the United States can produce using its available work force, the higher the standard of living all Americans can enjoy.

During the past two decades, productivity growth in the United States and in the rest of the industrialized world has slowed, and only part of this deterioration can be readily explained. If the United States has any hopes of raising its rate of productivity growth in the future, business managers, workers, and government policymakers must have a better understanding of the reasons why productivity growth over the last decade or more has been so disappointing.

This chapter focuses on American management. Although the evidence is far from complete, it suggests that a deterioration in the effectiveness of organizations and the quality of management played a role in the productivity slowdown. The challenge for policymakers in the coming years is to provide the appropriate climate and incentives to promote better management practices. And for American business, the important task will be to learn new management tools and make better use of old business methods to improve the performance of their organizations.

The Productivity Shortfall

Unlike unemployment or inflation, slow productivity growth from one year to the next often goes unnoticed as an economic problem. But over time, the cumulative effect of low rates of productivity advance can have

We would like to thank Hiranthi de Silva and Hensley Evans for research assistance.

Figure 6-1. *The Shortfall in Productivity from 1965 to 1987*

Index [a]

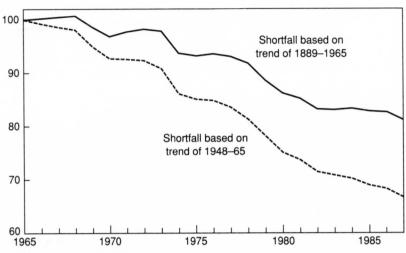

Source: Past trends are based on average annual growth rates of output per hour. For 1889–1948, based on private GDP per hour, from John Kendrick, *Productivity Trends in the United States* (Princeton University Press for National Bureau of Economic Research, 1961), pp. 298, 301, 311, 313, tables Aiii and Ax. For 1948–87, based on private business output per hour, from U.S. Department of Labor, Bureau of Labor Statistics, news release, USDL 87-436, October 13, 1987, and USDL 88-98, March 3, 1988.

a. Actual output per hour as a percent of level predicted by past trend growth.

a much bigger effect on average living standards than even a serious recession.

To illustrate, output in 1987 was only two-thirds of the level it would have attained if productivity had grown during the 1986–87 period as rapidly as it did during the 1948–65 period (figure 6-1). The picture is only a little brighter when the trend growth over the longer period, 1889–1965, is used. In this case, output in 1987 is about 80 percent of the level it would have reached had productivity grown at its prior historical pace. In other words, average American living standards could be 25 percent to 50 percent higher today if productivity growth had not slowed over the past twenty years.

The sharpest break in postwar productivity appears to have occurred in 1973, and using this benchmark, the United States has not been alone in the deterioration of productivity performance. The slowdown has been pervasive across countries. Table 6-1 shows that by three different measures—gross domestic product (GDP) per employed person, GDP per hour, and GDP per hour in manufacturing—the productivity slow-

Table 6-1. *Productivity Growth in Five Large Industrialized Countries, 1950–86*
Percent a year

Period	France	Germany	Japan	United Kingdom	United States
Growth of GDP per employed person					
1950–73	4.55	4.99	7.21	2.53	1.96
1973–79	2.65	2.78	2.87	1.30	0.03
1979–86	1.85	1.58	2.72	1.71	0.82
Growth of GDP per hour, total economy					
1950–73	5.01	5.83	7.41	3.15	2.44
1973–79	3.83	3.91	3.40	2.18	0.80
1979–84	3.24	1.88	3.06	2.95	1.09
Growth of GDP per hour, manufacturing sector					
1950–73	5.63	6.31	9.48	3.25	2.62
1973–79	4.90	4.22	5.39	0.83	1.37
1979–86	3.50	2.78	5.47	4.28	3.10

Source: Figures for GDP per employed person are from unpublished data, U.S. Department of Labor, Bureau of Labor Statistics, Division of Foreign Labor Statistics; for growth of GDP per hour worked, see Angus Maddison, "The Productivity Slowdown in Historical and Comparative Perspective" (Netherlands, University of Groningen, 1985); and for growth of manufacturing output per hour; see U.S. Department of Labor, Bureau of Labor Statistics, news release, USDL 87-237, June 15, 1987.

down since 1973 has been more severe in France, Germany, and Japan than in the United States.

In the United States the post-1973 productivity slowdown has also been pervasive across industries except for agriculture and nonelectrical machinery, where improvement has been driven by developments in the computer industry (figure 6-2). However, the pattern over time varies across sectors (figure 6-3). Productivity performance has partially recovered in goods production since 1979. Indeed, productivity in durable goods manufacturing and farming grew faster between 1979 and 1986 than before 1973. Output per hour in the mining sector fell rapidly during the 1973–79 period but has stabilized and grown a little since then. Construction productivity, however, has been falling since 1968 and has not made a recovery.

Productivity growth in the non-goods producing industries has been especially disappointing. From annual growth of 2.5 percent before 1965 (just a little less than manufacturing productivity growth), the rate of productivity advance in this sector dropped steadily after 1973, increasing by only 0.1 percent a year from 1979 through 1986. In this sector, post-1979 growth increased only in wholesale and retail trade; in other areas of the sector, the slowdown got worse after 1979.[1]

1. Although looking at productivity by industry provides valuable insights, Edward

Figure 6-2. *The Change in Labor Productivity Growth between 1948–73 and 1973–86, by Industry*

Annual percent change

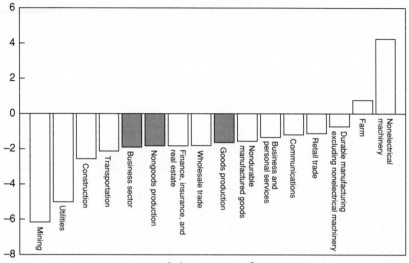

Industry or sector ᵃ

Source: Unpublished data from U.S. Department of Labor, Bureau of Labor Statistics.
a. The shaded bars indicate aggregates of industries, not individual industries. The business sector includes all industries shown. The goods-producing industries are manufacturing, mining, construction, and farming.

Several lessons can be drawn from this brief review of the data. First, the fact that the other major economies also experienced slowdowns suggests that some common factors were at work in several countries. Second, the fact that the post-1973 slowdown was common to so many industries suggests that one or more of the factors causing the slowdown were common not only to several countries but also to most industries. Third, the differences that emerge by industry, particularly those since 1979, indicate that not all of the causes of the slowdown had economywide impacts. Some special or industry-specific factors may also be at work.

Denison has cautioned against placing too much emphasis on industry-specific data. He notes that estimating industry productivity requires data on purchases and sales of intermediate goods and these data are weak. As a result, recent productivity growth in manufacturing may have been overestimated. See Edward F. Denison, *Estimates of Productivity Change by Industry: An Evaluation and an Alternative* (Brookings, forthcoming).

Figure 6-3. *The Change in Labor Productivity Growth between 1973–79 and 1979–86, by Industry*

Annual percent change

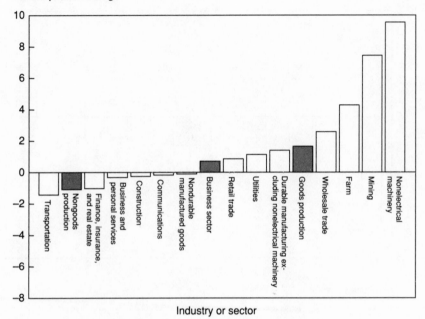

Industry or sector

Source: Unpublished data from U.S. Department of Labor, Bureau of Labor Statistics.

Explaining the Slowdown

Given its sizable impact, the 2.45 percentage point drop in U.S. productivity growth since 1973 clearly merits scrutiny. Several analysts have attempted to dissect the slowdown and to apportion the blame among certain identifiable causes. Edward Denison has provided perhaps the most detailed and complete effort in this area.[2]

Denison on the Causes of the Slowdown

Table 6-2 summarizes Denison's findings. Despite popular impressions to the contrary, Denison concludes that changes in the quality and educational level of the labor force have not seriously contributed to the

2. Edward F. Dension, *Trends in American Economic Growth, 1929–82* (Brookings, 1985), p. 37.

Table 6-2. *Causes of the Slowdown in Productivity Growth according to Denison*

Item	Effect of slowdown on post-1973 growth (percentage points)[a]	Percentage contribution to slowdown
Total slowdown	−2.45	100.0
Education	0.10	−4.1
Weather in farming	0.03	−1.2
Age-sex composition	−0.02	0.8
Inventories	−0.09	3.7
Nonresidential fixed capital	−0.06	2.5
Land	−0.02	0.8
Reallocation from farming	−0.19	7.8
Reallocation from nonfarm self-employment	−0.17	6.9
Pollution abatement	−0.10	4.1
Worker safety and health	−0.02	0.8
Dishonesty and crime	−0.05	2.0
Economies of scale	−0.15	6.1
Intensity of demand	−0.23	9.4
Unexplained slowdown	−1.47	60.0

Source: Edward F. Denison, *Trends in American Economic Growth, 1929–1982* (Brookings, 1985), p. 37.
a. Slowdown in growth of output per hour in nonresidential business, 1973–82 compared with 1948–73.

slowdown. The change in the age-sex composition of the labor force did slow growth, but only by a tiny amount.[3] In addition, since 1973 the labor force has become more educated, which should have boosted productivity growth. It is possible, however, as Richard Murnane discusses in chapter 7, that the quality of education has declined, pulling down the skills of new entrants to the work force. Denison does not specifically take account of this. But Martin N. Baily and, more recently,

3. Dale W. Jorgenson, Frank M. Gollop, and Barbara W. Fraumeni find a somewhat larger age-sex effect than Denison. In part, this is because they include changes in the mix of occupations as a change in labor quality. Changes in productivity resulting from alterations in the occupational structure of the labor force are counted in the residual in Denison's work. See Jorgenson, Gollop, and Fraumeni, *Productivity and U.S. Economic Growth* (Harvard University Press, 1987). Edwin Dean, Kent Kunze, and Larry S. Rosenblum of the Bureau of Labor Statistics (BLS) have also estimated changes in labor quality, based on age, sex, education, and experience, and they reach conclusions that are closer to Denison's. See "Productivity Change and the Measurement of Heterogeneous Labor Inputs," paper presented at the Conference on New Measurement Procedures for U.S. Agricultural Productivity, March 31–April 1, 1988, Washington, D.C.

John Bishop have explored this hypothesis and found that declining educational quality could not have contributed much to the post-1973 slowdown, although Bishop believes that the adverse impact of declining test scores between 1965 and 1979 may show up in still lower productivity growth in the future.[4]

Denison identifies four factors, however, that clearly contributed to the productivity slowdown. Two had fairly modest effects. Some believe, for example, that the decline in investment (measured by the growth of capital per worker) over the last fifteen years has greatly reduced productivity growth. But Denison calculates that a slower rate of advance in the capital-labor ratio accounted for just 7.0 percent, or about 0.17 percentage point, of the post-1973 drop in the productivity growth rate.[5] More intensive regulation of environmental and health and safety conditions is a second contributing factor, accounting for another 0.12 percentage point of the slowdown by Denison's estimation. Using a somewhat different methodology, Wayne Gray finds that regulation has exerted somewhat larger effects.[6] But even if Gray's estimates are more accurate, it is doubtful that stiffer regulation accounts for any more than 8 to 10 percent, or 0.20 to 0.25 percentage point, of the productivity deterioration.

4. Martin Neil Baily, "Productivity and the Services of Capital and Labor," *Brookings Papers on Economic Activity*, 1:1981, pp. 1–50. (Hereafter *BPEA*.); John Bishop, "Is the Test Score Decline Responsible for the Productivity Growth Decline?" Working Paper 87–05 (Cornell University, Center for Advanced Human Resource Studies, 1988). A variety of methods of testing general intellectual achievement show a long-term trend of rising scores. The rate of increase accelerated from 1957 to 1965 and then turned down until 1979. After that, growth resumed again. To the extent that this has had adverse effects, the timing does not fit as an explanation of the slowdown. The test scores of labor-force entrants in the 1970s were at or above their long-run trend. Bishop suggests that some adverse impact of the period of declining scores may show up in the next few years. See Richard Murnane's discussion of education in chapter 7 of this volume.

5. Dale Jorgenson and others attribute 46 percent of the growth in aggregate output over the period 1948–79 to the rise in capital input. This calculation gives a much larger weight to capital than does Denison, but the decline of the capital contribution during the 1973–79 period was fairly minor. See Jorgenson, Gollop, and Fraumeni, *Productivity*, p. 314.

6. Denison bases his estimate on the resources of capital and labor needed to meet regulation requirements, including estimates of specific legislation such as the Mine Safety Act. Wayne B. Gray uses a cross-section of manufacturing industries to estimate the productivity impact. See Gray, "The Impact of OSHA and EPA Regulation on Productivity," Working Paper 1405 (Cambridge, Mass.: National Bureau of Economic Research, 1984). (Hereafter NBER.)

More significant, in Denison's view, is the great drop after 1973 in the population shift from lower-productivity smaller farms to higher-productivity endeavors in self-employed businesses. Denison attributes 15 percent—or roughly 0.37 percentage point—of the slowdown to the ending of the gains from reallocation. He also finds that the 1973–75 and 1980–82 recessions dropped the productivity growth rate by 16.0 percent, or 0.38 percentage point.

In sum, Denison attributes only 0.97 percentage point of the total 2.45 percentage point slowdown in productivity after 1973 to identifiable causes. We could augment his calculations by adding a bit more to the capital effect or the effect of regulation, and we could take more account of the energy crisis, which Denison largely ignores. But even so, there remains an unexplained slowdown of at least 1.0–1.2 percentage points after 1973.

Measurement Error

It is conceivable that some portion of the slowdown is attributable to measurement error. Perhaps productivity growth is doing better than the official data series show. Martin Baily and Robert Gordon have recently investigated this idea, and they find that indeed there are serious problems with the way output and productivity are measured, but that, paradoxically, these problems do not help to explain much of the slowdown.[7]

Consider first some of the problem areas. The data on construction productivity prepared by the Bureau of Labor Statistics (BLS) indicate that output per hour in the industry has declined dramatically since 1968. Indeed, by 1986 average labor productivity in this industry reportedly was below the level of 1948. That seems implausibly low. In part, the BLS data may overstate the materials used in the industry, but this part of the error would then disappear in the productivity statistics for the economy as a whole. Errors may also arise in valuing the output of houses, office buildings, and other construction projects, which have no adequate price deflator. This may overstate inflation and hence understate real growth by as much as one-third.[8]

This understatement of productivity in construction is partly offset by

7. Martin Neil Baily and Robert Gordon, "Measurement Issues, the Productivity Slowdown, and the Explosion of Computer Power," *BPEA*, 2:1988 (forthcoming).
    8. Ibid.

the fact that productivity now seems to be overstated in the computer industry. Until the GNP revision of 1985, output in this industry was understated because the Bureau of Economic Analysis (BEA) took no account of the decline in computer prices that took place. The 1985 revisions, however, introduced a new price index for computers and office machinery. Based on this new index, advances in the computer industry have added 1 full percentage point to the productivity growth rate of manufacturing since 1982.[9]

Most observers agree that the price of computers has been declining over time. It is possible today to buy a computer for only a fraction of the cost of an equivalent computer ten years ago. But current BEA procedures may end up overstating the growth of real output in the industry and thus overstating the rate of productivity advance. Edward Denison suggests that computer price declines would be less substantial if BEA were to use the same methods as those traditionally used for producers' durable equipment.[10] Whether or not that is true, there is general agreement that the current methods of constructing constant-dollar output series give too much weight to industries or products whose prices are falling. This overweighting of computers will become more serious in future years and will artificially boost manufacturing productivity estimates.

Measurement problems in the service sector probably have resulted in an understatement of productivity growth, particularly since 1979. Figure 6-3 shows that in the four sectors in which measurement is especially poor—construction; transportation; finance, insurance, and real estate; and business and personal services—the slowdown proceeded at the same pace or intensified after 1979. Three of the four are service industries, where the intensification seems very implausible. Innovation and computerization have probably led to at least some improvements in efficiency in finance and in the provision of business services in recent years. It is also hard to believe that the decline of construction productivity has continued unabated.

The existence of these problem areas for measurement does not explain a large part of the *slowdown* for two main reasons. First, the industries in question sell much of their output to other businesses, so that measurement errors will have less effect on aggregate productivity

9. Denison, "Estimates of Productivity Change," p. 32.
10. Ibid., p. 30.

statistics than on the industry-specific figures. Productivity growth being missed in, say, the business-services industry should be picked up by productivity figures for the industries buying those services.

Second, there were measurement problems in earlier periods also. Growth is being understated now, but it was also being understated before.

This conclusion about the slowdown is reinforced by examining figure 6-2, which indicates that the post-1973 productivity slowdown in the four industries most likely to be plagued with measurement error was not more substantial than in other industries in which measurement problems are not so important.

In sum, the productivity slowdown is not simply a measurement phenomenon. At the same time further research into measurement issues would enable analysts and policymakers to have a better grasp on the underlying developments that affect the long-run performance of the economy.

Changes in Technology

Economists have attributed the extraordinary performance of productivity in the first twenty-five years after World War II to technological change, which increases the efficiency and productivity of capital and labor used in production. Perhaps the post-1973 productivity slowdown, therefore, has resulted from a collapse in the pace of technological change.

A slower pace of technological change is a likely cause of the productivity slowdown in countries other than the United States. Figure 6-4 illustrates, for example, that in the 1950s productivity in the European economies and Japan was very low compared with the United States, but that subsequently output per manhour in these countries converged to the U.S. level, though at a steadily diminishing pace.[11] This pattern was inevitable. Relative to other industrialized countries, the United States has been and remains a "frontier economy" whose growth depends on how fast technological change can push out the frontier. In contrast, other countries have had the advantage of being able to absorb U.S. technology gradually and thus grow at a more rapid rate—at least until they have caught up to the U.S. frontier.

But what about the frontier? Has it been moving out at a slower pace

11. See William J. Baumol, "Productivity Growth, Convergence and Welfare: What the Long-Run Data Show," *American Economic Review*, vol. 76 (December 1986), pp. 1072–85.

Figure 6-4. *Convergence of Productivity Levels in the United States,
Europe, and Japan*

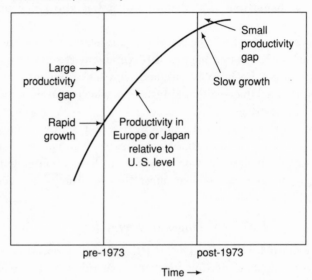

100 percent of
U. S. level of productivity

Large → productivity gap

Rapid → growth

Productivity in Europe or Japan relative to U. S. level

Small productivity gap

Slow growth

pre-1973   post-1973

Time →

in recent years? Baily and Chakrabarti find mixed evidence.[12] The pace
of new product and process development seems to have fallen off in the
chemical industry; and the gains from economies of scale have ended
both in chemicals and electric power. At the same time, however,
important new areas of technology development—notably in computers
and electronics—have opened up new avenues for productivity growth.

Rather than a slower movement of the frontier, the more important
problem may be that American business managers have not been taking
full advantage of the technological opportunities that already exist. In
part this problem could indicate a shortcoming of recent management.
But American managers have also had to operate in an increasingly
volatile macroenvironment in the last two decades—two energy crises
and serious recessions, bouts of double-digit inflation and interest rates,
and stiffer foreign competition—that could have diverted them from

12. Martin Neil Baily and Alok K. Chakrabarti, *Innovation and the Productivity Crisis*
(Brookings, 1988).

longer-run efforts to raise productivity. In short, one possible interpretation of the productivity slowdown in the United States and other industrial countries is that because of its failure to exploit fully the technological opportunities that already exist, the leader lost its capacity to lead. The other countries that have been followers have not yet been able to assume a leadership role. Given the large, unexplained portion of the productivity slowdown, it clearly seems appropriate to explore this hypothesis by examining the connection between management and productivity in the United States in greater detail.

Assessing American Management

Critics of U.S. business managers argue that they have abandoned their commitment to productivity and innovation and geared their decisionmaking to short-term profits.[13] Modern scientific management techniques, it is said, have deemphasized the benefits of hands-on experience and have promoted short-term cost-saving and financial manipulation instead.

The U.S. auto industry is the principal exhibit in the critics' case. In the early 1980s, William Abernathy and his colleagues at the Harvard Business School (HBS) contended that American auto companies had not displayed a commitment to excellence in product design, process technology, and manufacturing technique.[14] More recently, Kim Clark and his HBS associates found that both U.S. and European auto manufacturers used more labor and required longer lead times to develop new auto models than their Japanese counterparts.[15] The principal reason: compared with Japanese firms, which used a strong project leader and a lean team of development engineers, the U.S. and European companies put too many people on a project, were overbureaucratized, and failed to have a strong project leader.

Katz and his coanalysts at the Massachusetts Institute of Technology

13. For the most forceful academic indictment of U.S. business management, see Robert H. Hayes and William J. Abernathy, "Managing Our Way to Economic Decline," *Harvard Business Review*, vol. 58 (July–August 1980), pp. 67–77.

14. William J. Abernathy, Kim B. Clark, and Alan M. Kantrow, *Industrial Renaissance: Producing a Competitive Future for America* (Basic Books, 1983).

15. Kim B. Clark, W. Bruce Chew, and Takahiro Fujimoto, "Product Development in the World Auto Industry," *BPEA*, 3:1987, pp. 729–71.

automobile center have reached similar findings, showing that Japanese assembly plants have higher productivity than U.S. plants.[16] Significantly, American managers have had difficulty introducing Japanese-model team systems successfully, even though the Toyota-GM NUMMI plant in California managed by Toyota has done so. Indeed, using American workers, the NUMMI plant producing the Chevy Nova/Toyota Corolla has achieved productivity comparable to the Corolla plant in Japan.[17]

The criticism of American managers extends beyond the automobile industry. Lester Thurow, the dean of the Sloan School of Management, argues that American managers have failed to commercialize new technologies, pointing to the fact that U.S. companies missed out entirely on the VCR revolution, even though the original technology was developed in the United States.[18] More recently, many U.S. companies—in and outside the auto industry—have failed to adopt the Just-in-Time production system developed by Toyota, a system that is much more than a way of saving inventory; it is a cost-saving reorganization of the entire system of production that forces workers to become much more conscious of the quality of each component.[19]

These criticisms of American management are not universally shared. Defenders point out that U.S. exports have suffered in the 1980s largely because of an overvalued dollar. Moreover, export shares of American multinational companies have remained strong. Robert E. Lipsey and Irving B. Kravis supply the evidence: between 1966 and 1983 U.S. exports as a share of world exports dropped from 17.5 percent to 13.9 percent, but exports by U.S. parents and their majority-owned foreign affiliates maintained the same share of world exports in both years, 17.7 percent.[20] In their view, the ability of U.S.-owned enterprises to remain competitive throughout this period is a sign of healthy rather than deficient management. U.S.-based exports lost market share only because

16. Harry C. Katz, Thomas A. Kochan, and Jeffrey H. Keefe, "Industrial Relations and Productivity in the U.S. Automobile Industry," *BPEA*, 3:1987, pp. 685–715.

17. See chapter 7 by Richard Murnane in this volume for a discussion of the NUMMI project.

18. Lester C. Thurow, *The Zero-Sum Solution: An Economic and Political Agenda for the 80's* (Simon and Schuster, 1985), p. 54.

19. James C. Abegglen and George Stalk, Jr., *KAISHA: The Japanese Corporation* (Basic Books, 1985).

20. Robert E. Lipsey and Irving B. Kravis, "The Competitiveness and Comparative Advantage of U.S. Multinationals, 1957–1983," Working Paper 2051 (Cambridge, Mass.: NBER, 1986), pp. 4, 7.

the United States became a relatively less attractive place to locate plants, not because managerial quality at U.S. companies has deteriorated.

The continuing high level of productivity of the United States compared with other countries also is evidence of strong managerial performance. Combined data from the BLS and DRI, Inc. indicate that in 1986 output per hour in Japanese manufacturing was 83 percent of the U.S. level and in Germany the figure was 78 percent.[21] OECD data for 1984 suggest an even greater U.S. advantage: 69 percent of the U.S. level in Japan and 70 percent in Germany.[22]

The high level of U.S. manufacturing productivity is impressive because capital per worker in U.S. manufacturing is no higher than in Japan and Germany, nor is there reason to believe that production workers here are of a higher quality. Moreover, the United States has maintained a large productivity lead despite weaknesses in the American educational system, discussed more thoroughly in chapter 7.[23]

Finally, the fact that some U.S. industries have had trouble competing in world markets does not necessarily mean that American managers are deficient overall. For example, there are many industries—including agriculture, chemicals, and package express delivery—in which productivity in Japan is much lower than in the United States.

Assessing the Evidence

Who is right—critics or defenders of American management? It is useful to begin by assessing claims that center on the shares of world trade that are or are not captured by U.S. companies. Such statistics can be misleading. Given the enormous advantages that the United States had at the end of World War II, it was inevitable that other countries would catch up and expand their share of world trade, thereby decreasing the share of the United States. As a result, a declining U.S. share does not necessarily indicate declining U.S. performance.

21. Baily and Chakrabarti, *Innovation*, p. 9.
22. *OECD Economic Outlook*, vol. 42 (December 1987), p. 45. The OECD figures measure output per employee; since the Japanese work longer hours than U.S. workers, the gap in output per hour would be wider still.
23. Rohlen has compared Japanese and American school systems and notes that a higher percentage of students in Japan graduate from high school and that scores on achievement tests indicate that Japanese students have higher language and math skills than American students. Thomas P. Rohlen, *Japan's High Schools* (University of California Press, 1983).

The fact that world trade shares of multinationals have not changed, meanwhile, is difficult to interpret because of changes in the structure of trade and industry. Trade within Europe and trade between Canada and the United States are very large and have grown enormously. American multinationals clearly have been successful in participating in this growth, but much of this trade is analogous to trade across two state borders within the United States. Many American companies no longer manufacture whole product lines in each country in which the line is sold; they produce various components in several countries. This process raises their share of world trade but only because of a change in the internal organization of production rather than because of any particular success in world markets.

More generally, there is confusion in the public debate over U.S. competitiveness about what can be inferred from international trade patterns. As Robert Lawrence explains in chapter 2, trade balances are far more influenced by exchange rate movements and the relative amounts of national saving and investment than by any changes in the quality of management. Similarly, the shares of a country in world manufacturing trade have more to do with its trade policy, the diversity of its industry, and whether it has an endowment of natural resources. A country that is equally productive or equally unproductive at producing everything will not trade. Trade is stimulated when a country can sell what it is relatively good at producing and buy what it is relatively inefficient in making. A country that discovers oil (like Britain) will reduce exports of manufactured goods and its share of world trade in these goods. Conversely, when the United States began rapidly increasing its oil imports in the 1970s, it also began to increase exports of manufactured products, reversing for a while the downward trend in the U.S. share of world trade.

Accordingly, statistics on trade performance do not tell us how well U.S. managers are doing, so it is more useful to focus directly on productivity data and case studies for gaining insight into the debate over the quality of U.S. management. The high level of U.S. productivity clearly indicates that U.S. companies have been doing something right for a long time and that they still have significant advantages in comparison with other countries. But the superiority of U.S. industry in the past may have contributed to the problems found in the case studies and in the recent slow growth of productivity. U.S. companies may have become resistant to change and unwilling to learn from technological advances or improvements in work practices developed overseas. In contrast, foreign companies, especially those in Japan, have been able to assimilate U.S. technology and successful U.S. management practices with surprising ease. Even with its slowdown, productivity growth in Japan is still much faster than in the United States, as shown by table 6-1. And even at slower rates of growth, productivity levels in Japan could soon overtake those in the United States; in fact, in some major industries (steel) they already have.

To summarize, the evidence is not definitive in showing either that management quality deteriorated or that management caused the slowdown in U.S. productivity growth. But that does not mean that management problems should be ignored. There is no escaping the slowdown, the increasingly stiff competition from Japanese firms, and the evidence from case studies showing that certain leading industries have had difficulty organizing production or dealing with changes in markets or technology. These are reasons enough to look at the U.S. economic environment and see if it is offering the right incentives to ensure good management.

Incentives for Technology Development and Cost Reduction

Do the incentives in the United States encourage innovation and productivity improvement? Three important aspects of a nation's business environment can promote productivity growth: strong competition provides incentives for managers to lower the costs and improve the quality of what they sell; innovation by individual firms promotes the growth of national productivity and welfare; and a rapid diffusion of new ideas throughout many firms in the economy speeds up the growth in aggregate productivity.

The problem is that each of these factors interferes with the other two. If the advantage that a firm gains from an innovation can be quickly imitated by other firms, the incentives to innovate are sharply reduced, threatening the overall pace of innovation. Similarly, if aggressive price competition among a relatively small number of large firms characterizes the economy, the "supernormal" profits from innovation by any one firm will be ephemeral and that too may discourage new innovation. Conversely, if price competition is muted, so that firms can continue for long periods to enjoy the extra profits generated by an innovation, that same lack of competition may induce them to become lax about other aspects of the business, including the control of costs and quality. And if the exclusive right to one's own innovation is strongly protected by patent and copyright laws, the spur to innovation will be offset by a very slow spread of new ideas throughout the economy.

What then is the optimal mix of attributes to encourage innovation and productivity improvement? To gain insights into the answer, we will contrast the climate for competition and innovation in the United States and Japan.

Competitive Behavior

Michael E. Porter's book, *Competitive Strategy*, has become a bible for executives in major U.S. corporations.[24] Written with unusual clarity, perception, and organizational skill, it sets out the various market and technological circumstances a firm can find itself in and discusses what factors should be weighed in each case when making decisions about pricing, investment, and other strategic variables. The basic premise of how American companies should deal with competitors is discussed in chapter 5:

> In most industries a central characteristic of competition is that firms are mutually dependent: firms feel the effects of each others' moves and are prone to react to them. In this situation, which economists call an oligopoly, the outcome of a competitive move by one firm depends at least to some extent on the reactions of its rivals. "Bad" or "irrational" reactions by competitors (even weaker competitors) can often make "good" strategic moves unsuccessful. Thus success can be assured only if the competitors choose to or are influenced to respond in a non-destructive way.[25]

Porter argues that although firms can in principle improve their situations by aggressive competitive moves, in practice such behavior is counterproductive. "Cooperation" with rivals or "non-destructive responses" are contrasted with "bad" or "irrational" reactions, "narrow self-interest," or "squealing" on a friend.

Porter's approach to competition clarifies and promotes the philosophy that already existed, and although this philosophy may have worked well

---

24. Michael E. Porter, *Competitive Strategy: Techniques for Analyzing Industries and Competitors* (Free Press, 1980).

25. Ibid., p. 88.

in the past, it is in marked contrast to that of the leading Japanese companies described by Abegglen and Stalk.[26] These authors cite the example of competitive behavior followed by Yamaha and Honda in the market for motorcycles, which they argue is typical of Japanese manufacturing companies. Honda neglected its motorcycle business in the early 1970s in order to establish its automobile sales, and Yamaha used this opportunity to try and move ahead of Honda. The president of Honda responded by saying that his company would crush Yamaha and it almost did just that, initiating a war that cut prices by a third, to the point at which small motorcycles cost less than bicycles. As a result, Yamaha was pushed to the edge of bankruptcy.

Aggressive price-cutting tactics occur among Japanese manufacturers and are typical of Japan's strategy for moving into foreign markets. And this same aggressive strategy has been a source of increasing friction. Robert Lawrence has pointed out that Germany maintains a surplus in manufacturing trade that is larger than Japan's as a percent of GNP, and yet German competition has not generated within the United States and Europe anywhere near the same hostility.[27]

The differences in competitive behavior between American and Japanese firms are often described in relation to their time-horizons. It is argued that U.S. companies are short-sighted and use high discount rates in assessing investment projects. But even if true, this tendency is only part of the problem. U.S. companies have been willing to invest in very long-term technology development projects, but they have been unwilling to use price cutting as a form of investment to forestall the entry of rivals. A company that uses its cash flow to invest in new equipment or in research and development (R&D) can hope to receive a favorable response from the stock market. A company that suffers a loss in profits as a result of price cutting is signaling that it is in trouble.

In addition, opposition to aggressive competition is enshrined in U.S. law. Price cutting may lead to charges of predatory pricing. And when Japanese companies enter the U.S. market with low prices or cut price in the presence of excess capacity, U.S. companies often respond by pressing for trade restraints, arguing that the Japanese exporters have unlawfully "dumped" their goods or have benefited from export subsidies.

26. Abegglen and Stalk, *KAISHA*, pp. 48–49.
27. Robert Z. Lawrence, "Imports in Japan: Closed Markets or Minds?" *BPEA*, 2:1987, p. 519.

The current semiconductor accord—arranged after U.S. chip manufacturers lodged a dumping complaint against their Japanese competitors—is perhaps the clearest example of this approach.

Porter argues that price competition with rivals is undesirable and counterproductive. But that is not true for the society as a whole. Competition benefits consumers. By the same token, the absence of competition is harmful because it allows firms to charge prices that are too high and to produce at output levels that are too low. More important, when there is a climate of aggressive competition for market share, companies are forced to find ways of cutting costs, raising quality or both, or else they will go under. Indeed, this reality helps explain the strong rebound of manufacturing productivity in the United States in the 1980s. The overvalued dollar combined with a domestic recession in 1982 created an environment in which the survival of even large U.S. manufacturers was in question, and productivity improvement was thus essential. Aggressive competition from Japanese companies certainly contributed to the commitment by U.S. companies to raising productivity.

Technology Development and Competition

Many believe that U.S. companies, having established themselves as the preeminent economic powers after World War II, have since become complacent and thus easy targets for more aggressive competitors. Mancur Olson develops this theme in a different form and uses it to explain why Germany and Japan grew more rapidly than did Britain and the United States after World War II.[28] In stable economies, argues Olson, coalitions form among economic groups—oligopolies, labor unions, and so on—that have a strong interest in avoiding change. The defeat of Germany and Japan in World War II resulted in long-term economic benefits for both countries, by this logic, because it destroyed their antichange coalitions. In contrast, in the United States these coalitions have solidified and now act to limit competition and stifle change.

Although this line of argument is plausible, there is another reason why U.S. companies have been unwilling to be price cutters. Aggressive competition can also have a devastating effect on the incentives for major technology development. Suppose one firm develops a new product.

28. Mancur Olson, *The Rise and Decline of Nations: Economic Growth, Stagflation, and Social Rigidities* (Yale University Press, 1982).

Initially, it will have a monopoly and can set a high price for the product. After a while, however, other firms develop competing products, and the market is divided among several firms. Even if the price is kept high, this division of the market dilutes the return to the innovating company. But, potentially, the problem for the innovator can be even worse. When a new product is first introduced, its price is typically well above the cost of its production, so there will be considerable scope for price cutting once several firms enter the market. In fact, if the market behaves competitively, price will fall to the marginal cost of production. Aggressive price competition in the markets for new products will thus sharply reduce the return to innovation by eliminating any return in excess of the cost of production.[29]

In short, innovators can find it very difficult to capture, or appropriate, the full benefits of their innovations, and this situation occurs especially in a highly competitive environment in which rival firms can quickly copy from new technologies and products. In the language of economists, there are strong positive "externalities" from research and development, or discrepancies between the returns that innovation provides to society and the gains that accrue to the innovators. According to estimates made by Edwin Mansfield, the private rate of return to R&D activities has been high, on the order of 25 percent, but the social rate of return has been much higher, between 50 percent and 100 percent.[30] As a result, it is very much in a nation's interest to promote private sector efforts at innovation.

Patents and trade secrets law offer two such mechanisms by giving innovators property rights in their developments. Nevertheless, although in some cases patents allow an innovator to dominate a field for a long time (for example, photocopiers for Xerox), usually they provide only limited incentives. Mansfield has estimated that a patent raises the cost of imitation by only 10 percent outside the chemical industry.[31] This

---

29. One reason why price competition has traditionally been limited among American companies is that these firms try to recover the sunk costs of developing and introducing new products. They realize that if all the firms in an industry engage in fierce price cutting, then they will all lose money.

30. Edwin Mansfield, "Microeconomies of Technological Innovation," in Ralph Landau and Nathan Rosenberg, ed., *The Positive Sum Strategy: Harnessing Technology for Economic Growth* (National Academy Press, 1986), pp. 310–11.

31. Ibid., p. 314.

helps explain why in their recent survey of major corporations, Richard Levin and his colleagues at Yale found that patents are not the most important way of protecting the returns from innovations.[32]

Trade secrecy can have more powerful effects for process technology where access is limited, as indicated by DuPont's success in protecting its process technology for producing synthetic fibers. For U.S. companies in general, however, secrecy is of limited value. Information leaks out. Key employees leave and take their knowledge with them. American society is a very open one, and employees have a high degree of mobility.

Thus, in practice, neither patents nor secrecy solves the externality problem. This reality underscores the importance of the trade-off between competition and innovation. On the one hand, firms with market power may be lulled into complacency, failing to pursue new products and processes aggressively. On the other hand, some market power for at least a temporary period helps guarantee that innovators will reap the fruits of their labors. The difficulty is in striking the right balance between these extremes.

Japan's Approach to Competition and Innovation

In the past, Japanese firms relied on technology from the United States, and after World War II the United States encouraged this process. By borrowing technology from the United States, Japan avoided the trade-off between competition and innovation. Now, however, Japan spends heavily on R&D. How has Japan met the challenge of combining competition with innovation?

For one thing, the government limits competition. As Japan has put more resources into technology development, the government has intervened to direct competing firms. The Ministry on Industry and Trade (MITI) encouraged companies to allocate opportunities for technology development. One company would develop technology aimed for one part of the market, while another firm aimed at another part. This process increased the overall efficiency of R&D by reducing the duplication of research efforts and by allowing innovators to gain at least a temporary monopoly.

The industrial structure in Japan also mitigated some of the negative effects that competition otherwise would have had on innovation. Japanese

---

32. Richard C. Levin and others, "Appropriating the Returns from Industrial Research and Development," *BPEA*, 3:1987, pp. 783–820.

industry is organized into groups, and companies within each group support one another by giving loans, trading workers, sharing distribution facilities, and, in some cases, buying one another's products. The group structure reduces the risk of bankruptcy that occurs when companies develop new products or processes. For example, Mazda did not develop the rotary engine, but it gambled heavily on this technology, a gamble that failed. Its group gave loans and other support to the company.

Equally significant, Japanese companies have been able to appropriate more of the return to their R&D by directing a greater share to the development of new processes than their U.S. counterparts. Japanese firms have used and improved product innovations in the United States and Europe, thus manufacturing the same products at lower cost and, often, with higher quality. The externality problem is less severe for process innovation than for product innovation because it is easier to keep the details of a new process secret (and thus to keep technological developments from flowing back to the United States). In addition, successful process innovation encourages competition for market share. Thus Japanese firms have cut prices, expanded sales, and moved down the learning curve, thereby maintaining mark-ups despite the price cuts. Meanwhile, by operating in a high-saving, low rate-of-return economy, Japanese firms have operated with lower mark-ups and still earned the required rate of return on R&D and other investments.

Finally, in situations in which the Japanese groups have successfully limited their domestic competition, perhaps with help from MITI, companies have been able to earn their target rate of return on R&D at home. But then the government encourages Japanese companies to compete abroad. As a result, many Japanese firms enter the U.S. market by pricing at the marginal cost of production and undercutting American firms.

Not all of these approaches were equally important in any particular industry. Some did not succeed, some may not really have been tried. But Japan's ability to maintain the benefits of competition while still providing the incentives for investment offers important lessons. For example, Japan has taken advantage of ideas and technologies developed in the United States and in Europe. U.S. managers must emulate that practice by finding out about best-practice methods wherever they originate in the world economy.

Japan has encouraged an industrial structure in which groups of companies support one another, thereby limiting risk. U.S. antitrust administrators can learn that bigness is not bad in itself. The large scale of the U.S. economy and U.S. companies makes the United States well-suited to absorb risk, already a characteristic strength of the American economy.

Japan has found that when its companies compete in world markets, cost cutting and quality enhancement are encouraged. This lesson also applies to the United States. Those companies that have faced stiff foreign competition have become more efficient and productive. The Japanese have not allowed foreign competitors to enter their market freely, however, and this weakens their economy. Perhaps an economy with fledgling industries needs protection, but Japan is not in that position now. Average productivity and living standards in Japan remain well below those of the United States partly because of Japan's protectionist policies.

Japan has succeeded at times in directing traffic among competing companies and allocating directions for research. But such an industrial policy can fail badly if government policymakers misjudge market forces or misread where a country's comparative advantage lies. Policymakers in Britain before Mrs. Thatcher pursued an unsuccessful industrial policy. We need to know more about where the Japanese succeeded and where they failed and why. The gap between the private and social returns to innovation suggests a role for government, but one that should be cautious and restricted. Government should not usurp the market. Given U.S. institutions, U.S. policymakers should offer general support for technology development but not try to direct traffic. Ultimately the main response to the economic challenge must come from the private sector.

Takeovers and Economic Efficiency

As a result of important changes in the business environment—fluctuations in energy prices, interest rates and inflation, to name a few—American industry is restructuring. Companies are developing new lines of business, selling old plants, shifting production facilities overseas, and diversifying or consolidating. Much of this restructuring is being accomplished through mergers and acquisitions, friendly and hostile takeovers.[33]

33. The words "merger," "takeover," and "acquisition" are used interchangeably in

To some, the wave of takeovers demonstrates the strength of the market system as companies adjust to the new environment. This view holds that market incentives are working appropriately. Others believe, however, that the difficulties in American business management have been caused by takeovers. Under this view, the "market for corporate control" does not produce results favorable to the broader social interest.

Although corporate takeovers and mergers have been a feature of U.S. financial markets for nearly a century, the policy debate about their effects has only recently focused on their implications for the performance of managers. Corresponding to the contrasting views about the desirability of takeovers, two theories have developed about the relationship between takeovers and managerial performance. The older view argues that takeovers are, for the most part, nonproductive transactions undertaken by empire-building managers who have run out of (or failed to develop) attractive internal investment opportunities for their firms.[34] By this theory, takeovers, at best, have a neutral effect on the productivity of firms. At worst, managers of both the acquiring companies and of the companies that are the targets of their acquisitory ambitions are diverted from long-term efforts to enhance productivity and to develop new products.

A competing theory formed the basis for public policy toward takeovers under the Reagan administration.[35] This theory holds that takeovers discipline bad managers; unless subject to a takeover threat, managers

---

this chapter to refer to any transaction in which the ownership of a corporation or whole business unit, as opposed to the physical assets owned by that business unit, substantially or completely changes hands. A merger is often taken to mean a friendly transaction between two firms of roughly the same size in which either firm may wind up as the surviving firm, or a third entity may be created to encompass both merging firms. In a takeover or an acquisition, one of the firms, usually the larger of the two, is more clearly identified as the surviving firm. Takeovers may be hostile or friendly. A "spin-off" is a special case of takeover in which the unit being acquired was previously part of another firm rather than a separately trading entity. A "leveraged buyout" (LBO) is another special case in which the "acquired" firm ends up as a distinct, separately traded entity with a greatly altered capital structure, heavily weighted with debt. Some spin-offs are also LBOs, but the two categories are not identical. We use the word "takeover" to mean any of the preceding transactions.

34. The origins of this theory go back at least to Dennis C. Mueller, "A Theory of Conglomerate Mergers," *Quarterly Journal of Economics*, vol. 83 (November 1969), pp. 643–59.

35. For a statement of this policy and the theory behind it, see *Economic Report of the President, February 1985*, chap. 5.

will choose policies that serve their own best interests, rather than those that maximize the returns for shareholders.[36]

The Evidence

Which view of takeovers is correct? The available evidence produces ambiguous results, but it suggests two things: not all takeovers are alike, and the economic context in which takeovers occur is important to the outcome.

Defenders of takeovers have supported their case with a large number of "event" studies, which measure the effect of various takeover-related events on the stock prices of firms.[37] These studies consistently show that shareholders of acquired firms gain about 30 percent to 40 percent when their firms are taken over. Michael Jensen, a leading takeover theorist, estimates that shareholders have reaped nearly $350 billion (in 1986 dollars) for the ten years from 1977 through 1986 as a result of takeover activity.[38] Furthermore, he claims these are net social gains, not transfers from other parties involved in, or affected by, the strategies or day-to-day operations of the firms. Shareholders of acquiring firms do not do nearly as well; some studies suggest small gains, others small losses. But nowhere do the losses seem large enough to account for the large gains to target firm shareholders.

In contrast, critics of takeovers point out that no evidence indicates

36. Some theorists have gone even further and argued that takeovers should be encouraged because, without interference, the market will not produce enough takeovers. This is because the raiders, who do all the work to find target companies and devise new strategies for managing them, will not receive all of the gains from these transactions, but generally must share them with target company shareholders. Hence they will not undertake acquisitions whose private gains are not large enough to compensate them for their effort, even if the total social gains from the transaction would be positive. See especially, Sanford J. Grossman and Oliver D. Hart, "Takeover Bids, the Free-Rider Problem, and the Theory of the Corporation," *Bell Journal of Economics*, vol. 11 (Spring 1980), pp. 42–64.

37. See Michael C. Jensen and Richard S. Ruback, "The Market for Corporate Control: The Scientific Evidence," *Journal of Financial Economics*, vol. 11 (April 1983), pp. 5–50; Richard Roll, "Empirical Evidence on Takeover Activity and Shareholder Wealth," in John C. Coffee, Jr., Louis Lowenstein, and Susan Rose-Ackerman, eds., *Knights, Raiders, and Targets: The Impact of the Hostile Takeover* (Oxford University Press, 1987), pp. 241–52; and Greg A. Jarrell, James A. Brickley, and Jeffry M. Netter, "The Market for Corporate Control: The Empirical Evidence Since 1980," *Journal of Economic Perspectives*, vol. 2 (Winter 1988), pp. 49–68.

38. Michael C. Jensen, "Takeovers: Their Causes and Consequences," *Journal of Economic Perspectives*, vol. 2 (Winter 1988), p. 21.

that target firms are, in general, poorly managed or poor performers for any other reason.[39] Nor does the evidence show that takeovers improve the performance of either the target firms or the acquiring firms. In their detailed study, Ravenscraft and Scherer report that studies of the mergers and takeovers that occurred during the 1960s and 1970s yield a mixed record, with some suggesting that target firms are somewhat less profitable than comparable nonacquired firms while others indicate that targets tend to be more profitable.[40] Other studies using stock price data show clearer results—that hostile takeover bids are made on firms that are not performing well. Targets of hostile tender offers have low stock prices relative to nontargets. However, this is not necessarily because of bad management but because stock prices of firms in the targets' industries tend to be low.[41]

What happens after acquisition or merger? Does the acquired firm or line of business show improved performance under new management or ownership? Ravenscraft and Scherer conclude that the answer, on balance, is no. They find that while acquired lines of business still tend to be more profitable than average after acquisition, their profitability declines compared with their pretakeover levels. The target firms do not return sufficient gains to compensate their new parents for the large premiums paid to acquire them.[42]

Frank Lichtenberg and Donald Siegel reach a different result by using Census of Manufacturing data on individual plants rather than on entire

39. Except for the occasional instance in which a takeover serves as an alternative to bankruptcy for a failing firm.

40. See David J. Ravenscraft and F. M. Scherer, "The Profitability of Acquired Companies," *Mergers, Sell-Offs, and Economic Efficiency* (Brookings, 1987), chap. 3. They conclude that the ambiguous results arise from sample bias in most previous studies. Large acquisitions, and firms acquired in tender offers, may on average be somewhat less profitable than comparable firms in their industries, but a much larger number of acquisitions involve small, privately held firms not often included in these studies, and these targets are, on average, substantially more profitable than comparable firms in their industries.

41. See especially Joel Hasbrouck, "The Characteristics of Takeover Targets: 'q' and Other Measures," *Journal of Banking and Finance*, vol. 9, no. 3 (1985), pp. 351–62; and Randall Morck, Andrei Schleifer, and Robert W. Vishny, "Characteristics of Hostile and Friendly Takeover Targets," Working Paper 2295 (Cambridge, Mass.: NBER, 1987). The authors conduct their stock price analysis by using the "q" ratio, or the ratio of a firm's market value to the replacement cost of its assets.

42. Similarly, Dennis Mueller finds evidence that merged firms tend to lose market share in the wake of a merger. Dennis C. Mueller, "Mergers and Market Share," *Review of Economics and Statistics*, vol. 67 (May 1985), pp. 259–67.

firms.[43] In their study of more than 5,000 plant acquisitions during the 1970s, these authors find that the plants taken over often displayed declining productivity before their acquisition, but thereafter improved productivity for seven years, eventually reaching their industrywide average. Lichtenberg and Siegel suggest that many of the plants they studied had been acquired during the merger wave of the 1960s and then sold during the 1970s when firms were restructuring. Thus their finding may just reflect attempts to solve problems created by earlier takeover decisions. In addition, their sample may have been biased because it included only "surviving" plants and not plants that were acquired and later shut down. Accordingly, the improvements they find may stem partly from the effect of less efficient plants dropping out of the sample.

In sum, the empirical evidence on the consequences of takeovers leaves an important puzzle unresolved. Shareholders of acquired firms clearly benefit from takeovers, but takeovers do not seem to improve management or profitability, at least not in ways we have been able to measure.

Takeovers and Structural Change

Many theories have been advanced concerning why mergers and takeovers occur. Critics say that firms merge to enhance their market power, to build empires, to reap tax benefits, or to "milk" acquired firms as they generate cash. None of these motives allows for mergers to improve productivity. A contrary view is that mergers allow firms to realize economies of scale and scope, to rationalize duplicative facilities, and to replace poor management, thereby improving productivity.

This debate will probably never be resolved, because it is likely that different mergers stem from different motives. As a result, in some cases, mergers will not yield productivity gains; in others, they will.

Nevertheless, as already highlighted, takeovers as a group have produced substantial gains for the shareholders of target firms without apparently producing noticeable improvements in profitability. What accounts for the apparent inconsistency? Where do the gains for shareholders come from?

43. Frank R. Lichtenberg and Donald Siegel, "Productivity and Changes in Ownership of Manufacturing Plants," *BPEA,3:1987*, pp. 643–73.

Andrei Schleifer and Lawrence Summers argue that target shareholders benefit at the expense of other parties. Raiders may close plants or lay off workers, thereby breaking explicit or implicit contracts between the target firm and its workers, suppliers, and local communities. The gains from the contract renegotiations accrue to target shareholders.[44]

A more benign variation of the same theme is that takeovers are a mechanism for structural adjustment in an industry or economy that is experiencing slower growth and more intensive competition. Mergers, especially large ones, are critical events in the lives of the firms, which can fundamentally change their identity and character. These changes facilitate the process of devising new strategies, renegotiating internal and external contracts, and adapting to new ways of doing business. Thus the gains to shareholders could include an improvement in performance that cannot be accurately measured because the before and after circumstances of the firm have changed so dramatically. Or they could reflect a reversal of what would otherwise have been a deterioration in performance.

The notion that takeovers are often part of larger structural changes affecting firms helps explain why mergers tend to occur in "waves." Figures 6-5 and 6-6 illustrate that the U.S. economy is currently in the midst of its fourth great merger wave of this century. Yet the causes and consequences of these waves remain largely a mystery.[45] Indeed, it is not clear whether the four big surges in activity are related by similar underlying causes, or whether their causes and purposes have been fundamentally different.

The first merger wave in the 1890s was the mechanism by which large corporate organizations as we know them today came into existence. Many of the consolidations of that period produced firms that monopolized their industries. The merger wave of the 1920s resulted in the formation of large second- and third-ranked companies in many of those same industries. George Stigler has summarized the effects of these two merger

---

44. See Andrei Schleifer and Lawrence H. Summers, "Breach of Trust in Hostile Takeovers," in Alan J. Auerbach, ed., *Corporate Takeovers: Causes and Consequences* (University of Chicago Press for National Bureau of Economic Research, 1988), pp. 33–67.

45. Brealy and Myers, in their widely used textbook on corporate finance, list a "general hypothesis explaining merger waves" as one of the "ten unsolved problems in finance." See Richard A. Brealy and Stewart Myers, *Principles of Corporate Finance* (McGraw-Hill, 1984).

Figure 6-5. *Real Value of Mergers, 1895–1986*

Billions of constant dollars

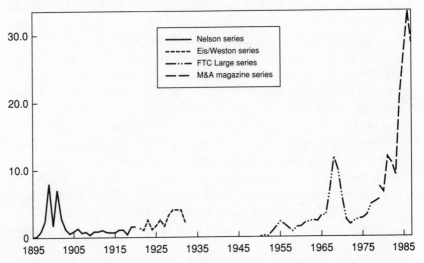

Sources: The Nelson series is from Ralph L. Nelson, *Merger Movements in American History, 1895–1956* (Princeton University Press, 1959), p. 60; Eis/Weston is from Carl Eis, "The 1919–1930 Merger Movement in American History" (Ph.D. dissertation, City University of New York, 1968) and from J. Fred Weston, *The Role of Mergers in the Growth of Large Firms* (University of California Press, 1953), both reprinted and expanded in Federal Trade Commission, *Economic Report on Corporate Mergers: Staff Report* (Washington, D.C., 1969), p. 665; the FTC Large series is from the Federal Trade Commission, *Statistical Report on Mergers and Acquisitions, 1979* (Washington, D.C., July 1981); and the M&A series is taken from various issues of *Mergers & Acquisitions* magazine. This publication collects data on mergers and takeovers in all sectors of the economy and began breaking the totals out by industry in 1984. The ratio of mining and manufacturing mergers to all mergers 1984–87 was used to estimate mining and manufacturing totals before 1984, so that data from this source are approximately comparable to the other sources shown here. All of the value series were originally reported in current dollars but have been deflated here by an all-commodities producers' price index issued by the Bureau of Labor Statistics using 1967 as the base year.

waves by noting that the first consisted largely of "mergers for monopoly," while the second consisted mostly of "mergers for oligopoly."[46]

The formation of large conglomerates dominated the merger wave of the 1960s, as some firms acquired others in new and unrelated businesses. In the 1970s, merger activity in general slowed down, but the number of spin-offs rose dramatically as firms began to rethink their strategies for diversification. Data published by W. T. Grimm and Co. indicate that 40 firms were divested during the 1970s for every 100 firms that were acquired.[47] Using more detailed data gathered at the level of individual lines of business, Ravenscraft and Scherer find in their sample

46. George J. Stigler, "Monopoly and Oligopoly by Merger," *American Economic Review*, vol. 40 (May 1950, *Papers and Proceedings, 1949*), pp. 23–34.

47. W. T. Grimm and Co., *Mergerstat Review* (Chicago: Grimm, 1985), and *Mergerstat Review* (1986), p. 92.

Figure 6-6. *Number of Mergers, 1895–1986*

Number

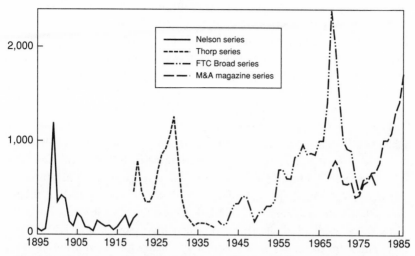

Sources: For Nelson series, see figure 6-5; for Thorp series, see Willard Thorp and others, "The Merger Movement," in U.S. Temporary National Economic Committee, Investigation of Concentration of Economic Power, *The Structure of Industry*, Senate Committee Print, 76 Cong. 3 sess. (Washington, D.C., 1941); the FTC Broad series is from FTC, *Economic Report on Corporate Mergers: Staff Report* and for 1970–79, from Devra L. Golbe and Lawrence J. White, "A Time-Series Analysis of Mergers and Acquisitions in the U.S. Economy," in Alan J. Auerbach, ed., *Corporate Takeovers: Causes and Consequences* (University of Chicago Press for National Bureau of Economic Research, 1988), pp. 265–302; and for M&A series, see figure 6-5.

of large firms that between 20 percent and 46 percent of the acquisitions were later reversed through divestiture.[48]

Since 1980, takeover activity has surged again. The value of assets acquired through merger or takeover rose each year in this decade to a peak of $190 billion in 1986. Merger activity slowed to $160 billion in 1987 but has continued at a very high level in 1988. Even discounted for inflation, these levels still represent a larger amount of asset trading than in any previous wave. Moreover, the "hostile" takeover has emerged as a new phenomenon in this wave. Prior to the 1980s, takeovers were almost never consummated without the consent of the target management. But in recent years, new financing techniques such as junk bonds have made it possible for raiders, often operating from a very small base, to marshal enough resources to tender for controlling interests in much larger firms. Data assembled for one study show that of a sample of 454

48. Ravenscraft and Scherer, *Mergers, Sell-Offs, and Economic Efficiency*, pp. 164–65.

firms that were in the *Fortune* "500" in 1980, the ownership of 82 changed hands from 1981 to 1985. Of these transactions, almost half were instigated by raiders and resisted by managers of the acquired firms.[49]

From a long-run perspective, it is apparent that new organizational forms have emerged in each of the four distinct merger waves. Presumably these new institutions responded to a new set of opportunities or threats in each wave. In some cases, the results have been positive; in others not. The key lesson for policymakers is that blanket policies toward mergers are likely to be counterproductive in many cases.

For example, Michael Jensen has argued that one of the benefits of takeovers is that they may alter the constraints and incentives facing the firm and force it to pay out a larger share of its cash flow in dividends or debt service. Commitments to high levels of payout can force firms to adopt cost-cutting, belt-tightening, attention-to-detail operating procedures that focus management's attention on the niches it can serve best. Thus the overall productivity of the firm increases. Moreover, forcing companies to pay out their cash flow constrains them from making potentially wasteful acquisitions. This result may benefit the economy as a whole. In fact, Ravenscraft and Scherer find that firms that made acquisitions during the conglomerate merger wave of the 1960s and 1970s, for the most part, failed to sustain the growth rates of the businesses they acquired, and a large share of the acquisitions were later spun off. A McKinsey and Company study done in the early 1980s concluded that nearly seven out of ten acquisitions undertaken during the 1960s and 1970s were failures.[50] And Alfred Chandler, the business historian at Harvard Business School who documented the rise of big corporate organizations as an innovative and productive force in the years prior to World War II,[51] now believes that the conglomerate merger movement of the 1960s was a massive experiment in organizational strategy that often failed.[52]

49. Morck, Schleifer, and Vishny, "Characteristics of Hostile and Friendly Takeover Targets," p. 3.

50. Based on an internal McKinsey and Co. study using some client-sensitive information. While the conclusions have been publicized, the study itself is not public.

51. See Alfred D. Chandler, Jr., *The Visible Hand: The Managerial Revolution in American Business* (Belknap Press, 1977).

52. See Alfred D. Chandler, Jr., *Scale and Scope: The Dynamics of Managerial Capitalism* (Harvard University Press, forthcoming).

But "back to the wall" management and payout strategies may be desirable only in certain environments. It does not make sense for firms with abundant and attractive investment opportunities to rely heavily on debt. If firms that should be reinvesting are being restructured and leveraged up to force the payout of cash flow, such strategies will only hasten their decline. In short, payout strategies can be a way of ceding the game, which may be appropriate for some firms in some industries, but would have devastating consequences if undertaken across too many sectors of the economy at once.

Moreover, while forcing companies to increase their payouts to creditors and shareholders may enhance productivity in the short run, it can reduce productivity in the long run if it discourages employees of the firm, both managers and workers, from developing firm-specific human capital. Although not yet well studied by economists and organizational theorists, it is nevertheless likely that firms that are too "lean and mean," as the popular phrase goes, may not elicit the loyalty needed to encourage employees to learn new skills or look for more efficient ways of doing things or build a new service-oriented relationship with a customer.

In sum, takeover research has resulted in some apparently confusing inferences because takeovers and mergers are heterogenous, with a range of motives and potential outcomes. Consequently, it is unwise to extrapolate from what may be very peculiar transactions to draw implications for all mergers and takeovers. Having said this, the weight of the evidence suggests that takeover transactions are an institutional response to profound change in the operating environments of firms.[53] In some cases, postmerger performance of the firms—and by implication of the economy as a whole—may improve; in others, the transaction may produce a worse result. However mixed the outcomes, the policy implications seem clear. Given the diversity of possible outcomes and the uncertain state of our knowledge, it would be a mistake to block the takeover process. To do so runs the risk of locking firms into old ways of doing things just when they most need to be flexible.

53. Michael Gort postulated an "economic disturbance" theory of mergers nearly twenty years ago, but his arguments were intended to explain discrepancies in the value placed on firms by different potential owners, rather than the need for institutional change in the firms. See Gort, "An Economic Disturbance Theory of Mergers," *Quarterly Journal of Economics*, vol. 83 (November 1969), pp. 624–42.

The Policy and Research Challenge

If the U.S. economy is to provide expanding opportunities for its citizens, the nation must somehow achieve a stronger growth rate of productivity. This enormous challenge requires efforts along two dimensions.

First, the United States is still the largest economy and the world leader in science and technology. The nation must find ways of pushing out the frontier of technical knowledge at a faster rate. Second, the United States must learn to make better use of the technology already available. The cultural values and institutional arrangements that have served the country well in the past may no longer be the most appropriate. U.S. firms have been at the forefront of new, high-technology product markets, but then lost their position because they were not as skilled at setting and maintaining standards for manufacturing quality and efficiency. American firms have not determined what customers want and then made the necessary incremental innovations to satisfy those tastes. In these tasks the United States must learn from others, as well as remain a good leader.

Competition and Cooperation

How can the United States meet the challenge of achieving a stronger growth rate of productivity? Priority should be given to research that can help us understand the effects of organizational form and competitive environment on productivity performance. Academic research on market structure and competition to date has been based primarily on the economic theory of games. Unfortunately, this approach can prove almost anything. One strand of analysis has argued that companies compete ferociously even when there are very few of them. Indeed, some say that even potential competition is adequate to ensure that prices are cut to the level of marginal costs. An alternative strand of the literature sees monopoly everywhere. The development of new technology is seen as an instrument to maintain monopoly power.

Research must be brought more into line with the empirical realities of the current environment. It is not enough to know that certain kinds of behavior are theoretically possible; we need to know which ones are relevant today. Clearly, a comparison of the industrial organizations of the United States and its major competitors is vital. Earlier, this chapter listed several mechanisms by which Japan has apparently been able to combine cooperative research and adequate competition. We need to know more about these strategies, where they have succeeded and failed, and whether similar strategies could work in the U.S. business environment.[54] And Japan's example is hardly the only important one. France has used directive economic policies that look very counterproductive, and yet France's productivity growth has been surprisingly strong. Germany has organized joint research efforts among small companies that have been highly successful.

The U.S. commitment to competition and the market has been a big reason for our nation's economic success. And the failures of the planned economies have offered new evidence for the advantages of the market. Yet the highly successful economies of Asia and Europe have organized their markets in ways that differ from ours, and we need to learn how their markets work to make their industries successful.

Encourage Efficient Organizations

The analysis presented in this chapter suggests that if there is a problem with American management, it is not that managers have become less competent, but that old organizational forms and old strategies are not working as well as they once did. The wave of takeovers, reorganizations, and restructurings suggests that a great deal of institutional experimentation is under way. But here, again, theoretical and empirical understanding of what is happening, of what works, and what does not work, and why, is lagging far behind the reality of ideas being tried. Although many new organizations will succeed, many others will undoubtedly fail. In general, experimentation is healthy and should not be discouraged. The role for the public sector in this process is primarily to set the rules of the game to prevent fraud or coercion. Within these broad parameters, investors, managers, entrepreneurs, workers, suppliers, financiers, and communities interested in economic development should have wide latitude to recontract freely among themselves. At the same time, we need to continue basic research into organizational behavior to learn more about what forms work under what circumstances and how these restructurings are changing the way work gets done.

When it is shown that some parties are harmed by restructurings, consideration should be given to policies that ease the pain for the injured

---

54. In work being prepared for the Brookings Papers conference in December 1988, David Teece is making a comparison of U.S. and Japanese industrial organizations.

parties. Workers, especially, may need help to make the necessary transitions. Economists are used to thinking of capital as the "fixed" factor of production and labor as "variable." But the worker may not see his or her skills as so flexible. Policies that help workers relocate or retrain when the skills they have, or the plants they work in, become obsolete, are, first of all, humane and fair. But they also contribute to long-run productivity growth by making an important resource more mobile, flexible, and responsive to rapidly changing markets.

The resources for retraining and providing favorable tax incentives for reeducation should be increased. Legislation similar to the Pension Reform Act of 1973 should be considered to require firms to provide transferable health care coverage and other benefits. And requiring advance notice of plant closings and large layoffs seems both fair and sensible. In return, the mobility of capital can be enhanced with generous depreciation schedules.

Remove the Obstacles to Commercialization

At one time the United States was proud of the Yankee ingenuity that borrowed technology from Europe and improved on it. Today, Rosenberg and Steinmueller ask: "Why are Americans such poor imitators?"[55] They identify three reasons, each of which can guide future U.S. efforts.

First, in line with our earlier discussion, Japanese firms in the 1950s saw U.S. technology that was well ahead of theirs, so they developed a comparative advantage in adaptation. The United States should learn this same lesson. U.S. firms need to devote greater efforts to borrowing other countries' technology and improving on it for use in the United States.

Second, there is too much incentive for R (research) in America and not enough for D (development). Government resources are channeled into research but not into its applications. Private companies also neglect to integrate R&D and engineering and production facilities.

Greater incentives for development and commercialization can be offered in several ways. The federal government currently supports little technology outside the context of defense. This emphasis can be changed by greater government funding for technological experimentation. In

---

55. Nathan Rosenberg and W. Edward Steinmueller, "Why Are Americans Such Poor Imitators?" *American Economic Review*, vol. 78 (May 1988, *Papers and Proceedings, 1987*), pp. 229–34.

addition, the current tax credit for private research and development should be retained. New proposals in Congress have suggested revisions to the credit that can make it more effective by removing disincentives for firms that, for one reason or another, have been performing too poorly to steadily increase their R&D commitments.

Third, the United States tends to look for important breakthroughs in technology, whereas productivity advances and commercial success come far more from the incremental innovation that follows a big breakthrough. The technology leader is often left behind by new entrants because the early models of a new technology are crude and unreliable, and the leader neglects the essential improvements in the product. U.S. firms would benefit by paying closer attention to incremental improvements, as their Japanese counterparts do.

Rosenberg and Steinmueller's reasons are plausible and intriguing, but they immediately raise the question as to why the United States is failing in the ways described. Why does the United States have these blind spots and what can be done to change? Here again, research into organizational behavior might help answer these questions.

Promote Competition and Protect Intellectual Property

Good management practices and efficient organizations are fostered by an environment that punishes forcefully those companies that allow costs to rise and quality to fall and that fail to take advantage of new technology. Vigorous worldwide competition is the best means to achieve the necessary enforcement in industries in which products are traded internationally. Hence, avoiding protectionism is important.

Despite the political concerns about direct foreign investment in the United States, foreign investors can provide Americans with a double advantage. When foreign companies set up in the United States, using U.S. workers and operating under U.S. rules, direct management-to-management competition occurs. In addition, such plants offer a direct conduit for the transmission of foreign technology and the best foreign management practices to the United States. We can make the externalities in technology development work more to our advantage.

If the United States is to promote a more vigorous competition, a serious review of the mechanisms that protect intellectual property is needed. There are signs that the existing methods are not working as well as they should. Is this perception really true, and, if so, how can the United States assess alternative methods of protection? The trade-off between incentives to innovate and the benefits of diffusion must be kept in mind.

As noted earlier, an important survey of U.S. companies by a group from Yale University found that patents were not the primary mechanism used to protect intellectual property.[56] In fact, the main mechanisms listed by the survey respondents suggest that companies mostly rely on getting a head start on competitors. But the increase of competition from worldwide sources is reducing the period during which companies can earn rewards from innovation. Perhaps we need new copyright instruments besides conventional patents or a new way of assessing patent application to ensure that the United States receives its due as the technology leader.

Conclusion

The United States has suffered a slowdown in the growth of productivity since 1973, and much of this slowdown remains unexplained. This chapter suggests that part of the reason for the slowdown, thus far underemphasized by many researchers, may be found in managerial practices. It does little good, however, to debate whether managerial quality has declined or whether serious uncertainties in the business climate have been responsible for the contribution that managerial decisions may have made to the slowdown. The key challenge for policymakers is to ensure that incentives are offered in the future to encourage firms to innovate, to commercialize their innovations, and to search for and implement measures to raise productivity.

56. See Levin and others, "Appropriating the Returns."

CHAPTER SEVEN

Education and the Productivity of the Work Force: Looking Ahead

Richard J. Murnane

ONCE AGAIN, the performance of the American educational system has become a serious public concern. Both private and public reports have sounded the alarm that the nation is at risk because of the inadequacies of American education. These studies, in turn, have prompted observers to conclude that deterioration in America's schools has been a significant cause of the drop in the productivity growth rate over the past fifteen years.

That conclusion is almost certainly not true. The productivity decline, especially the dramatic drop beginning in 1973, was too precipitous to blame on relatively slow-moving changes such as a possible reduction in the quality of the work force. There were some declines in scores on tests administered to elementary and secondary school students during the late 1960s and 1970s that are not well understood,[1] but a large part of the decline in the Scholastic Aptitude Test (SAT) scores, the measures of educational performance given the most attention in the media, is due to an increase in the number of students with relatively low ability who are taking the test.[2] Perhaps most important, the rate of labor productivity growth has also fallen in other countries, including France, Germany,

Richard Berry, Sue Berryman, John Bishop, David Cohen, Michael Feuer, Howard Gordon, Patricia Graham, Eric Hanushek, Jay Hubert, Harold Howe, Carl Kaestle, Francis Keppel, Daniel Koretz, Henry Levin, Charles Lindblom, Philip Moss, Jerome Murphy, Richard Nelson, Edward Pauly, and Judah Schwartz contributed helpful comments on earlier drafts. I would also like to thank David Johnson and David Title for research assistance.

1. Daniel M. Koretz, *Educational Achievement: Explanations and Implications of Recent Trends* (Washington, D.C.: Congressional Budget Office, 1987).

2. College Entrance Examination Board, *On Further Examination: Report of the Advisory Panel on the Scholastic Aptitude Test Score Decline* (New York: College Board, 1977).

Britain, and Japan, since 1973.[3] It is not sensible to conclude that changes in the quality of U.S. education played a large role in the productivity decline that affected many countries.

The critical question for Americans concerned about their educational system, however, relates not to the economic effects of education in the past, but to linkages between education and productivity in the future. That is the subject of this concluding chapter.

Education in Perspective

Economists typically characterize education by measuring the "output" of the educational system, either by the number of years of schooling completed by labor force entrants or by the scores achieved on standardized tests designed to measure certain cognitive skills such as thinking, reasoning, and reading ability. They then show that these measures of educational achievement are positively related to a measure of labor productivity. That research, some of which is discussed in this chapter, is interesting and demonstrates that educational achievements are related to labor productivity. Such evidence is not sufficient, however, to guide educational policymaking. To evaluate the potential effectiveness of alternative educational policies, it is necessary to go beyond the typical measures of education. One must discover what types of skills are most important in fostering productivity and what types of policies enhance development of those skills.

Of course, raising workers' productivity should not be the only goal of American education. There are many other important objectives, including fostering creativity and appreciation of the arts, and teaching students the rights and obligations of citizenship in a democratic and pluralistic society. At the same time, the stability of American democracy may depend on how well the nation permits minority groups to share more fully in the country's economic wealth. In this way, the enhancement of productivity growth may very much be linked to social values.

Linkages between education and economic performance also run in both directions, that is, not only does the quality of education have economic effects, but the operation of the economy influences the effectiveness of the educational system. In particular, the incentives for

3. Martin Neil Baily and Alok K. Chakrabarti, *Innovation and the Productivity Crisis* (Brookings, 1988).

minority youth living in inner cities to work hard in school are greatly diminished when there are few well-paying jobs available to them when they graduate.[4] This reality underscores the need to find ways of raising productivity growth—and hence income growth—for the nation as a whole.

Home Experiences Influence the Acquisition of Skills

While the United States has looked primarily to the schools to solve a variety of social problems, including the low skill levels of many labor force entrants, it has long been known that the family background of American children is a stronger predictor of their cognitive skill levels than are variables depicting school quality.[5] Said differently, family stresses and the lack of learning resources that accompany poverty reduce children's cognitive skills.[6] These effects are particularly severe for children who live in areas of concentrated poverty, where they encounter few, if any, successful role models.[7] Moreover, the effectiveness of schooling depends on the quality of the home environment, and this condition becomes more important as children age.[8]

Accordingly, the United States cannot rely solely on improvements in formal education to improve the cognitive skills of the children who will enter the work force in the years to come. If the nation is seriously concerned about the skills and attitudes of the work force of the future, it must focus attention and resources on the quality of the lives children lead outside of school. This concern is critical at this time when one American child in five lives in poverty.[9]

Many Factors Influence Labor Productivity

The productivity of the labor force, defined as the output produced by each hour of work, does not depend solely on the skill levels of

4. William J. Wilson, *The Truly Disadvantaged: The Inner City, the Underclass, and Public Policy* (University of Chicago Press, 1987).

5. James S. Coleman and others, *Equality of Educational Opportunity,* Office of Education (Washington, D.C.: U.S. Department of Health, Education, and Welfare, 1966).

6. Lisbeth B. Schorr, *Within Our Reach: Breaking the Cycle of Disadvantage* (Anchor Press/Doubleday, 1988).

7. Wilson, *Truly Disadvantaged,* pp. 56–57.

8. Jeanne Chall and Catherine Snow, *Families and Literacy: The Contribution of Out-of-School Experiences to Children's Acquisition of Literacy* (Harvard University Graduate School of Education, 1982).

9. Frank Levy, *Dollars and Dreams: The Changing American Income Distribution* (New York: Russell Sage Foundation, 1987).

workers. Many other factors contribute heavily to labor productivity, including the quantity and quality of the capital equipment with which the labor force works, the pace and character of technical change, and the way that labor is organized in the production process.[10]

The importance of workplace organization is highlighted by the recent General Motors-Toyota NUMMI automobile project. In this joint venture, the Toyota management system was introduced to a GM plant in Fremont, California, that had been closed, partly because of low productivity. Eighty percent of the labor force used in the joint venture consisted of workers previously laid off by GM. The Toyota management system involved serious changes in the way workers were utilized, including use of worker teams responsible for quality control, a just-in-time inventory system, and team standardization of tasks. Within two years, productivity in the plant rose close to levels achieved by Toyota plants in Japan. In other words, the introduction of the Toyota management system resulted in a dramatic increase in labor productivity, using essentially the same work force that GM had labeled as seriously deficient.[11]

The GM-Toyota experience demonstrates that the productivity of the work force depends critically on *how* workers are used, not only on the skills that workers bring to the job. While this notion plays a role in many theoretical treatments of labor productivity,[12] it is missing from most empirical investigations of the relationship between education and productivity, and from documents such as *A Nation at Risk*, which criticizes the quality of American education.[13] It is important, therefore, that policymakers concerned with raising productivity pay as much

10. Edward F. Denison, *Trends in American Economic Growth, 1929–1982* (Brookings, 1985).

11. Clair Brown and Michael Reich, "When Does Union-Management Cooperation Work? A Look at NUMMI and GM-Van Nuys," paper prepared for the conference, "Can California Be Competitive and Caring?" UCLA, May 6, 1988; and John F. Krafcik, "Learning from NUMMI," International Motor Vehicle program, Working Paper (Massachusetts Institute of Technology, 1986).

12. See, for example, Finis Welch, "Education in Production," *Journal of Political Economy*, vol. 78 (January 1970), pp. 35–59; and Richard R. Nelson and Edmund S. Phelps, "Investment in Humans, Technological Diffusion, and Economic Growth," *American Economic Review*, vol. 56 (May 1966), pp. 69–75.

13. National Commission on Excellence in Education, *A Nation at Risk: The Imperative for Educational Reform*, a Report to the Nation and the Secretary of Education (Washington, D.C., 1983).

attention to promoting the more effective use of existing labor force skills as they do to raising the skills that workers bring to their jobs.[14]

Education-Related Productivity Problems in the Years Ahead

Productivity growth cannot be enhanced by improving educational quality without knowing what skills are most important to job performance, as well as which skills are most likely to foster growth in a dynamic, changing economy. As it turns out, there is research on both these issues that can guide policymakers to identify problems in the current educational system that are likely to be linked to future productivity performance.

Cognitive Skills and Worker Productivity

Several studies, most conducted by industrial psychologists, report positive, statistically significant correlations between workers' scores on tests of cognitive skills and their performances on the job.[15] These results need to be interpreted with caution, however. The sizes of the correlations depend on the way job performance is measured, and the scores on the pencil-and-paper tests measure at most only a few of the many types of skills that affect job performance.[16] The test scores do not provide good measures of the ability to solve ill-structured, ambiguous problems,[17] and they provide no information about individuals' ability to work cooperatively in a group. Nonetheless, the studies do suggest that cognitive skills definitely influence the productivity of workers in a wide range of jobs.

Among the most interesting research in this area is a recent study by

14. Manufacturing Studies Board, *Human Resource Practices for Implementing Advanced Manufacturing Technology* (National Academy Press, 1986).

15. John Bishop, "Information Externalities and the Social Payoff to Academic Achievement," Working Paper 87-06 (Cornell University, Center for Advanced Human Resource Studies, 1987), and "Why High School Students Learn So Little and What Can Be Done About It," Working Paper 88-01 (Cornell University, Center for Advanced Human Resource Studies, New York State School of Industrial and Labor Relations, 1988); and John E. Hunter, "Cognitive Ability, Cognitive Aptitudes, Job Knowledge, and Job Performance," *Journal of Vocational Behavior*, vol. 29 (December 1986), pp. 340–62.

16. Henry M. Levin, "Ability Testing for Job Selection: Are the Economic Claims Justified?" in Bernard R. Gifford, ed., *Testing and the Allocation of Opportunity* (Boston: Kluwer Academic Publishers, forthcoming).

17. Norman Frederiksen, "The Real Test Bias: Influences of Testing on Teaching and Learning," *American Psychologist*, vol. 39 (March 1984), pp. 193–202.

John Bishop reporting that workers' scores on tests of mathematical skills are more highly correlated with supervisors' assessments of workers' productivity than are scores on tests of verbal skills.[18] One reason why mathematics skills may be particularly important is that they give information about workers' ability to follow directions, since mathematics depends on the use of algorithms. Since mathematical ability is cumulative, scores on math tests may reflect the ability of workers to accumulate knowledge in school, and later, on the job. Both of these skills—following directions and learning cumulatively—are critical to the effectiveness of on-the-job training.

Education and Employment in a Changing Economy

For many years, economists have hypothesized that the rate of technical change in an economy not only influences the rate of productivity growth directly, but also influences the value of education in fostering productivity growth.[19] The logic is as follows. In an economy in which production techniques change only very slowly, and most work is carried out by virtually the same techniques for lengthy periods of time, skills can be transferred from one generation to the next through apprenticeships and other modes of on-the-job training without reliance on the general skills provided by formal schooling. When techniques are changing rapidly, however, then general skills typically learned in school, such as the ability to follow written directions, are especially valuable in fostering productivity.

Over the last twenty years, several studies have provided empirical evidence to support this hypothesis. For example, it has been shown that the rate of return to investment in the education of farmers (one measure of the productivity gains associated with education) is positively related to the rate at which new agricultural techniques are being developed.[20] Another study has shown that highly educated workers (defined as workers with more than a high school education) have a comparative advantage over less educated workers in the implementation of new technology in the manufacturing sector.[21] These studies support

18. Bishop, "Why High School Students Learn So Little."
19. Nelson and Phelps, "Investment in Humans."
20. Welch, "Education in Production."
21. Ann P. Bartel and Frank R. Lichtenberg, "The Comparative Advantage of Educated Workers in Implementing New Technology: Some Empirical Evidence," *Review of Economics and Statistics*, vol. 69 (February 1987), pp. 1–11.

the hypothesis that education is particularly important in fostering productivity growth when production processes are changing and new technologies are being introduced.

Education can also help ease job displacement. In a dynamic economy, the demand for labor will always grow relatively more rapidly in some sectors than in others, creating the need for workers to change jobs in order to adjust to changes in the structure of demand. This response was particularly true during the 1970s, when the decline in manufacturing, precipitated by the 1973 oil crisis, displaced many workers from their jobs.[22] Significantly, among the many workers displaced by the decline in manufacturing during the 1970s, better educated workers experienced the shortest spells of unemployment.[23] In other words, better educated workers were more successful in making the transition from jobs in one industry to jobs in another. One potential explanation is that the costs of training workers with relatively high education levels are lower than the costs of training less educated workers.

Technological change in the future will continue to cause turbulence in the labor market. Ensuring that workers have the skills to make transitions to new types of work will not only foster growth but will also ease pressure for legislation and regulation that protect jobs in dying industries at the expense of creating jobs in growing sectors of the economy.

A somewhat different view of the relationship between technical change and the labor force is presented in *Workforce 2000*, a recent report prepared for the Department of Labor.[24] This study argues that the structure of the economy is changing in a manner that is eliminating employment opportunities for relatively low-skilled workers. Accordingly, skill requirements for workers are projected to "escalate" in the future; those without the necessary skills simply won't get jobs.

There is certainly merit in the view that the skill levels of the labor force will matter in the years ahead, but there are reasons to be skeptical

22. Frank Levy and Richard C. Michel, "Individual Earnings by Sex, Education, and Age: Recent U.S. Trends," prepared for the Joint Economic Committee of the U.S. Congress, Washington, D.C., 1988.

23. Richard M. Cyert and David C. Mowery, eds., *Technology and Employment: Innovation and Growth in the U.S. Economy* (Washington, D.C., National Academy Press, 1987); and Jacob Mincer, "Education and Unemployment" (Columbia University, National Center on Education and Employment, 1987).

24. William B. Johnson and others, *Workforce 2000: Work and Workers for the 21st Century* (Indianapolis, Ind.: Hudson Institute, 1987).

of the findings of the *Workforce 2000* report. The projections that support the conclusion about skill escalation simply extrapolate sectoral growth rates, taking account of the education distribution of the labor force within each sector. This procedure can be misleading. Projections of the demand for workers with different education levels are very sensitive to various methodological decisions, including the level to which data are aggregated. A number of studies that use an approach similar to that used in *Workforce 2000*, but differing in methodological details, report projections that show no skill escalation.[25]

The *Workforce 2000* report implicitly assumes that the way work is done in each sector will not change. In fact, the way work is organized is very likely to be determined by the quality of the work force. For example, the perception that workers will have the skills to follow directions, to solve problems, and to work cooperatively in groups may encourage management to give small groups of workers considerable autonomy in organizing production, as has been done in the NUMMI experiment. The increasing use of microchip technology also increases the potential to organize work in different ways. Chip technology can reduce the time involved in carrying out secretarial tasks such as typing and filing and permit workers to take on a wider range of problem-solving responsibilities. At the same time, chips can also be used to "dumb down" jobs and to monitor electronically workers' performances in carrying out routinized tasks. In short, the quality of the work force may influence the character of technological change.[26]

My point is that the importance of education to the operation of the economy does not depend on projections of the skill levels that will be required in the jobs of the future. Even if U.S. manufacturing makes a comeback, which would lead to a projection of many new jobs for high school educated workers, the issue of the design of work would remain. More than the quality of work life is at stake; the level of wages hangs

25. Cyert and Mowery, *Technology and Employment*; Levin, "Ability Testing"; Russell W. Rumberger and Henry Levin, "Forecasting the Impact of New Technologies on the Future Job Market," *Technological Forecasting and Social Change*, vol. 27, no. 4 (1985), pp. 399–417; Levin and Rumberger, "Educational Requirements for New Technologies: Visions, Possibilities, and Current Realities," *Educational Policy*, vol. 1, no. 3 (1987), pp. 333–54; and Martha F. Riche, "America's New Workers," *American Demographics*, vol. 10 (February 1988), pp. 34–41.

26. U.S. Congress, Office of Technology Assessment, *Technology and the American Economic Transition: Choices for the Future*, OTA-TET-238 (Washington, D.C.: Government Printing Office, 1988).

in the balance. Among the consequences of the increased competition from abroad is a decline in manufacturing wages. The manufacturing sector can no longer remain competitive in world markets while paying premium wages to workers carrying out routine tasks. High wages in the future will require the high levels of productivity associated with a NUMMI-like work structure. This conclusion is as true for workers on the shop floor as it is for highly educated workers, such as engineers. The concern with educational quality goes beyond James Conant's call for a more able scientific elite and extends to the entire work force.[27]

Required Skills

What types of cognitive skills have the greatest impact on workers' productivity? Those that seem particularly important are the ability to understand directions (even when the manuals are poorly written), to ask questions, to assimilate and synthesize unfamiliar information, and to identify and solve problems that occur during the normal working day; in short, literacy and problem-solving skills in specific contexts.[28]

Problem solving in specific contexts is especially important because of evidence that experienced workers routinely perform computation tasks in the context of their jobs that they cannot do on written tests like those administered in school.[29] Thus students' skills in carrying out arithmetic computations outside of the specific contexts with which they are familiar may be a poor test of the skills that workers need to function effectively in the labor force. As a result, students' scores on tests that assess their ability to follow directions related to a specific context and to solve problems related to particular applications will be better predictors of productivity in the labor force than are scores on tests that measure ability to decode words and carry out arithmetic computations devoid of context.

How high must skill levels be? While there is insufficient evidence to

27. James B. Conant, *The American High School Today: A First Report to Interested Citizens* (McGraw-Hill, 1959).

28. Richard L. Venezky, Carl F. Kaestle, and Andrew M. Sum, *The Subtle Danger: Reflections on the Literacy Abilities of America's Young Adults* (Princeton, N.J.: Educational Testing Service, 1987).

29. Sylvia Scribner, "Thinking in Action: Some Characteristics of Practical Thought," in Robert J. Sternberg and Richard K. Wagner, eds., *Practical Intelligence: Nature and Origins of Competence in the Everyday World* (Cambridge University Press, 1986), pp. 13–30.

answer this question definitively, the best available information indicates that enhancing productivity growth will require that all students be provided with threshold levels of literacy and problem-solving skills, as measured on pencil-and-paper tests. Extremely high scores on the types of standardized tests typically used in schools to measure cognitive skills may not be necessary for productive performance in the labor force. Effective workers in many jobs are those who learn to solicit helpful advice from fellow workers—a practice common in the workplace but not encouraged or even permitted in most school settings.[30] Moreover, even the best pencil-and-paper tests of literacy and problem-solving skills cannot provide as rich a context for problem solving as is present in most real jobs.[31] And there is reason to be concerned that many new entrants to the labor force today and in the future do not and will not possess threshold levels of literacy and problem-solving skills. These new workers will be needed in the labor-scarce economy of the 1990s.

Providing all students with threshold levels of critical skills is not a modest goal. Most American schools have found it easier to offer excellent instruction to a subset of motivated students preparing for elite colleges than to help all students acquire threshold levels of literacy and problem-solving skills.[32]

Trends in the Cognitive Skills of American Students

One must be careful in assessing the cognitive skills of American students and new labor force entrants because many sets of scores are available and the patterns vary across the tests.[33] Several tests, however, seem to give reliable information about the distribution of literacy and problem-solving skills.

In 1986 the National Assessment of Educational Progress (NAEP) examined the literacy skills of young American adults, aged 21–25.[34] This study found that more than 90 percent of young adults could follow

30. Lauren B. Resnick, "Learning in School and Out," *Educational Researcher*, vol. 16 (December 1987), pp. 13–20.

31. Howard Gardner, "Assessment in Context: The Alternative to Standardized Testing," (University of California at Berkeley, School of Education, Commission on Testing and Public Policy, 1988).

32. Arthur G. Powell, Eleanor Farrar, and David K. Cohen, *The Shopping Mall High School: Winners and Losers in the Educational Marketplace* (Houghton Mifflin, 1985).

33. Koretz, *Educational Achievement.*

34. I. Kirsch and A. Jungeblut, *Literacy: Profiles of America's Young Adults: Final Report* (Princeton, N.J.: Educational Testing Service, 1986).

simple directions, solve single-step problems, and make inferences when all of the necessary information appears in a single sentence. However, more than 30 percent of the sample had difficulties gathering information from several sentences and "analyzing nonroutine or multistep problems."[35] Analysis of the item scores indicated that the problem was not basic reading skills but rather the ability to use reading to solve multistep problems.

The 1986 NAEP literacy assessment of young adults also gave information on the average literacy skills of young adults with different amounts of education. Not surprisingly, the number of years of school completed was a strong predictor of young adults' literacy skills. This is consistent with the evidence that "higher educational attainment was associated with shorter spells of unemployment after displacement."[36] But these favorable results concerning length of schooling should not be interpreted to mean that students graduating from high school tend to have the literacy skills needed to function productively in the workplace. While graduates have higher average skills than high school dropouts, a disturbingly high proportion of the graduates are weak in literacy skills and problem-solving skills.

Recent studies indicate that American students' math skills—a proxy from problem-solving skills—are comparable to their literacy skills. For example, the summary report of the 1986 NAEP mathematics assessment concluded: "The fact that nearly half of the 17-year-olds do not have mathematical skills beyond basic computation with whole numbers has serious implications. With such limited mathematical abilities, these students nearing graduation are unlikely to be able to match mathematical tools to the demands of various problem situations that permeate life and work."[37]

The 1986 NAEP literacy and mathematics assessments show strong relationships between family background and children's skills. For example, parents' educational attainments are strong predictors of their children's literacy and mathematical skills.[38] Several factors seem responsible for this correlation; parents' educational attainment is strongly associated with the availability of literacy materials in the home, the

35. Venezky, Kaestle, and Sum, *Subtle Danger*, p. 22.

36. Cyert and Mowery, *Technology and Employment*, p. 60.

37. John A. Dossey and others, *The Mathematics Report Card: Are We Measuring Up?* Report 17-M-01 (Princeton, N.J.: Educational Testing Service, 1988), p. 41.

38. Ibid.; and Venezky, Kaestle, and Sum, *Subtle Danger*.

probability that children choose a college-preparatory curriculum in high school, and children's educational attainments.

The recent national assessments also indicate that minority group members have much lower skills on average than do young white Americans. While part of the reason is found in differences in educational attainments, minority group members still have much lower average literacy and problem-solving skills than do their white counterparts with the same amount of formal education—a pattern related to the higher incidence of poverty among minority group families.

Thus the evidence from the 1986 NAEP literacy and mathematics assessments reveals that a significant proportion of young adults lack what appears to be threshold levels of problem-solving skills—skills that are important in adapting to new technology and in learning the skills needed in new jobs. Especially distressing is the evidence that members of minority groups and young adults who grew up in poverty tend to lack these skills. This is important because an increasingly large proportion of American children (the labor force entrants in the coming years) are minority group members and individuals growing up in low-income families.

On the surface, it may seem that the key to improving the levels of critical skills is finding ways to make teachers and students work harder. Current efforts in this direction include increased use of standardized tests to monitor students' performance, with poor performance jeopardizing school administrators' job security and students' promotion and graduation. Accountability through testing creates incentives for teachers to focus instruction on the arithmetic computation skills and word recognition skills that are emphasized on standardized tests to the neglect of the more difficult-to-assess problem-solving and literacy skills. The National Science Board attributes improvements in U.S. students' performance on routine computations between 1978 and 1986, as well as the decline in their mathematical problem-solving skills, to such a focus by teachers.[39] Similarly, an analysis of the NAEP literacy assessment concluded that a "casual inspection of the most popular basal reading programs used by elementary schools and of the standardized achievement tests most often used for district and state testing shows that . . . [attention to multiple text features and the integration of information

39. National Science Board, *Science and Engineering Indicators, 1987* (Washington, D.C., 1987).

over many sentences] are skills that are rarely taught except in relation to narrative tests, and rarely tested with forms, charts, and other non-prose texts."[40]

In short, what is emphasized in state testing programs influences what is emphasized in the classroom (the de facto curriculum) and what students learn. Accordingly, in designing policies to improve skill levels it is critical to go beyond shibboleths about more effort by school personnel and greater accountability. The educational system must work smarter rather than just work harder. It is possible that some recent state school reform efforts have failed this test. They have hurt the development of the skills most needed in the labor force.

It is also important to focus reform efforts at an early stage in the schooling system. As already noted, math skills tend to be especially highly related to on-the-job productivity. Recent studies comparing the mathematics skills of American middle-class children with middle-class children growing up in Japan and Taiwan indicate similar skill levels among first graders, but markedly lower performance by American fifth graders.[41] As a result, in evaluating school-based strategies to improve the literacy and problem-solving skills of American children, it is important to focus attention on what can be done to develop the crucial skills of elementary school-aged children in particular.

The Changing Demographics of American Students and New Labor Force Entrants

Increasingly, the students in American schools and the new entrants to the U.S. labor force will be individuals with characteristics that historically have been associated with low literacy and problem-solving skills. One such group is children living in poverty. In 1986, 20 percent of the population under aged 18 lived in families classified as poor, an increase from 16 percent in 1979.[42] Moreover, poverty is an enduring condition for many children. For example, Bane and Ellwood estimate

---

40. Venezky, Kaestle, and Sum, *Subtle Danger*, p. 44.

41. Harold W. Stevenson, Shin-Ying Lee, and James W. Stigler, "Mathematics Achievement of Chinese, Japanese, and American Children," *Science*, vol. 231 (February 14, 1986), pp. 693–99.

42. U.S. Bureau of the Census, "Poverty in the U.S.: 1985," *Current Population Reports*, series P-60, no. 158 (Washington, D.C.: Department of Commerce, 1987), table 2.

that "the average poor black child today appears to be in the midst of a poverty spell which will last for almost two decades."[43]

There is a great deal of evidence that children who grow up in poverty typically do poorly in school and encounter difficulties in the labor market.[44] Contributing reasons are the lack of educational resources in the home, the stresses within families associated with low income, and the lack of access to high-quality schools.

A second group whose representation in the school-aged population is increasing rapidly consists of minority group members, especially Hispanic children. As the recent NAEP literacy and mathematics assessments document, children from minority groups historically have had lower achievement levels on average than have white children. One compelling reason is the greater incidence of poverty among minority group families. In 1983, 40 percent of minority group children lived in poverty, compared with 14 percent of nonminority children.[45]

The poor lifetime job prospects of children from minority groups and among children who grow up in poverty raise important issues of equity. In the years ahead, these concerns about equity will be joined with concerns about the productivity of the economy. During the 1970s, the labor force grew at an annual rate of 3 percent—a consequence of the baby boom cohorts completing their schooling and entering the work force. During this period of rapid labor force growth, there were many qualified applicants for most entry-level jobs. As a result, many poorly skilled workers were unemployed or employed in low-skill jobs.

In contrast, the 1990s are projected to be a period in which the labor force will grow at an annual rate of only 1 percent.[46] Accordingly, the decade ahead is likely to be marked by a labor *shortage* in which all workers will be needed in the labor force, including minority group members and the large number of new entrants who spent a significant part of their lives in poverty. The skill levels of these new entrants may

43. Mary Jo Bane and David T. Ellwood, "Slipping Into and Out of Poverty: The Dynamics of Spells," *Journal of Human Resources*, vol. 21 (Winter 1986), p. 21.

44. Chall and Snow, *Families and Literacy*; and Venezky, Kaestle, and Sum, *Subtle Danger*.

45. Harold L. Hodgkinson, *All One System: Demographics of Education, Kindergarten through Graduate School* (Washington, D.C., Institute for Educational Leadership, 1985), p. 8.

46. Office of Technology Assessment, *Technology and the American Economic Transition*, p. 364.

have a significant impact on the productivity of the economy in the years ahead.

Thus the challenge for policymakers is to improve the skill levels of new entrants to the labor force, those who bring to the schools and later to the labor force characteristics that have historically been associated with low achievement. The policy recommendations discussed later in the chapter should help meet this challenge. But it is important to keep in mind that the roots of the low achievement of many American children lie in the circumstances of poverty in which they live. Consequently, educational policy changes not accompanied by policies that significantly reduce the poverty that dominates many children's lives will have only modest influences on their academic achievements.

The Federal Policy Dilemma

In the United States, responsibility for elementary and secondary education has traditionally been left primarily to the states, which in turn delegate an extraordinary amount of authority to 15,000 local school districts. As a result, the governance structure for education is extremely decentralized, and the federal role is limited. In 1986 the federal government's expenditures for public elementary and secondary education were only 6.2 percent of total expenditures, down from 9.2 percent in 1979.[47]

The modest size of the federal contribution to public education, however, does not totally reflect the federal impact. In particular, Supreme Court decisions and federal legislation have significantly influenced children's educational opportunities. Of particular importance are the 1954 Supreme Court decision in *Brown* v. *Topeka Board of Education* that ruled segregated education to be inherently unequal; the Elementary and Secondary Education Act of 1965 that provided the first significant federal funds for the education of disadvantaged children; and the 1975 Education for All Handicapped Children Act (PL94–142) that guaranteed all handicapped children a free and appropriate public education. Thus the federal government has significantly influenced the extent to which children with different characteristics attend school together. At the same

47. U.S. Bureau of the Census, *Statistical Abstract of the United States, 1988* (Washington, D.C.: Department of Commerce, 1987), p. 119.

time, federal influence on how teachers and students spend their time in school has been small.

In contrast, state governments have been extremely active in recent years in attempting to influence what happens in schools. The states have used a number of policy instruments, including stiffer teacher certification requirements, higher teacher salaries, tougher high school graduation requirements, and extensive testing of students in a variety of subjects at a number of grade levels. While some of the effects of these policies can be predicted—higher salaries increase the lengths of time that teachers stay in teaching—it is still too early to determine the effects that the combination of new state policies will have on public education.[48]

Still, the state role in influencing the direction of public elementary and secondary education almost certainly will continue to grow. What then is left for the federal government? Only federal authorities can ensure that national priorities are not neglected by the states. And they can do so by exerting leverage on the decentralized system of public education.

A Role for Federal Education Policy

Earlier the discussion pointed to the importance of having all entrants to the labor force possess literacy and problem-solving skills above the threshold necessary to learn specific skills needed in particular jobs. Are the states neglecting this priority? Clearly, there is no single answer, since there are significant state-to-state differences in educational reform programs, and the influences of any one state program will vary among school districts and among schools. However, there are two reasons why the various state reforms now under way may not be providing all labor force entrants with literacy and problem-solving skills.

First, tightening high school graduation requirements and increasing the number of required mathematics and science courses may increase the proportion of students who drop out of school and consequently enter the labor force with very low cognitive skill levels.[49]

48. Richard J. Murnane and Randall J. Olsen, "Factors Affecting Length of Stay in Teaching: Evidence from North Carolina," paper delivered at the April 1988 meetings of the American Educational Research Association, New Orleans, La.; and Murnane and Olsen, "The Effects of Salaries and Opportunity Costs on Duration in Teaching: Evidence from Michigan," *Review of Economics and Statistics*, in press.

49. Hodgkinson, *All One System*, pp. 12–13.

Second, to the extent testing programs give weight to skills such as arithmetic computation instead of multistep problem solving, teachers' rational responses to the accountability pressure may be to further emphasize drill and practice of arithmetic skills at the cost of instruction in problem-solving strategies. As mentioned, the National Science Board suggests that this phenomenon may explain why students' skills in computation increased between 1978 and 1986, while skills in problem solving decreased during this period. Similarly, the use of basic readers that do not integrate charts and graphs with prose, when coupled with minimum-competency tests geared to the content of the reading programs, reduces incentives for teachers to focus attention on these skills.[50]

The Leverage Dilemma

Historically, state reform efforts have attempted to prescribe how schools should operate. Particular textbooks and curricula are often required. The evidence is quite clear that such top-down prescriptive programs do not consistently improve the educational achievement of children. In fact, the thrust of much recent writing on school improvement is that these "command-and-control" efforts are counterproductive because they reduce the authority and the discretion of the only people who can ultimately improve the performance of schools, namely, their faculties and administrations. Of course, the corollary of these findings is that schools cannot be improved unless their faculties are given the resources and autonomy to design and implement instructional programs tailored to their needs and circumstances.[51]

It would be a mistake, however, to infer that the federal government should therefore entrust individual school faculties with developing their own programs without federal support and influence. School faculties in many states are under significant pressures from state-imposed minimum competency tests to focus instruction on the skills measured on the tests, which typically emphasize lower order skills, such as knowledge recall, and arithmetic computation, and give little weight to the critically

50. Venezky, Kaestle, and Sum, *Subtle Danger*, p. 44.

51. John E. Chubb, "Why the Current Wave of School Reform Will Fail," *The Public Interest*, vol. 90 (Winter 1988), pp. 28–49; Gerald Grant, *The World We Created at Hamilton High* (Harvard University Press, 1988); Linda M. McNeil, *Contradictions of Control: School Structure and School Knowledge* (New York: Routledge and Kegan Paul, 1986); and Arthur E. Wise, "The Two Conflicting Trends in School Reform: Legislated Learning Revisited," *Phi Delta Kappan*, vol. 69 (January 1988), pp. 328–32.

important, but difficult-to-assess, skills of literacy and multistep problem solving. In addition, the faculties of many schools, perhaps because they have been operating so long under the pressure of district and state mandates, have few ideas about how to improve curricula, especially in mathematics. For example, nearly one-quarter of the teachers in the U.S. elementary schools that were included in a recent comparison of U.S. and Japanese schools had no ideas about how to change the curriculum if they were free to do so. The two most common suggestions teachers did make were to increase emphasis on "basics" and to devote more time to reading, spelling, and language instruction. Only one teacher suggested spending more time on mathematics.[52]

Thus the challenge is to design federal policies that emphasize the goal of providing all students with literacy and problem-solving skills, while respecting, and even nurturing, the flexibility in schools and classrooms that seems necessary for effective schooling.

Suggestions for Federal Education Policies

Two types of policy suggestions can improve educational quality in a way that enhances productivity. In one category are proposals that the federal government should not encourage. In the other are affirmative measures the federal government can and should take.

Policies That the Federal Government Should Not Encourage

At least three popularly discussed proposals for improving the quality of public schooling in fact hold little or no promise of improving the productivity of students after they leave school: merit pay for teachers, longer schooling periods, and more extensive use of computer-based instruction.

Merit pay plans that tie teachers' compensation to supervisors' evaluations of performance have a long history in the United States. Thousands of school districts have adopted these schemes over the last seventy years. The vast majority of districts dropped merit pay within five years, however, and did so well before teachers' unions gained their present power. While the reasons vary, a common theme is that the plans were expensive to administer, did not increase effort levels by individual teachers, and mitigated against the teamwork that is a critical component

52. Stevenson, Lee, and Stigler, "Mathematics Achievement," p. 698.

of effective schooling. In fact, there is no evidence that any urban school district has improved its educational performance by adopting a merit pay plan. The few districts that have had long-lived "merit pay plans" are those that add merit pay to exceptionally high uniform salary scales, that serve middle-class student populations, and that tend to award merit pay more for extra work than for superior teaching performance.[53]

Another often-discussed educational reform measure is to lengthen the school day or school year. Available evidence indicates, however, that this approach to improve educational quality would not be cost effective. Recent estimates suggest that a 10 percent increase in the amount of time in school leads to an improvement in student achievement of only 1.5 to 2.0 percent.[54] The reason for the small effect of a longer schooling period is that teachers and students reduce the intensity of their efforts in order to pace themselves over the longer period of instruction.

It is nevertheless possible that a longer school day or school year could be used to achieve new curricular goals that inherently require more instructional time. But such programs can only work if school faculties are committed to the notion that a longer period of instruction is necessary to teach new material rather than simply to cover existing material more intensively. Thus initiatives for a longer period of instruction should come from school facilities, not from federal or state government.

Still another popularly mentioned reform measure is to emphasize greater use of electronic technology to improve student learning. The weakness of this strategy is that almost all existing educational software consists of drill and practice programs that are of little value in enhancing literacy and problem-solving skills. Existing software cannot substitute for the scarce resource, effective teachers. In fact, the evidence indicates that existing technology enhances learning only when effectively incorporated into resourceful teachers' instructional programs.[55]

53. Richard J. Murnane and David K. Cohen, "Merit Pay and the Evaluation Problem: Why Most Merit Pay Plans Fail and a Few Survive," *Harvard Educational Review*, vol. 56 (February 1986), pp. 1–17.

54. Henry M. Levin and Mun C. Tsang, "The Economics of Student Time," *Economics of Education Review*, vol. 6, no. 4 (1987), pp. 357–64.

55. Michael W. Apple, "Teaching and Technology: The Hidden Effects of Computers on Teachers and Students," *Educational Policy*, vol. 1, no. 3 (1987), pp. 135–57; David K. Cohen, "Educational Technology, Policy, and Practice," *Educational Evaluation and Policy Analysis*, vol. 9 (Summer 1987), pp. 153–70; and Office of Technology Assessment, *Technology and the American Economic Transition*.

In short, devoting more resources to the purchase of computer hardware and software is no substitute for staffing the schools with teachers who understand the importance of enhancing children's literacy and problem-solving skills and have the resources and support to engage in this challenge. (This argument does not imply that there is no federal role in supporting development of new technology; to the contrary, the federal government can be an important catalyst in the development of new testing and instructional programs.)

Merit pay, longer school periods, and more technology are only three examples of a wide variety of top-down prescriptive policies that recently have been suggested to improve schools. The evidence does not support the efficacy of any of these prescriptive policies, as they have traditionally been framed.

Areas of Possible New and Renewed Policy Initiatives

Fortunately, a number of initiatives promise significant improvement in educational quality. Several, such as preschool programs for disadvantaged children and compensatory education efforts, have already been tried, but on the basis of past performance warrant expansion and additional resources. Others, such as incentives for math teachers and better tests, grow naturally out of the foregoing diagnosis of the current problems in the American educational system.

PRESCHOOL PROGRAMS FOR DISADVANTAGED CHILDREN. Over the last twenty-five years, several experimental programs have been initiated to provide 3- to 5-year-olds from disadvantaged families with education, health, and nutrition services, combined with social services for participants' families. Research indicates that many of these programs, including the well-known Perry Preschool program, had significant long-term benefits for their intended beneficiaries: lower school dropout rates, placement rate in special education classes, teenage pregnancy rates, unemployment rates, and crime rates. In addition, these programs enhanced college attendance and participation in post-high school training programs.[56] Most important, the dollar value of these benefits outweighed their costs. Moreover, the evidence suggests that 80 percent of the

---

56. John R. Berrueta-Clement and others, *Changed Lives: The Effects of the Perry Preschool Program on Youths through Age 19* (Ypsilanti, Mich.: High/Scope Press, 1984); and Schorr, *Within Our Reach*.

benefits of the Perry Preschool program accrued not to participants themselves but to society in general in the form of higher tax payments, lower transfer payments, and reduced crime.[57] Clearly, therefore, preschool programs for disadvantaged children seem to be an important target of opportunity for federal educational policy.

Since the mid-1960s, the federal government has funded preschool programs under the Head Start program. Many evaluations of Head Start have been conducted, and the results are encouraging, suggesting that the program has improved participants' chances of succeeding in school.[58] However, no careful evaluation of the long-term effects of Head Start has been conducted. Consequently, it is not known whether the program, which currently serves 450,000 children, is as effective as the Perry Preschool program, the evaluation of which was based on a group of fifty-eight participating children.[59] Among the reasons that Head Start might be less effective than the Perry Preschool program is that the funding level for each student is lower, and consequently, in most sites, the program is less of an immersion experience for participants.

Currently, Head Start serves less than 20 percent of the 2.4 million children living in poverty who are eligible for the program. Extending Head Start coverage to all eligible children whose parents desire participation holds great promise. The cost of extending coverage to half of the eligible population is estimated to be an additional $2.5 billion.[60] While extending coverage is an important goal, it is important that available funds not be spread so thinly that the program becomes merely a shadow of the demonstration projects such as the Perry Preschool program that have had marked influences on children's lives.

It is also important to conduct research that will provide more evidence about the long-term effects of Head Start programs, particularly the extent to which the effects are sensitive to funding levels for each participant. Such research should examine a variety of long-term outcomes. This is critical because no preschool programs, not even the Perry

57. Edward M. Gramlich, "Evaluation of Educational Projects: the Case of the Perry Preschool Program," *Economics of Education Review*, vol. 5, no. 1 (1986), pp. 17–24.

58. Carol E. Copple, Marvin G. Cline, and Allen N. Smith, *Path to the Future: Long-Term Effects of Head Start in the Philadelphia School District* (Washington, D.C.: Department of Health and Human Services, 1987).

59. Koretz, *Educational Achievement*, pp. 92–94.

60. Children's Defense Fund, *A Call for Action to Make Our Nation Safe for Children: A Briefing Book on the Status of American Children in 1988* (Washington, D.C., 1988).

Preschool program, have had sustained effects on the most commonly used measure of outcomes, namely, IQ and achievement test scores.[61]

CHAPTER 1. Title 1 of the Elementary and Secondary Education Act of 1965 gave school districts federal funds for compensatory education. In 1981 the program was reauthorized as Chapter 1 of the Education Consolidation and Improvement Act. Title 1 and Chapter 1 regulations specify that only low-achieving children in schools serving a higher proportion of poor students than the district average are eligible for the program. Currently, more than 14,000 school districts receive Chapter 1 funds, most of which are used to provide supplementary reading instruction to primary school-aged children.

Two flaws in the Chapter 1 program, however, have limited its effectiveness. First, a key consequence of the current Chapter 1 funding formula is that some elementary schools with high poverty rates by national standards are not served because they are located in districts with such high poverty rates that these schools do not serve the poorest student populations in the district. Second, Chapter 1 regulations specify that the funds must be used exclusively for eligible children and not to provide supplementary instruction to a whole class of children, only some of whom are eligible for Chapter 1. As a result, the common way of providing compensatory education is in "pull-out" programs, under which eligible children are taken from their regular classes to work in small groups with teachers paid from Chapter 1 funds.[62] This feature of the program has made it difficult to measure its effectiveness and conceivably has detracted from its potential benefits.

As it is, the quantitative evaluations conducted thus far indicate that Chapter 1 programs are not as effective as Head Start. However, many analysts question the reliability of these evaluations.[63] One reason is that no analyses of the long-term effects of Chapter 1 on schooling or postschooling outcomes have been conducted. A second reason is that because virtually all school districts in the country receive Chapter 1

61. Koretz, *Educational Achievement*, pp. 92–94.

62. Beatrice F. Birman and others, *The Current Operation of the Chapter 1 Program* (Washington, D.C.: Department of Education, Office of Educational Research and Improvement, 1987).

63. Carl F. Kaestle and Marshall S. Smith, "The Federal Role in Elementary and Secondary Education, 1940–1980," *Harvard Educational Review*, vol. 52 (November 1982), pp. 384–408.

funds, it is difficult to find schools without Chapter 1 programs serving children with the same characteristics as those in schools served by Chapter 1. As a result, evaluations of the Chapter 1 programs are typically conducted by comparing the achievement within the same school of children who do and do not participate. This approach is flawed because even those children who do not participate in a Chapter 1 program in fact receive additional attention when their class size is reduced by the pull-outs of Chapter 1 children. Thus the achievement of the "control group" children may rise as a result of the indirect influence of Chapter 1.

The evaluations of Chapter 1 are also inconsistent with the findings from the National Assessment of Educational Progress (NAEP), which indicate that the gaps between the average reading and mathematics skills of nine-year-old black children and white children have closed over time, as have the gaps between the skill levels of children from low-income and more affluent families. While the narrowing of these differentials cannot definitively be attributed to Chapter 1, no compelling alternative explanation has been given. In fact, one explanation for the relative improvement in the reading achievement of low income and minority group children over the last fifteen years is that Chapter 1 stimulated awareness of the needs of disadvantaged children and increased the attention paid to them in school.[64] Chapter 1 also funded a core of professionals who acted as advocates for the program.[65]

In sum, the available evidence suggests that the Chapter 1 program be retained, but that new ways be found to make it more effective in enhancing the skill levels of disadvantaged children. Several changes that are included in the recently enacted Elementary and Secondary School Improvement Amendments of 1988 hold promise.

First, the legislation authorizes a funding increase of $500 million a year for each of the next five years. The projected 1993 funding level of approximately $6.8 billion (the current funding level of $4.3 billion plus an additional $2.5 billion) is estimated to support funding for all eligible children. Second, the new legislation provides modest additional funds to local school districts in counties with especially high concentrations of children from low-income families. Third, schools serving attendance areas in which 75 percent of the children are from low-income families

---

64. Ibid.
65. Paul E. Peterson, Barry G. Rabe, and Kenneth K. Wong, *When Federalism Works* (Brookings, 1986).

may use Chapter 1 funds to upgrade the entire educational program for all students.

The concentration of grants and the support of school-wide initiatives in schools serving high percentages of children eligible for Chapter 1 may increase the effectiveness of the program in two ways. First, they permit schools to end pull-out programs that often result in fragmented instruction. Second, they provide additional resources that faculties may use to devise enriched curricula.

Since the legislation reauthorizing Chapter 1 was enacted in the spring of 1988, it will be several years before it is known whether the authorized increases in funding levels will be appropriated and whether the revised regulations alter the content of the Chapter 1 program. Whatever funding levels are approved, however, the program cannot be effective in improving the achievement of disadvantaged children without continued enforcement of Chapter 1 regulations, especially the requirement that local school districts use Chapter 1 funds to supplement local funds rather than to substitute for them.

STEP, A SUPPORT PROGRAM FOR AT-RISK YOUTH. According to U.S. census data, approximately 14 percent of American adolescents do not complete high school. The percentages of black youth and Hispanic youth—groups with growing representation in the student population— who drop out and do not return to school are higher, 20 percent and 30 percent respectively.[66] Dropouts typically lack the skills needed to work productively in the labor market. This explains, at least in part, why in 1986 the average earnings of male high school dropouts, aged 20-24, were 37 percent lower than the average earnings of male high school graduates in the same age group.[67] Finding ways to encourage at-risk youth to complete school and to acquire the skills needed to function in the labor force is an important national priority.

One promising demonstration program entitled STEP (summer training and education program) offers a combination of academic instruction and work opportunity over two consecutive summers to dropout-prone youth, aged 14 and 15. During each summer, STEP participants receive ninety

66. William T. Grant Commission on Work, Family, and Citizenship, *The Forgotten Half: Non-College Youth in America* (Washington, D.C., 1988), p. 11. Estimates of dropout rates tabulated from Census data are considerably lower than estimates calculated from other sources.

67. Ibid., p. 21.

hours of remedial instruction in reading and math, work for eighty hours, and attend eighteen hours of instruction in "life skills and opportunities," aimed at promoting responsible decisions in the areas of sexual behavior and drug use. Participants are paid the minimum wage for the time spent both in class and at work. During the school year, STEP participants meet regularly with counselors who offer tutoring, monitor school attendance, and offer encouragement for staying in school.

Clearly, the key question about STEP concerns its long-term effects on participants' lives. Since the program, which costs $1,587 a participant more than publicly funded summer jobs, only started in 1985, it will be several years before it is known whether its effects on school completion and performance in the labor market justify the cost. The results of the program's short-term consequences are encouraging, however. STEP participants show gains in both reading and math over the summer, while control group youth who receive summer jobs but no academic instruction or counseling experience losses. STEP youth also report increased knowledge of the consequences of teenage parenting and increased use of contraception.[68]

SUMMER TRAINING FOR MATHEMATICS TEACHERS. Not only is it difficult for students to master the skills needed to solve problems requiring several steps, it is also difficult to teach these skills. Partly as a result of staffing adjustments made during the period of decline in student enrollments—adjustments that resulted in layoffs of many young teachers certified in mathematics—many schools lack faculty who can develop curricula emphasizing problem-solving skills. One recently resuscitated program that may alleviate this problem somewhat is the set of summer training institutes for mathematics and science teachers sponsored by the National Science Foundation. This program, which was first introduced in 1954, terminated in 1983, and then reintroduced in 1984, provides summer stipends and training for secondary school

---

68. Cynthia L. Sipe, Jean B. Grossman, and Julita A. Milliner, *Summer Training and Education Program (STEP): Report on the 1986 Summer Experience* (Philadelphia: Public/Private Ventures, 1987). Part of the test score gains was probably the result of the control group having more practice in test taking over the summer. However, as yet unpublished research by Public/Private Ventures indicates that several months after the summer, a significant portion of the test score differential between treatment and control groups remained.

mathematics and science teachers. Participants are chosen on a competitive basis.

Unfortunately, no rigorous evaluations were done to determine whether the institutes in the 1960s and 1970s led to improved student achievement.[69] However, the program has two characteristics that make it potentially attractive as a modest strategy to improve mathematics instruction. First, the program is not intrusive on schools because participation is voluntary. Second, the voluntary nature of the program attracts teachers interested in improving the quality of their instruction.

For these reasons, the summer institutes should be continued and even extended. In particular, efforts should be made to recruit participants from schools serving large percentages of disadvantaged students—the students who are least likely to acquire the threshold levels of problem-solving skills needed to become productive members of the labor force. The program should also be extended on a pilot basis to include teachers of mathematics in junior and upper primary schools. The reason is that international comparisons of test scores reveal that the mathematics weaknesses of American students relative to those in Japan are already pronounced at the fifth grade level.[70] Finally, small grants should be made available on a competitive basis to the institute's graduates to improve mathematics curricula in their schools. Available evidence supports the effectiveness of such small grants programs in fostering teacher initiative.[71]

INCENTIVES TO BECOME TEACHERS. As student enrollments in the nation's public schools begin to climb, concerns about the possibility of teacher shortages once again arise. Three dimensions of the potential teacher shortage problem are particularly relevant to the focus of this chapter. The first is a shortage of qualified mathematics teachers, precipitated by significant differentials between the salaries of teachers and those of college mathematics majors who enter business or industry.

69. U.S. General Accounting Office, *New Directions for Federal Programs to Aid Mathematics and Science Teaching*, GAO/PEMD-84-5 (Washington, D.C., 1984); Hillier Krieghbaum and Hugh Rawson, *An Investment in Knowledge* (New York University Press, 1969); and Victor L. Willson and Antoine M. Garibaldi, "The Association between Teacher Participation in NSF Institutes and Student Achievement," *Journal of Research in Science Teaching*, vol. 13, no. 5 (1976), pp. 431–39.

70. Stevenson, Lee, and Stigler, "Mathematics Achievement."

71. Lorraine M. McDonnell and Milbrey W. McLaughlin, *Program Consolidation and the State Role in ESEA Title IV*, R-2531-HEW (Santa Monica, Calif.: Rand Corp., 1980).

For example, in 1986, the average twelve-month starting salary paid by business and industry to college math majors was 48 percent above the average salary paid to beginning teachers. In contrast, the analogous differential for college graduates trained in the humanities was 17 percent.[72] Second, urban school districts serving large percentages of disadvantaged students typically find it more difficult to staff their schools with qualified teachers than do suburban school districts.[73] Third, the percentage of minority teachers is declining, a disturbing trend since minority teachers can serve as effective role models for minority students, helping them to develop self-confidence and acquire skills.

For these reasons, the federal government should offer incentives that will ease these three dimensions of the potential teacher shortage. In the past, a number of approaches have been tried, including loan forgiveness for college graduates who become teachers. Available evidence indicates that a more effective strategy is to provide grants for college expenses to academically able college students and demand in return a number of years of service teaching in urban schools.[74] Places in such a program could be reserved for academically able minority group members and for students with significant training in mathematics. The U.S. experience with the Teacher Corps, a Great Society program that in the years from 1966 to 1975 focused on recruiting teachers for service in poverty areas, provides several lessons for the design of a new federal initiative in this area.[75]

CURRICULUM DEVELOPMENT AND TEST CONSTRUCTION. Administering achievement tests to students on a regular basis and reporting the average scores of students in each school is a powerful instrument

---

72. Data on teaching salaries came from National Education Association surveys; data on nonteacher salaries came from College Placement Council surveys.

73. David Greenberg and John McCall, "Teacher Mobility and Allocation," *Journal of Human Resources*, vol. 9 (Fall 1974), pp. 480–502.

74. David M. Arfin, "The Use of Financial Aid to Attract Talented Students to Teaching: Lessons from Other Fields," *Elementary School Journal*, vol. 86 (March 1986), pp. 405–23.

75. James J. Bosco and L. Richard Harring, "Afloat on the Sea of Ambiguity: The Teacher Corps Experience," *Education and Urban Society*, vol. 15 (May 1973), pp. 331–49; and H. Jerome Freibert, "The Federal Government as a Change Agent: Fifteen Years of the Teacher Corps," *Journal of Education for Teaching*, vol. 7 (October 1981), pp. 231–45.

for influencing educational practice. Administrators in high-achieving schools find new opportunities open to them, whereas administrators in schools where student scores are consistently low find their positions in jeopardy. As a result, tests encourage administrators to urge teachers to focus instruction on the skills emphasized on the tests.

Whether accountability through test scores constitutes good educational policy depends critically on the content of the tests. As discussed, minimum competency tests introduced recently in many states may create pressures on teachers to emphasize arithmetic computation rather than problem solving in mathematics,[76] and narrowly defined reading skills at the expense of literacy skills involving logic, inference, and synthesis.[77] This trend is troubling given the likelihood that most states will make greater use of accountability through testing in the years to come.

An important role for federal educational policy is to support the development of assessment instruments that more effectively measure students' literacy and problem-solving skills, and to encourage the use of such instruments in state and school district testing programs. One potentially promising approach is for the federal government to fund the development of exemplary grade-specific curricular frameworks in literacy and problem solving, and simultaneously to fund the development of a very large number of test exercises that measure the extent to which students have mastered the literacy and problem-solving skills consistent with the exemplary curricula.[78] The new assessment exercises could be indexed and placed on large-capacity computer disks, and subsets of items could be made available through computer technology to states, school districts, and individual school faculties for use in curriculum development, assessment of student skills, and for inclusion in accountability testing programs. It is important that the assessment exercises be available to the general public for scrutiny concerning quality and potential bias. One way to encourage the development of high-quality assessment exercises is to make public the name of the individual who prepared each exercise. The indexing system could permit consumers to gain access to exercises developed by specific authors. This would permit

76. National Science Board, *Science and Engineering Indicators, 1987*, p. 21.
77. Venezky, Kaestle, and Sum, *Subtle Danger*, pp. 43–44.
78. Richard J. Murnane and Senta A. Raizen, eds., *Improving Indicators of the Quality of Science and Mathematics Education in Grades K-12* (National Academy Press, 1988).

users to evaluate the quality of different exercises. The indexing system would also allow users to access exercises dealing with particular skills, and using particular contexts. This would permit the faculty of a school that decided to focus curricular reform on the development of a particular type of problem-solving skills or particular contexts to have access to a large number of exercises related to their focus of instruction.[79]

Better tests could also lead to compensatory education programs, such as Chapter I and STEP, which have been criticized for an overemphasis on teaching reading and arithmetic computation. Evaluating the effectiveness of these programs by students' scores on tests that measure literacy and problem-solving skills may create incentives for focusing instruction on these critical skills.

Federal leverage to change the orientation of school curricula and testing is needed because the development of high-quality exercises that test problem-solving skills is difficult and expensive. In addition, there is likely to be a "market failure" in the development of high-quality assessment exercises because it is difficult for for-profit organizations to recoup the cost associated with their development. This problem is particularly severe if the exercises are made available to school personnel, who can then make multiple copies of the exercises.

Federal policy should help support the development of new computer software that can enhance student learning in ways that existing commercially available drill and practice software does not. Federal support should also help develop computer technology, possibly based on concepts of artificial intelligence, that can assess students' literacy and problem-solving skills more accurately than pencil and paper test exercises do. There seems to be considerable potential for advances in both of these areas. For example, the Defense Department and a number of private corporations have used computer simulations to improve employees' performances on a variety of tasks.[80] Computer simulations may prove to be a powerful way to teach problem-solving skills in the classroom. Given the "public good" nature of much research on developing computer technology to teach and assess problem-solving skills, rapid progress will

79. David N. Perkins, Judah L. Schwartz, and Martha Stone-Wiske, "Toward Teaching for Understanding: Assessment, Computer-based Coaching, and Classroom Implementation," proposal submitted by Harvard University Educational Technology Center, July 1988, to the Ford Foundation.

80. Office of Technology Assessment, *Technology and the American Economic Transition*, pp. 242–45.

require federal support. Such support is merited so long as it is directed toward pushing out the frontier of what can be done with computers in the classroom and is not used to support the development of more drill and practice software.

KEEPING TRACK OF PROGRESS. Over the last twenty years significant progress has been made in developing improved indicators of the skills of American students. Of particular importance is the National Assessment of Educational Progress, which periodically evaluates the skills of American students in various subject areas. The NAEP test exercises are subject to many of the same criticisms leveled at state-sponsored minimum competency tests. It is critical in the years ahead to develop test exercises for inclusion in the NAEP testing program that provide detailed information on the literacy and problem-solving skills of American students. The 1984 NAEP literacy survey of young adults is a good start in this direction.

It is also important to include tests of literacy and problem-solving skills in the design of the federally sponsored longitudinal data sets providing information on the schooling and subsequent work experiences of American students. This would provide important new opportunities to learn whether these skills, as opposed to simpler skills such as reading and arithmetic computation, are especially critical in influencing the experiences of new entrants to the labor force.

Summary

Several key lessons emerge from the foregoing overview of U.S. educational policy, as it relates in particular to productivity growth:

—The cognitive skills of American workers are only one of many factors influencing their productivity. Attempts to improve the productivity of the labor force should also focus on other contributing factors, including the systems of management under which workers are utilized.

—Educational reform measures alone can only have marginal success in raising the educational achievements of children from low-income families. The problems of poverty must be attacked directly.

—School curricula must not only be aimed at raising children's reading and arithmetic computation skills. The key objective for raising productivity growth lies in raising literacy and problem-solving skills.

—The ultimate challenge for federal educational policymakers is to promote the development of threshold levels of literacy skills and problem-solving skills for all children, and to do so in a manner that respects and supports the initiatives of individual school faculties. Taken together, several modest policies—Head Start, Chapter I, STEP, teacher recruitment, summer training, and test development—offer an economical way to focus federal resources in ways that will contribute to productivity growth.

Index